MISSION TRENDS NO. 5

MISSION TRENDS NO. 5

Faith Meets Faith

Edited by
Gerald H. Anderson
and
Thomas F. Stransky, C.S.P.

PAULIST PRESS
New York/Ramsey/Toronto
and
WM. B. EERDMANS PUBLISHING CO.
Grand Rapids

Copyright © 1981 by
Paulist Fathers, Inc.
and Wm. B. Eerdmans Publishing Co.

Library of Congress
Catalog Card Number: 81-80983

Published by Paulist Press
545 Island Road, Ramsey, N.J. 07446

ISBN: 0-8091-2356-8

and
Wm. B. Eerdmans Publishing Co.
255 Jefferson, S.E., Grand Rapids, Mich. 49502

ISBN: 0-8028-1821-8

Printed and bound in the
United States of America

Contents

The Editors

GERALD H. ANDERSON, director of the Overseas Ministries Study Center in Ventnor, New Jersey, is editor of the *International Bulletin of Missionary Research*, and vice-president of the International Association for Mission Studies. He was formerly professor of church history and ecumenics, and academic dean of Union Theological Seminary, Manila, Philippines, and president of Scarritt College for Christian Workers, Nashville, Tennessee.

THOMAS F. STRANSKY from 1970 to 1978 was president of the Paulist Fathers, the first missionary society of priests founded in the United States (1858). He is a member of the Joint Working Group between the World Council of Churches and the Roman Catholic Church, an official consultant to the Vatican Secretariat for Promoting Christian Unity, and a participant in the Scholars' Group sponsored by the Southern Baptist Convention and the U.S. Catholic Bishops' Ecumenical Commission. In 1979–1980 he was Visiting Professor in Missions and Ecumenics at Princeton Theological Seminary in New Jersey, and at The Washington Theological Union in Washington, D.C.

Both editors participated in the World Council of Churches' World Conference on Mission and Evangelism at Melbourne, Australia (May 1980) and in the Lausanne Committee's Consultation on World Evangelization at Pattaya, Thailand (June 1980). They have also co-edited *Christ's Lordship and Religious Pluralism* (Maryknoll, N.Y.: Orbis Books, 1981).

Foreword

Since World War II, Christians have been aware that the Church has become in fact a *worldwide* religious family, yet more and more a *minority* community. Instead of occupying a massive, majority position in the West, from which Christian churches and groups reach out to "occupy" the rest of the world, they form almost everywhere only a minority of committed faithful. Even in North America and Europe, the freedom of religious choice or decision no longer remains in the context of Christian faith and Christian community or church. Everywhere major world religions and new spiritual movements have become more widespread and explicitly missionary. Like it or not, the whole world has become a conscious religious marketplace in which faith meets faith, or no-faith.

No wonder, then, that a dominant missionary and pastoral issue in the remaining years of the twentieth century is the relation of Christian faith to religious pluralism. No other period in church history—with the possible exception of its early centuries—has seen as much theological ferment regarding the attitude and approach of Christians to people of other faiths as we are experiencing today. No wonder, also, that the issue itself is already intensely debated within and between Christian churches and traditions. Specifically, what is the meaning of communal and personal confessing of biblical faith in Jesus Christ, the only name by which we must be saved (cf. Acts 4:12)?

As in previous *Mission Trends*, we bring together representative voices of the Protestant, Roman Catholic, and Orthodox traditions that reflect recent literature on the theme. The authors are from four continents and include lay persons, educators, a journalist, missionaries, church leaders—and statements from the Vatican, the World Council of Churches, and an evangelical seminary faculty. All essays are intentionally *from* Christians *for* Christians, to encourage them in their contacts and meetings with people of other faiths to reflect and act responsibly—with courage, gentleness, and reverence (1 Peter 3:15). The attitude and approach of Christians to Marxists, Maoists, and those of secular ideologies are not included here, but will be dealt with in future volumes.

We are gratified by the apparent wide usage of the *Mission Trends* series in college and seminary classes in several parts of the world and across a broad theological spectrum. We are dependent, of course, on the generous cooperation of the authors, and of the editors and publishers who have permitted our reprinting of articles and statements on which they have the copyright. Reactions and recommendations from our readers are welcome as we prepare *Mission Trends No. 6,* which will deal with mission priorities and strategies in the decade ahead.

GERALD H. ANDERSON
THOMAS F. STRANSKY, C.S.P.

I: Mission and Religious Pluralism

The Gospel Among the Religions

Lesslie Newbigin

If the Christian meets a neighbor of another faith on the basis of a commitment to Jesus Christ as the true light and true life, what understanding of other faiths is implied by the Christian in such a meeting?

Lesslie Newbigin, former missionary bishop of the Church of South India, samples and evaluates various Christian answers. They range from "Other religions and ideologies are wholly false and the Christian has nothing to learn from them" to "Non-Christian religions are the means through which God's saving will reaches those who have not yet been reached by the gospel" to "Leave ultimate salvation questions to the wise mercy of God."

Newbigin argues that in dialogue the Christian meets the person of another faith without prior knowledge of ultimate destinies. "I meet him simply as a witness, as one who has been laid hold of by Another and placed in a position where I can only point to Jesus as the one who can make sense of the whole human situation which my partner and I share as fellow human beings." Furthermore, says Newbigin, the Christian should engage in dialogue not "as one who possesses the truth and the holiness of God but as one who bears witness to a truth and holiness which are God's judgment on him and who is ready to hear the judgment spoken through the lips and life of his partner of another faith."

The purpose of dialogue, then, suggests a trinitarian model. It is "obedient witness to Jesus Christ . . . who is glorified as the living Holy Spirit takes all that the Father has given to humankind . . . and declares it to the church as that which belongs to Christ as Lord." Bishop Newbigin concludes that "In this encounter the church is changed, the world is changed, and Christ is glorified."

Lesslie Newbigin was former Associate General Secretary of the World Council of Churches, and Professor of Mission at Selly Oak Colleges in Birmingham, England. This essay is from his book, *The Open Secret: Sketches for a Missionary Theology*, published and copyrighted by Wm. B. Eerdmans Publishing Co. (Grand Rapids, Mich., 1978), pp. 190–206.

The Christian goes to meet his neighbor of another religion on the basis of his commitment to Jesus Christ. There is no dichotomy between "confession" and "truth-seeking." His confession is the starting point of his truth-seeking. He meets his partner with the expectation and hope of hearing more of truth. But inevitably he will seek to grasp the new truth offered him by means of those ways of thinking and judging and valuing which he has already learned and tested. The presuppositions which shape his thinking will be those which he draws from the gospel. This must be quite explicit. He cannot agree that the position of final authority can be taken by anything other than the gospel—either by a philosophical system, or by mystical experience, or by the requirements of national and global unity. Confessing Christ—incarnate, crucified, and risen—as the true light and the true life, he cannot accept any other alleged authority as having right of way over this. He cannot regard the revelation given in Jesus as one of a type or as requiring interpretation by means of categories based on other ways of understanding the totality of experience. Jesus is for the believer the source from whom his understanding of the totality of experience is drawn and therefore the criterion by which other ways of understanding are judged.

In this respect the Christian will be in the same position as his partners in dialogue. The Hindu, the Muslim, the Buddhist, the Marxist—each has his distinctive interpretation of other religions, including Christianity, and the faith of each provides the basis of his own understanding of the totality of experience and, therefore, the criterion by which other ways of understanding, including that of the Christian, are judged. The integrity and fruitfulness of the interfaith dialogue depends in the first place upon the extent to which the different participants take seriously the full reality of their own faiths as sources for the understanding of the totality of experience.

I

If this is the basis upon which the Christian participates in the dialogue, what understanding of other faiths does this imply? Many different answers have been given and are given to this question. Many volumes would be needed to state and examine them. The following is only a sample of answers for the purpose of orientation.

1. Other religions and ideologies are wholly false and the Christian has nothing to learn from them. On this three things may be said.

(a) The sensitive Christian mind, enlightened by Christ, cannot fail to recognize and to rejoice in the abundant spiritual fruits to be seen in the lives of men and women of other faiths. Here we must simply appeal to the witness of Christians in all ages who have lived in friendship with those of other faiths.

(b) In almost all cases where the Bible has been translated into the languages of the non-Christian peoples of the world, the New Testament word *Theos* has been rendered by the name given by the non-Christian peoples to the one whom they worship as the Supreme Being. It is under this name, therefore, that the Christians who now use these languages worship the God and Father of Jesus Christ. The very few exceptions, where translators have sought to evade the issue by simply transliterating the Greek or Hebrew word, only serve to prove the point; for the converts have simply explained the foreign word in the text of their Bibles by using the indigenous name for God. (I owe this piece of information to a conversation with Dr. Eugene Nida.) The name of the God revealed in Jesus Christ can only be known by using those names for God which have been developed within the non-Christian systems of belief and worship. It is therefore impossible to claim that there is a total discontinuity between the two.

(c) John tells us that Jesus is the light that lightens every man. This text does not say anything about other *religions,* but it makes it impossible for the Chistian to say that those outside the church are totally devoid of the truth.

2. The non-Christian religions are the work of devils and their similarities to Christianity are the results of demonic cunning. This view is stated by Justin in his *Apology* and is linked by him with the assertion that the Logos speaking through Socrates and others sought to lead men to the light and away from the work of demons—the Logos who was made man in Jesus Christ. A sharp distinction is here drawn between pagan religions (the work of demons) and pagan philosophy (in which the Logos was shedding his light). Two points should be made regarding this view.

(a) It would be wise to recognize an element of truth here: the sphere of religions is the battlefield *par excellence* of the demonic. New converts often surprise missionaries by the horror and fear with which they reject the forms of their old religion—forms which to the secularized Westerner are interesting pieces of folklore and which to the third-generation successors of the first converts may come to be prized as part of national culture. Religion, including the Christian religion, can be the sphere in which evil exhibits a power against which human reason and conscience are powerless. For religion is the sphere in which a man surrenders himself to something greater than himself.

(b) Even the strange idea that the similarities to Christianity in the non-Christian religions are evidences of demonic cunning points to an important truth. It is precisely at points of highest ethical and spiritual achievement that the religions find themselves threatened by, and therefore ranged against, the gospel. It was the guardians of God's revelation who crucified the Son of God. It is the noblest among the Hindus who most emphatically reject the gospel. It is those who say, "We see," who seek to blot out the light (John 9:41).

3. Other religions are a preparation for Christ: the gospel fulfills them.[1] This way of understanding the matter was strong in Protestant missionary circles in the early years of this century and is fully expressed in the volume of the Edinburgh Conference of 1910 on *The Missionary Message*. The non-Christian religions can be seen as preparation for the gospel, either as the "revelation of deep wants of the human spirit" which the gospel satisfies, or as partial insights which are corrected and completed by the gospel.[2] Obviously such a view can be discussed only on the basis of an intimate and detailed knowledge of mankind's religions. There is indeed a vast missionary literature, mainly written in the first half of this century, which studies the religions from this point of view. Briefly, one has to say that this view had to be abandoned because, in R. Otto's phrase, the different religions turn on different axes. The questions Hinduism asks and answers are not the questions with which the gospel is primarily concerned. One does not truly understand any of the religions by seeing it as a preparation for Christianity. Rather, each religion must be understood on its own terms and along the line of its own central axis.

4. A distinct but related view of the matter, the one dominant at the Jerusalem Conference of 1928, seeks "values" in the religions and claims that while many values are indeed to be found in them, it is only in Christianity that all values are found in their proper balance and relationship. The final statement of the council lists such spiritual values—"the sense of the Majesty of God" in Islam, "the deep sympathy for the world's sorrow" in Buddhism, the "desire for contact with ultimate reality" in Hinduism, "the belief in a moral order of the universe" in Confucianism, and "disinterested pursuit of truth and of human welfare" in secular civilization—as "part of the one Truth."[3] And yet, as the same statement goes on to say, Christ is not merely the continuation of human traditions: coming to him involves the surrender of the most precious traditions. The "values" of the religions do not together add up to him who alone is the truth.

5. A different picture of the relation between Christianity

and the other religions is given in Pope Paul VI's encyclical *Ecclesiam Suam* (1964). Here the world religions are seen as concentric circles having the Roman Catholic church at the center and other Christians, Jews, Muslims, other theists, other religionists, and atheists at progressively greater distances. In respect of this proposal one must repeat that the religions cannot be rightly understood by looking at them in terms of their distance from Christianity. They must be understood, so to speak, from within, on their own terms. And one must add that this model particularly fails to do justice to the paradoxical fact central to the whole issue that it is precisely those who are in one sense closest to the truth who are in another sense the bitterest opponents of the gospel. Shall we say that the priest and the Levite, guardians of God's true revelation, are nearer to the center than the semipagan Samaritan?

6. Recent Roman Catholic writing affirms that the non-Christian religions are the means through which God's saving will reaches those who have not yet been reached by the gospel. Karl Rahner argues as follows: God purposes the salvation of all men. Therefore he communicates himself by grace to all men, "and these influences can be presumed to be accepted in spite of the sinful state of men." Since a saving religion must necessarily be social, it follows that the non-Christian religions have a positive salvific significance. In this respect they are parallel to the Judaism of the Old Testament, which, though it was a mixture of truth and error, was until the coming of Christ "the lawful religion willed by God for them." The adherent of a non-Christian religion is thus regarded as an anonymous Christian. But a Christian who is explicitly so, "has a much greater chance of salvation than someone who is merely an anonymous Christian."[4]

This scheme is vulnerable at many points. The devout adherent of another religion will rightly say that to call him an anonymous Christian is to fail to take his faith seriously. The argument from the universal saving purpose of God to the salvific efficiency of non-Christian religions assumes, without proving, that it is religion among all the activities of the human spirit which is the sphere of God's saving action. The unique revelation to Jesus Christ of the Old Testament is not adequately recognized.

Its most serious weakness, however, is one which is shared in some degree by the other views we have examined: it assumes that our position as Christians entitles us to know and declare what is God's final judgment upon other people. On the question of the ultimate salvation of those who have never heard the gospel, most contemporary Protestant writers are content to say that it is a matter to be left to the wise mercy of God. Some contemporary Roman Catholics (Hans Küng, for example) rebuke the attitude as a failure to do one's theological duty. Küng even uses the word "supercilious" to characterize this unwillingness to announce in advance the outcome of Judgment Day.[5] I must confess, on the other hand, that I find it astonishing that a theologian should think he has the authority to inform us in advance who is going to be "saved" on the last day. It is not accidental that these ecclesiastical announcements are always moralistic in tone: it is the "men of good will," the "sincere" followers of other religions, the "observers of the law" who are informed in advance that their seats in heaven are securely booked. This is the exact opposite of the teaching of the New Testament. Here emphasis is always on surprise. It is the sinners who will be welcomed and those who were confident that their place was secure who will find themselves outside. God will shock the righteous by his limitless generosity and by his tremendous severity. The ragged beggars from the lanes and ditches will be in the festal hall, and the man who thought his own clothes were good enough will find himself thrown out (Matt. 22:1–14). The honest, hard-working lad will be out in the dark while the young scoundrel is having a party in his father's house (Luke 15). The branch that was part of the vine will be cut off and burned (John 15). There will be astonishment both among the saved and among the lost (Matt. 25:31–46). And so we are warned to judge nothing before the time (I Cor. 4:1–5). To refuse to answer the question which our Lord himself refused to answer (Luke 13:23–30) is not "supercilious"; it is simply honest.

This is not a small matter. It determines the way in

which we approach the person of another faith. It is almost impossible for me to enter into simple, honest, open, and friendly communication with another person as long as I have at the back of my mind the feeling that I am one of the saved and he is one of the lost. Such a gulf is too vast to be bridged by any ordinary human communication. But the problem is not really solved if I decide from my side of the abyss that he also is saved. In either case the assumption is that I have access to the secret of his ultimate destiny. If I were a Hindu, I do not think that even a decision by an ecumenical Christian council that good Hindus can be saved would enable me to join in ordinary human conversation with a Christian about our ultimate beliefs. All such pronouncements go beyond our authority and destroy the possibility of a real meeting. The truth is that my meeting with a person of another religion is on a much humbler basis. I do not claim to know in advance his ultimate destiny. I meet him simply as a witness, as one who has been laid hold of by Another and placed in a position where I can only point to Jesus as the one who can make sense of the whole human situation which my partner and I share as fellow human beings. This is the basis of our meeting.

II

How, from this starting point, do I begin to understand the religion of my partner?

1. Believing that in Jesus God himself is present in the fullness of his being, I am committed to believing that every part of the created world and every human being are already related to Jesus. John expressed this by saying that Jesus is the Word through whom all things came to be, that he is the life of all that is, and that he is the light that gives light to every man. To say this is to affirm that the presence and work of Jesus are not confined within the area where he is acknowledged. John also says, in the same breath, that the light shines in the darkness and that the darkness has not mastered it. His whole Gospel is the elucidation of that statement in terms of actual history. This is not a sort of Christ-monism:

there is light and there is darkness. But light shines on the darkness to the uttermost; there is no point at which light stops and darkness begins, unless the light has been put under a bushel. When the light shines freely one cannot draw a line and say, "Here light stops and darkness begins." But one can and must say, "There is where the light shines; go towards it and your path will be clear; turn your back on it and you will go into deeper darkness." One can and must do what John the Baptist did; one can and must "bear witness to the light."

The Christian confession of Jesus as Lord does not involve any attempt to deny the reality of the work of God in the lives and thoughts and prayers of men and women outside the Christian church. On the contrary, it ought to involve an eager expectation of, a looking for, and a rejoicing in the evidence of that work. There is something deeply wrong when Christians imagine that loyalty to Jesus requires them to belittle the manifest presence of the light in the lives of men and women who do not acknowledge him, to seek out points of weakness, to ferret out hidden sins and deceptions as a means of commending the gospel. If we love the light and walk in the light we will also rejoice in the light wherever we find it—even the smallest gleams of it in the surrounding darkness.

Here I am thinking, let it be clearly understood, not only of the evidences of light in the religious life of non-Christians, the steadfastness and costliness of the devotion which so often puts Christians to shame; I am thinking also of the no less manifest evidences of the shining of the light in the lives of atheists, humanists, Marxists, and others who have explicitly rejected the message and the fellowship of the church. "The light" is not to be identified with the religious life of men; religion is in fact too often the sphere of darkness, Christian religion not excluded. The parable of the Good Samaritan is a sharp and constantly needed reminder to the godly of all faiths that the boundary between religion and its absence is by no means to be construed as the boundary between light and darkness.

Christians then, in their dealing with men and women

who do not acknowledge Jesus as Lord, will meet them and share with them in a common life, not as strangers but as those who live by the same life-giving Word, and in whom the same life-giving light shines. They will recognize and rejoice in the evidences they find of a response to the same God from whom alone life and light come. They will join with their non-Christian neighbors in all that serves life against death and light against darkness. They will expect to learn as well as to teach, to receive as well as to give, in this common human enterprise of living and building up a common life. They will not be eager to have their particular contributions to the common human task separately labeled as "Christian." They will be happy only if what they do can serve the reign and righteousness of the Father of Jesus who loves all, gives life to all, and purposes the blessing of all.

2. But having said this, having joyfully and gratefully acknowledged all the goodness to be found in every part of the whole human family, it is necessary to go on to say that there is a dark side to this bright picture. The most dark and terrible thing about human nature is our capacity to take the good gifts of God and make them into an instrument to cut ourselves off from God, to establish our independence from God. All the impulses towards good, all the experiences of God's grace, and all the patterns of conduct and of piety which grow from these, can be and have constantly been made the basis for a claim on our own behalf, a claim that we have, so to speak, a standing in our own right. And so, in the name of all that is best in the moral and spiritual experience of the race, we cut ourselves off from the life which God intends for us—a life of pure and childlike confidence in the superabundant kindness of God. This is the tragic story which was enacted in the ministry of Jesus, when—in the name of all that was best and highest in the law and piety of the time—the incarnate Lord was rejected and condemned to death. This is the story which Paul repeats in many different ways, and above all in three chapters (9–11) of the letter to the Romans. It is the story which has been constantly re-peated in the history of the church when Christians believe they have, in virtue of their faith and baptism, a claim upon

God which others do not have and when they refuse to accept the plain meaning of the teaching of the apostle that there is no distinction between Christian and pagan because the same Lord is Lord of all and bestows his riches upon all who call upon him (Rom. 10:12).

The cross of Jesus is on the one hand the exposure of this terrible fact and, on the other hand, God's way of meeting it. For, as Paul teaches in many places, while at the cross our human righteousness and piety found themselves ranged in murderous enmity against the God whom they proposed to honor, in that same deed we were offered another kind of righteousness—the righteousness which is God's gift, the relationship of total reconciliation with God present in his own person in the one who is condemned and crucified by our righteousness. This unique historic deed, which we confess as the true turning point of universal history, stands throughout history as witness against all the claims of religion—including the Christian religion—to be the means of salvation. Contrary to much of the teaching we have reviewed, we have to insist that religion is *not* the means of salvation. The message of Jesus, of the unique incarnate Lord crucified by the powers of law, morals, and piety and raised to the throne of cosmic authority, confronts the claim of every religion with a radical negation. We cannot escape this. Jesus comes to the representatives of the highest in human spirituality, as he came to Saul of Tarsus, as one who threatens the most sacred ground on which they stand. He appears as the saboteur, the subverter of the law. It is only after his unconditional claim has been accepted that a man in Christ, like Paul the apostle, can look back and see that Christ has not destroyed the law but fulfilled it.

The experience of Paul is mirrored in that of many converts from Hindu and Muslim faith with whom I have discussed this matter. At the point of crisis Jesus appeared to them as one who threatened all that was most sacred to them. In the light of their experience of life in Christ they now look back and see that he has safeguarded and fulfilled it. To put the matter in another way: the revelation of God's saving love and power in Jesus entitles and requires me to believe that

God purposes the salvation of all men, but it does not entitle me to believe that this purpose is to be accomplished in any way which ignores or bypasses the historic event by which it was in fact revealed and effected.

3. The accomplishment of this saving purpose is to be by way of and through a real history—a history whose center is defined by the events which took place "under Pontius Pilate." The end envisaged is the reconciliation of all things in heaven and earth in Christ (Col. 1:20), the "summing up of all things in Christ" (Eph. 1:10), the liberation of the entire creation from its bondage (Rom. 8:19-21). The object to which God's purpose of grace is directed is the whole creation and the whole human family, not human souls conceived as billions of separate monads each detached from its place in the whole fabric of the human and natural world. To think in this way and then to engage in speculations about which of these monads will finally reach the goal and which will not is to distort the biblical picture out of all recognition. The salvation which is promised in Christ and of which his bodily resurrection is the firstfruit, is not to be conceived simply as the fulfillment of the personal spiritual history of each individual human being. To speak in this way is to depart both from Scripture and from a true understanding of what it is to be a person. We are fully persons only with and through others, and in Christ we know that our personal history is so rooted in Christ that there can be no final salvation for each of us until he has "seen of the travail of his soul" and is satisfied (Isa. 53:11). The New Testament itself suggests at many points the need for the patience this requires (Heb. 11:39-40; Rev. 6:9-11). The logic which leads the writer to the Hebrews to say of the saints of former days that "apart from us they should not be made perfect" surely did not cease to operate with the first century. We must equally say that we, and all who are called to the service of God's universal promise of blessing, cannot be made perfect, cannot be saved apart from all who have not yet had the opportunity to respond to the promise. This is the theological context, surely, in which we should try to understand the place in God's purpose of all

those millions who have lived and died out of reach of the story which we believe to be the clue to universal history.

4. Because this salvation is a real consummation of universal history and not simply the separate consummation of individual personal lives conceived as abstracted from the public life of which they are a part, it follows that an essential part of the history of salvation is the history of the bringing into obedience to Christ of the rich multiplicity of ethical, cultural, and spiritual treasures which God has lavished upon mankind. The way in which this is to be understood is shown in the well-known verses from the fourth Gospel.

> I have yet many things to say to you, but you cannot bear them now. When the Spirit of truth comes, he will guide you into all the truth; for he will not speak on his own authority, but whatever he hears he will speak, and he will declare to you the things that are to come. He will glorify me, for he will take what is mine and declare it to you. All that the Father has is mine; therefore I said that he will take what is mine and declare it to you (John 16:12-15)

We can spell out what is said here in a threefold form.

(a) What can be given to and grasped by this group of first-century Jews is limited by the time and place and circumstances of their lives. It is true knowledge of the only true God and in that sense it is the full revelation of God (John 17:3, 6). But it is not yet the fullness of all that is to be manifested.

(b) It will be the work of the Holy Spirit to lead this little community, limited as it now is within the narrow confines of a single time and place and culture, into "the truth as a whole" and specifically into an understanding of "the things that are to come"—the world history that is still to be enacted.

(c) This does not mean, however, that they will be led beyond or away from Jesus. Jesus is the Word made flesh, the Word by which all that is came to be, and is sustained in being. Consequently, all the gifts which the Father has lavished on mankind belong in fact to Jesus, and it will be the work of the Spirit to restore them to their true owner. All these gifts will be truly received and understood when the Holy Spirit takes them and declares their true meaning and use to the church.

We have here the outline of the way in which we are to understand the witness of the church in relation to all the gifts which God has bestowed upon mankind. It does not suggest that the church go into the world as the body with nothing to receive and everything to give. Quite the contrary: the church has yet much to learn. This passage suggests a trinitarian model which will guide our thinking as we proceed. The Father is the giver of all things. They all belong rightly to the Son. It will be the work of the Spirit to guide the church through the course of history into the truth as a whole by taking all God's manifold gifts given to all mankind and declaring their true meaning to the church as that which belongs to the Son. The end to which it all looks is "a plan for the fulness of time, to unite all things to him, things in heaven and things on earth" (Eph. 1:10). The apostle, looking at the marvelous events by which the Gentiles who were outside of the covenant have been brought into it and made members of the household of God, can see in them the signs of the accomplishment of this purpose. As we, from a longer experience of the church's mission to all the nations, look back upon the story of the church and trace its encounter first with the rich culture of the Hellenic world and then with one after another of the cultures of mankind, we can see, with many distractions and perversions and misunderstandings, the beginnings of the fulfillment of this promise.

5. The church, therefore, as it is *in via*, does not face the world as the exclusive possessor of salvation, nor as the fullness of what others have in part, the answer to the questions they ask, or the open revelation of what they are anonymously. The church faces the world, rather, as *arrabōn* of that salvation—as sign, firstfruit, token, witness of that salvation which God purposes for the whole. It can do so only because it lives by the Word and sacraments of the gospel by which it is again and again brought to judgment at the foot of

the cross. And the bearer of that judgment may well be and often is a man or woman of another faith (cf. Luke 11:31–32). The church is in the world as the place where Jesus, on whom all the fullness of the godhead dwells, is present, but it is not itself that fullness. It is the place where the filling is taking place (Eph. 1:23). It must therefore live always in dialogue with the world, bearing its witness to Christ but always in such a way that it is open to receive the riches of God which belong properly to Christ but have to be brought to him. This dialogue, this life of continuous exchange with the world, means that the church itself is changing. It must change if "all that the Father has" is to be given to it as Christ's own possession (John 16:14–15). It does change. Very obviously the church of the Hellenic world in the fourth century was different from the church which met in the upper room in Jerusalem. It will continue to change as it meets ever new cultures and lives in faithful dialogue with them.

6. One may sum up—or at least indicate the direction of—this part of the argument by means of a picture. We have looked at and rejected a series of models which could be expressed in pictures. We will suggest (following Walter Freytag) a simple sketch which may serve to indicate the true basis for dialogue between Christians and those of other faiths.[6] It will be something like this:

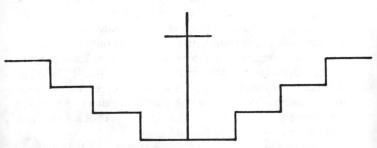

The staircases represent the many ways by which man learns to rise up towards the fulfillment of God's purpose. They include all the ethical and religious achievements which so richly adorn the cultures of humankind. But in the middle of them is placed a symbol which represents something of a different kind—a historic deed in which God exposed himself in a total vulnerability to all our purposes and in that meeting exposed us as the beloved of God who are, even in our highest religion, the enemies of God. The picture expresses the central paradox of the human situation, that God comes to meet us at the bottom of our stairways, not at the top; that our real ascent towards God's will for us takes us further away from the place where he actually meets us. "I came to call not the righteous, but sinners." Our meeting, therefore, with those of other faiths, takes place at the bottom of the stairway, not at the top. "Christianity" as it develops in history takes on the form of one of those stairways. The Christian also has to come down to the bottom of his stairway to meet the person of another faith. There has to be a *kenosis*, a "self-emptying." The Christian does not meet his partner in dialogue as one who possesses the truth and the holiness of God but as one who bears witness to a truth and holiness which are God's judgment on him and who is ready to hear the judgment spoken through the lips and life of his partner of another faith.

III

On the basis which has been laid down one can speak briefly of the purpose with which the Christian enters into dialogue with people of other faiths. This purpose can only be obedient witness to Jesus Christ. Any other purpose, any goal which subordinates the honor of Jesus Christ to some purpose derived from another source, is impossible for the Christian. To accept such another purpose would involve a denial of the total lordship of Jesus Christ. A Christian cannot try to evade the accusation that, for him, dialogue is part of his obedient witness to Jesus Christ.

But this does not mean that the purpose of dialogue is to persuade the non-Christian partner to accept the Christianity of the Christian partner. Its purpose is not that Christianity should acquire one more recruit. On the contrary, *obedient* witness to Christ means that whenever we come with another person (Christian or not) into the presence of the cross, we are prepared to receive judgment and correction, to find that our Christianity hides within its appearance of obedience the reality of disobedience. Each meeting with a non-Christian partner in dialogue therefore puts my own Christianity at risk.

The classic biblical example of this is the meeting of Peter with the Gentile Cornelius at Caesarea. We often speak of this as the conversion of Cornelius, but it was equally the conversion of Peter. In that encounter the Holy Spirit shattered Peter's own deeply cherished image of himself as an obedient member of the household of God. ("No, Lord; for I have never eaten anything that is common or unclean.") It is true that Cornelius was converted, but it is also true that "Christianity" was changed. One decisive step was taken on the long road from the incarnation of the Word of God as a Jew of first-century Palestine to the summing up of *all things* in him.

The purpose of dialogue for the Christian is obedient witness to Jesus Christ, who is not the property of the church but the Lord of the church and of all people and who is glorified as the living Holy Spirit takes all that the Father has given to humankind—all people of every creed and culture—and declares it to the church as that which belongs to Christ as Lord. In this encounter the church is changed, the world is changed, and Christ is glorified.

NOTES

1. Perhaps the best-known example is J. N. Farquhar, *The Crown of Hinduism* (Madras: Oxford Univ. Press, 1915).

2. *The Missionary Message* (New York: Revell, 1910), p. 247.

3. Jerusalem Report I, p. 491.

4. Karl Rahner, *Theological Investigations* (London: Darton, Longman & Todd, 1966), vol. 5, *Later Writings*, pp. 115-34.

5. Hans Küng, *On Being a Christian* (Garden City, N.Y.: Doubleday, 1976), pp. 99.

6. Walter Freytag, *The Gospel and the Religions* (London: SCM Press, 1957), p. 21.

Christ's Lordship and Religious Pluralism

Pietro Rossano

At the close of the Second Vatican Council in 1965, the
Roman Catholic Church promulgated the "Declaration
on the Relation of the Church to Non-Christian Religions." A decade and a half later, Pietro Rossano, Secretary of the Vatican Secretariat for Non-Christians, reflects on the same theme in the light of the Vatican
Council statement, further theological insights, and practice. He analyzes the persistent religious quest and the
resulting plurality of religions "as socio-cultural structures with doctrines, moral and ritual elements." He
bases his evaluation of human religious phenomena on
Christ as the perfect image of the perfect human. And he
emphasizes that the biblical data include not only God's
actions toward Jews and Christians, but also his universal actions described by "Wisdom economy." Rossano,
an Italian scholar, then outlines new Roman Catholic
theological stances toward the world religions, as well as
the questions which remain. This was originally a lecture
presented at a consultation held at Union Theological
Seminary in Richmond, Virginia in October 1979, and
was published—along with responses from other
scholars and a reply by Msgr. Rossano—in the volume
of proceedings from the conference, *Christ's Lordship
and Religious Pluralism*, edited by Gerald H. Anderson
and Thomas F. Stransky (Maryknoll, N.Y.: Orbis
Books, 1981).

As a representative of the Vatican Secretariat for Non-
Christians, I shall relate my comments to what was stated in
the Second Vatican Council and in the subsequent documents
of the Roman Catholic Church, from Paul VI's 1975 Exhorta-

tion on Evangelization (*Evangelii Nuntiandi*) which resulted from the 1974 Synod of Bishops, to John Paul II's 1979 Encyclical on the Redemption of Man (*Redemptor Hominis*).

I. From the Religious Quest to Religions

In its declaration *Nostra Aetate* the Second Vatican Council started from the existential religious quest that today, as in the past, springs up in the human heart: "What is man? What is the meaning, the purpose of life? What is the moral good and what is sin? Whence suffering, and what purpose does it serve? Where lies the path to true happiness? What is the truth about death, judgment and retribution beyond the grave? What, finally, is that ultimate inexpressible mystery which encompasses our existence: whence do we come, and where are we going?" (n. 1).[1]

Clement of Alexandria (ca. 150–215) saw these same questions raised in his own time,[2] and that they were formulated in the same terms some centuries before Christ in the *Svetasvatara Upanishad* (1, 1). Such questions have not ceased; today they have become more acute by developments in science and technology.[3]

These universal questions are rooted in the very structure of man, and therefore reveal a specific dimension of the human person. Psychologists speak of "psychogenous" or spiritual needs, before which "science" is impotent. Such questions contain a spectrum of elements and different nuances according to different ethnic and cultural families. But they also indisputably reveal convergent and analogical features: a search for origins, for the ultimate cause and final destiny; a reaching out beyond what is visible and transient; a flight from the river of suffering to reach the banks of quiet and peace; an aspiration towards a highest Good that does not deceive or disappoint; a search for what is permanent amid the contrasts of change; a thirst for a life that is fulfilling and happy; a desire for perfect relationship and for social and cosmic harmony; a fleeing from fear, frustration in the face of death and unavoidable evil; a longing for protection and security; an unspoken expectation of liberation and salvation; a rebellion against limits and injustice; the torment of being torn between the experience of transcendence and the experience of finitude, between the good that one wishes to do and the evil to which one is inclined; the thirst for communication with a perfect Thou. The human person searches for more, for a "*novum*" that liberates and heals, develops and fulfills.

The Christian pursues this religious quest in common with Muslims and Buddhists, with Taoists and with the followers of the African religions; in fact, with every human being, even with those who declare themselves alien to any religious faith.

From the religious quest it is but a small step to the religions as socio-cultural structures with doctrinal, moral, and ritual elements. These religions represent the social and ritual codification of the replies to the existential quest of entire generations. They are the "accumulated traditions" on which the "personal faith" of individuals rests.[4] To the variety of religious quests there corresponds a plurality of replies. It is here that the plurality of religions is born. The history and phenomenology of religions are concerned with their distinction and classification. One evident distinction is between the religions of historical-prophetic monotheism (Judaism, Christianity, Islam), and those of a monistic nature, with their theo-cosmo-anthropic character. One could also speak of religions of self-realization (Hinduism, Buddhism), of cosmic and social integration (Taoism, Confucianism, Shintoism, African religions), and of submission to and dialogue with God (Judaism, Christianity, Islam).

Historically, whence does this plurality of religions arise? Besides the very complexity of the religious quest, itself the bearer of a multitude of particular queries, we should consider the ethnic particularity (the so-called "genius" or character of each people), the variety of ecological, historical and cultural experiences, the elusiveness of the goal and of the object pursued, and the limitations of the human subject. But, in answer to that question, we must not undervalue the crucial importance of religious founders and leaders, whose experience has become the paradigm for innumerable numbers of followers. Here the aphorism "*paucis vivit genus humanum''* is apt: the entire human family lives under the influence of a few persons.

II. Religious Pluralism and the Search for Truth

The experience of the variety of religious traditions creates a great problem for every human conscience. This pluralism is, in fact, irreducible. It is marked by exclusions, contrasts, jealousies, absolutisms, all of them well known to the science of religions. They have drawn upon religions the accusation of being elements of division in the human family. Sometimes they have aroused contempt and scepticism towards the religions themselves.

The problem must not be minimized. Despite every attempt at establishing the union and harmonization of religions, it is scientifically certain that the Christian ''way'' is different from the Buddhist ''path''; that Hindu ''liberation'' is not the ''submission'' of Islam; that the ''life'' sought in African religious practices is not comparable to that offered by Gnostic or tantric traditions; that the aim of *bhakti* is not that of Zen; and so on. To this historical-phenomenological diversity one must add that every religious tradition has its own way of evaluating other religions. Each has its own ''theology of religions''; they stretch from writing-off and rejecting all others as aberrant, to the legitimization of all, as with Hinduism (although by doing this, Hinduism imposes its own specific dogma of the equivalence of every religion).[5]

A reasonable person concludes that systems of such diversity and contrast cannot possibly be considered equally valid and true. In fact, from the very origins of the Church, the enquiry concerning the true religion and the true worship of God (*de vera religione; de vero Dei cultu*) has been a feature of the Christian conscience. The religious journeys of Justin, Augustine, Hilary of Poitiers, to name only a few, are widely known. Nor can the quest for truth along the human religious pilgrimage be disregarded today even in the name of a legitimate pluralism in the social field. The person is bound to search for truth as it affects both one's manner of life and one's destiny.

That is why at the beginning of its *Declaration on Religious Freedom,* the Second Vatican Council states: "All are bound to seek the truth, especially in what concerns God and his Church and to embrace the truth they come to know, and hold fast to it. . . . It is in accordance with their dignity as persons . . . that all should be at once impelled by nature and also bound by moral obligation to seek the truth, especially religious truth. They are also bound to adhere to the truth, once it is known, and to order their whole lives in accord with the demands of the truth. . . . Truth, however, is to be sought after in a manner proper to the dignity of the human person and his social nature. The inquiry is to be free."[6]

III. For the Christian, Christ is the Religious Truth

For the Christian, the truth is Christ who is "the way, the truth and the life" (Jn. 14:6), "the center of the universe and of history."[7] The Christian is obliged to justify rationally and historically his act of faith in Christ, in whom "one finds the fullness of religious life,"[8] the "*novum*" that God the Creator has given and offers to human beings within their history, and the key to decipher all the religious traditions of humankind.

In fact, the New Testament bears witness to a significant process of development in the Christian's knowledge of Christ. This begins with the amazement of the crowds and the disciples (the "pre-Easter" period, cf. Mk. 1:27–28), then moves on to the Easter faith that acknowledges Him to be Lord and God (cf. Jn. 20:28–29), and further on to the proclamation of Him as the sole mediator of salvation (cf. Acts 4:12). Then later, in the apostolic age, Christian reflection begins to unravel the implications of what faith in Him involves in the context of Jewish monotheism and the religious traditions of the time. The Prologue of John, the Christology of the Letters to the Ephesians and to the Colossians, and of the Book of Revelation, speak of the universal sovereignty of Christ over time and history. He is "the Alpha and the Omega, the first and the last, the beginning and the end" (Rev. 22:13; cf. 1:17–18). He is "the Lamb, slain before the foundation of the world'' (Rev. 13:8; cf. 1 Pt. 1:19–20; Rom. 16:25–26), the Lamb slain and victor, who holds the scroll of the historical events (Rev. 5:6–8); "in Him we have been chosen before the foundation of the world'' (Eph. 1:4). St. Paul identifies Christ with the Wisdom of God (1 Cor. 1:24–30). In Paul's catechesis, as reflected in the Letter to the Romans (2:9–11, 28–29), in the Pastoral Letters (1 Tim. 2:5; Tit. 2:11) and in the discourses recounted in Acts (14:15–17; 17:22–28), he recognizes the universal dimensions of the salvific action of God centered in Christ.

The New Testament thus furnishes authoritative premises for a reflection on the universal sovereignty of Christ over history and over the world religions. Such premises gave rise to a difficult but fruitful development in the first five centuries of the Church. This reflection was later halted by an historically understandable religious isolationism, and emerged only in some outstanding figures who, as it were, passed on the torch through the centuries: from the philosopher Justin Martyr, who recognized in Christ a spiritual sovereignty over humankind even before His appearance in history, to Irenaeus, Clement, Origen, Augustine, the Pseudo-Dionysius, and Basil. Later we find the solitary figures of Raymond Lull, Bonaventure, Nicholas of Cusa, Thomas More, Matteo Ricci, John Henry Newman, J. N. Farquhar, Otto Karrer, until such time as the change in the historical situation urgently called Christians courageously to resume their reflection on Christ, "the center of the universe and of history." Such mediation sees Christ as Him in whom all things were created; to whom all is directed; in whom all subsists (Col. 1:16–17); in whom God will reconcile all things with Himself (Col. 1:16, 17–20); Christ who comes into the world where His light is already present (Jn. 1:1–10); Christ the same today as He was yesterday and will be for ever (Heb. 13:8); in whom every person finds salvation, whether one lived before or after Him.[9] As John V. Taylor, the Anglican Bishop of Winchester, incisively observes, this means that "from the beginning the world was held in existence by the Redeemer who was to die. . . . Being forgiven is therefore a more primary condition of man than being a sin-

ner. Being in Christ is a more essential human state than
being in ignorance of Christ."[10]

IV. The Religions in the Light of Christ Pantokrator

For the Christian, every theological evaluation of the
human religious phenomenon is based on this image of
Christ. It was already delineated in the New Testament and
then developed in the early centuries when the churches were
confronted with the religious traditions prevalent in the
Mediterranean area. Today as we face the immense problem
of the religious pluralism of humankind, let us see what can
be drawn from this same image of Christ.

Above all, this Christology allows us theologically to
interpret and appreciate the religious quest. This religious
search, a constant feature of the human heart, is perceived
as the expression and existential epiphany of the creature-
hood of man and of his being called to Christ. God moves
men and women to seek Him, and, it may be, to touch and
find Him, though He is not far from any of them (Acts
17:27). This "instinct of the inviting God"[11] is Christocentric because Christ is the future of man, the image of the
perfect human on whom we are modelled (1 Cor. 15:48–49;
cf. 2 Cor. 3:18). The unity and the variety of the religious
quest are thus seen as the fruit of the inexhaustible riches of
the human family which the creative wisdom of God has
apportioned among individuals, families, and nations. The
Christological hymn of the Letter to the Colossians (1:15–20)
turns on the axis "He-and-all," namely, the multiplicity of
creatures, and their origin and destiny in Christ.

In the light of Christ Pantokrator a theological understanding of the religions in their diversity, continuing presence and vitality, becomes possible. If it is historically true
that the variety of religions depends on the particular genius
and character of each people, and on their history and existential situation, one may also theologically assert that each
religion represents the traditional manner of response of a
given people to the gift and enlightenment of God. It is a

response given with a particular frame of culture and language, which often makes extremely difficult the relation and communication of religions among themselves.

By stating this we do justice both to the divine and to the human element present in each religion. In his Encyclical *Redemptor Hominis* (no. 12), Pope John Paul II writes of religions in this sense as the "marvellous heritage of the human spirit," and of their values as "the work of the Spirit of God who breathes where he will" (Jn. 3:8). The assertion does not imply that the religions contain different revelations of God, as if God had revealed Himself in one way to one people and in another way to another. The historical revelation in Jesus Christ is one thing, the "light that enlightens every man" (Jn. 1:9) is another.

If the illumination given by the Word is the same, the responses are different. An analogy may be found in the colors that shimmer on a surface touched by the same ray of light, or in the different sounds which come from various musical instruments in the hands of the same musician. From the striking polyvalence or difference of the human subject there is born the variety of human response. But this is also the consequence of that transcendence and immeasurability of the light of the Word: no human language or culture can express or reflect it in an adequate way.

Yet the human person can also resist, even refuse the inner action of the Spirit. One is capable of disobeying God and turning in on oneself, even to the point of subordinating religion to one's ego. "Both the obedience and the disobedience gets built into the tradition and passed on to later generations. And they, in their turn, may respond more readily to the unceasing calls and disclosures of the Spirit, and so be moved to reform some part of the tradition."[12] The religions in history are in a continual process of transformation, of progress and reform, of conservation and development, both under the influence of circumstances and, at best, under the action of the Spirit of Christ active in their adherents. As for the salvific function of these religions, namely, whether they are or are not paths to salvation, there is no doubt that "grace and truth" are given through Jesus Christ and by his Spirit (cf. Jn. 1:17). Everything would lead one to conclude, however, that gifts of "grace and truth" do reach or may reach the hearts of men and women through the visible, experiential signs of the various religions. The Second Vatican Council is explicit on this point.[13]

A more problematic area is the theological judgment on the significance and role of spiritual leaders and the founders of religions. In the light of Christ, Lord of the universe and of history, spiritual gifts may be given to individual people at particular moments of history and society, in order that they may give witness to and promote values which are fundamental to man's ultimate good. Such values may be the primacy of God, detachment from self and from worldly values, ascesis and mastery over body and spirit, submission to the will of God, the law of conscience, the urgency of seeking salvation, the practice of justice, the upholding of harmony and order in family and society, methods of truth and nonviolence, and so on.

In the biblical tradition, personalities who have the characteristics of religious leaders, such as Melchisedech, Job, and Cyrus, are related to Christ as signs and images of His coming. The seer of the Book of Revelation sees underneath the altar of heaven, along with the souls of those martyred "for the word of God," also those witnesses who gave their life "for the witness they bore" (Rev. 6:9). Could it not be that he is speaking of those who have struggled and suffered in order to affirm spiritual and moral values among men and women?[14]

V. A Universalist Reading of the Bible

There is a further step. Contemporary experience of religious pluralism not only stimulates Christians to meditate on the vast horizons of Christology, but invites them to reread the Bible itself from Genesis to the Book of Revelation, and so to discern the divine plan in universal history. It is often said that the Bible is ethnocentric because its dominant theme is the action of God towards the Jews and towards Christians.

This is true, but the very experience of our age calls us to rediscover also the universal perspectives of the Bible.

The Vatican Council's *Dei Verbum* and *Nostra Aetate* distinguish two dimensions, or if one prefers, two moments in God's action towards men and women. Both moments are documented in the sacred books: a universal aspect and a Jewish-Christian aspect. There is the economy of the covenant granted to Israel and to the Christians, and there is the sapiential economy in which all people are embraced. The Priestly Code already recognized a plurality of covenants, and the rabbis distinguished between the covenant of Moses, established with the Israelites, and that of Noah, a covenant which embraces all the peoples of the earth.

By "sapiential economy" I refer to the action of God through Wisdom. This is described in the great collection of the so-called Wisdom literature, but also in the first chapters of Genesis, in parts of Deuteronomy, in the prophets, and in the New Testament writings. Both economies, that of the Mosaic covenant and that of Wisdom, are, in a New Testament perspective, joined and fused in Jesus. He is the "elect," the "beloved of God," and the "son," in whom Israel is resumed. But he is also the "Wisdom of God," present throughout the universe. We could say that in one hand Jesus holds the children of Israel, and in the other hand, all the peoples of the earth.

This is not the place to develop and illustrate the Wisdom economy in any detail. I only present it as the backdrop upon which the Jewish-Christian economy with its own function and specific purpose is woven, and I emphasize that the significance and value of the religious traditions of humankind are illuminated by it. Wisdom is with God and proceeds from God (Prov. 2:6; 8:22–23; Sir. 24:1–3, 9; Wis. 7:25–26; 8:4; 9:4); Wisdom is present throughout all creation, among every people and nation, and rejoices to dwell among human beings (Prov. 8:23–31; Sir. 24:6; Wis. 8:1). Indeed Wisdom is given to every one as the "eye of God in the heart," (Sir. 17:6–8) and in every generation "she passes into holy souls and makes them friends of God and prophets" (Wis. 7:27).[15] She

is the source of right and perfect conduct because she teaches
fear of God and justice towards men and women (Prov. 3:7;
8:13; Sir. 17:14). Wisdom is the source of salvation for those
who welcome her and brings assurance of immortality near
to, and in friendship with God (Wis. 6:19-20, 24; 7:14;
8:27-28). She is life for the person who finds her (Prov.
8:35), and her fruits are virtues (i.e. the virtues of the Greeks:
self-control and prudence, justice and courage, cf. Wis. 8:7).
However, Wisdom is incarnated in a special way in the Torah
of Israel (Sir. 24:8-11; Bar. 4:37-38). The Bible sees, then, a
link between Wisdom and the ethical religious life of humankind.

I mentioned that besides the Wisdom economy, a reread-
ing of the Scriptures with the plurality of religions in mind
throws light on other aspects which are useful for a theological evaluation of these same religions. For example, from
Genesis to the Book of Revelation, the covenant and revelation—namely the relationship of God with His people—
are regularly presented according to the categories and
religious forms of the milieu (Mesopotamian, Egyptian,
Canaanian, Hellenistic), and Israel responds to the covenant,
positively or negatively, in the framework of the religious
psychology of the time.

Thus, the religions as such do not appear in antithesis to
God's self-communication but as the providential means, the
concrete and historical instruments of the God-man relationship in the Bible, even if many of their elements clearly
require purification and transformation before being assumed
or taken up. Friedrich Heiler observed that in the biblical
tradition the religious nature feasts (*Naturfeste*) were transformed into celebrations of the history of salvation (*Heils-
geschichtliche Feste*) without, however, entirely losing their
original meaning: thus the Sabbath, the Pasch, Pentecost,
the feast of the Tabernacles, the feast of Purim, the Hanuk-
ka, and, we could add, the Christian Christmas. At this
point we are confronted by one of "the greatest revolutions in
the history of religions."[16] According to the biblical tradition, therefore, a bond and a theological relationship exist
between religious expressions and the historical event of sal-

vation. Examples could be multiplied both for the Old and the New Testament. We may conclude that the creating and enlightening Word, present in history even before His Incarnation, secretly prepares, sustains, purifies, and finally takes up what humanity achieves in its laborious search for the absolute and for salvation.

The Bible appears to be hostile towards the religions only when they represent a threat to the covenant, or assume forms of a cosmic and vitalistic monism, or draw people to worship idols and thus substitute the creature for the Creator. But when the Bible encounters forms of pure religion or forms that are reconcilable with faith in the God of the Covenant, it welcomes them and takes them up. One need only refer to the cases of Melchisedech, or Jethro and of Job; these are non-Jewish religious personalities who are nevertheless recognized and praised for their faith.

VI. A New Attitude of the Church Toward the Religions

At this point a query arises on the relationship of the Church to the religions. *Nostra Aetate* represents the first time in its history that the Roman Catholic Church has faced this question in such an official way. This Declaration in many ways implies a new mentality, and in it we can distinguish two approaches. There is, first of all, a global approach to the world religions. In comparison with the attitude prevalent in many past centuries, this approach is certainly new and uses such terms as *esteem, respect, dialogue, proclamation, witness*. Secondly, there is a differentiated approach to the individual religions according to the nature of each; this had already been delineated in *Lumen Gentium* (n. 16).

What is the global approach? It can be summed up in two words: *proclamation* and *dialogue*. Proclamation is something the Church cannot deny itself. The very reason for the Church's existence is to proclaim the marvelous deeds of God (*mirabilia Dei*) in history, which culminate, in the "fullness of time," in the death and resurrection of Christ. In Pauline terminology, the purpose of the Church is to proclaim, announce, make known, manifest, tell, enlighten, teach[17] the *mysterion* hidden through previous centuries but now revealed and made known so that it may be proclaimed to all peoples and nations. In the context of religious pluralism, this proclamation must be carried out with fidelity and frankness.

But every time that the Vatican Council documents mention mission or proclamation, they also speak of esteem and respect for the religions, and of dialogue. Dialogue means that the herald of the Gospel should know the persons to whom one speaks and to respect them in their cultural and religious identity. This requires a high degree of listening to the other in depth, to let oneself be judged by the other and to understand the other's objections towards ourselves. It also means we give an account for the hope that is in us (1 Pt. 3:15), putting forward the Gospel in its own identity, free from the cultural accretions with which it is clothed in ourselves, and offering it not as a destructive force but as liberating and perfecting the values the other already possesses.

Dialogue thus requires a long and thorough hermeneutical effort both to enter into the other's horizon of meaning and to be able to point out the meaning the message has for him. As a consequence, dialogue brings the happy experience that every opening to the values and objections of the other implies a deepening and a fuller knowledge of the very message that the Church proclaims.[18] That is why, in the context of dialogue, among all the images used to designate the Gospel I find the most inspiring are those which refer to it as "little seed," "leaven," "salt," "graft," "unction," "seal"; namely the Gospel as a principle which does not destroy but "conserves, purifies and perfects," "heals, ennobles and perfects," as key expressions of Vatican II's vocabulary put it.[19] "Mission and dialogue," as the Protestant scholar Horst Bürkle observes regarding this couple that constantly recurs in the documents of the Vatican Council, "are so related to one another as to constitute a reciprocal guarantee against possible abuses: that the missionary effort does not become a plagiarism of Western type Christianity, and that dialogue does not degenerate into the exercise of making sterile historical comparison."[20]

While I have referred to the global approach of the

Council towards the religions, I must immediately add that the Church's approach varies in tone and emphasis in relation to particular religions. The Church stands in a different existential relationship with each: *Nostra Aetate* moves from the simpler and less structured religions to Hinduism, Buddhism, Islam, and to the Jewish people with whom there is a unique "spiritual bond." *Lumen Gentium* (n. 16) begins with "the people from whom Christ was born according to the flesh," and goes on to the Muslims who adhering to the faith of Abraham "along with us adore the one and merciful God, who on the last day will judge humankind." The document then speaks of those who seek an unknown God "in shadows and images," then concludes with those "who have not yet arrived at an explicit knowledge of God, but who strive to live a good life, thanks to His grace."

Each religion is seen in terms of its specific relationship to the Church: the relationship with Judaism which was her forerunner, expressed her and then rejected her, but which still accompanies her in history in accordance with "a mystery" of God; the relationship with Islam, with which the Church is linked by faith in Abraham and the prophets, by faith in Jesus, son of the Virgin Mary, word and spirit of God, and judge of history; the relationship with Hinduism in its numerous historical expressions, some of them clearly influenced by Christianity; the relationship with Buddhism in its journey towards the Permanent; the relationship with Confucianism, Taoism, and the African religions.

In each of these religious groupings the Christian finds various values, and responds to them accordingly in a process of give-and-take. A consequence of the mutual presence of mission and dialogue in the Church is that Christians find themselves in the uncomfortable but stimulating situation of being at one and the same time heralds and disciples, pilgrims and eschatological witnesses, people-with-others and people-for-others. Christians journey with others, seek with others, are enriched together with others, enrich others, and are enriched by them, by their anthropological, metaphysical, ascetical, mystical, and ritual values, "to share with them" in the Gospel of Christ (cf. 1 Cor. 9:23).

This twofold fidelity of the Christian to the "riches of creation" and to the Gospel message, to the religious traditions of humankind and to the Christ-event, depends ultimately on the acceptance of the universal sovereignty of Christ: Christ is the Word of God already "present in the world" and yet who "comes into the world," as we see in the double image of John's Prologue, to give to all "the power to become children of God" and to walk in His light (Jn. 1:12; Rev. 21:23–24; cf. AG 1).

In this perspective we can conclude by saying that Christ is seen as the origin, center, and destiny of the various religions, as He who brought them to birth, takes them up, purifies them, and fulfills them in order to take them to their eschatological goal, so that "God may be all in all" (1 Cor. 15:28; cf. LG 17; AG 11). This does not mean that our journey will be easy or that we can see the route it will take. There remain many difficult and complex questions to which Christians must devote attention and energies. For example, how in practice may the universal nature of the Christian message be reconciled with a respect for the spiritual traditions of others? If and how can fidelity to Christ and a particular religious tradition be reconciled? What is the relationship between the universal gift of God to those of goodwill and that communicated in the faith and sacraments of the Church community? How are we to relate what is received through faith in Christ with what was given previously? What is the relationship between the universal enlightenment through the Word and the historical revelation of the Gospel? How can a religious tradition be called a vehicle of the grace of God if it appears to be alien to Him and even opposed to Him? What is the real contribution of various religions to the Christian message if it only means our making explicit what is already in them?

This is why the Christian's attitude to the religions of the world is one both of humility and respect, and of frankness in giving witness to Christ, the Word that enlightens every person, *paratus semper nuntiare, paratus semper doceri,* always ready to announce, always ready to be taught.

NOTES

1. The Second Vatican Council documents are here quoted by abbreviating the first two Latin words which are each document's official titles. Thus,

NA: *Nostra Aetate* (On the Relation of the Church to Non-Christian Religions)

LG: *Lumen Gentium* (On the Church)

GS: *Gaudium et Spes* (On the Church in the Modern World)

DH *Dignitatis Humanae* (On Religious Freedom)

AG: *Ad Gentes* (On the Missionary Activity of the Church)

DV: *Dei Verbum* (On Divine Revelation)

The numbers refer to the document's paragraphs.

2. *Excerpts from Theodotus,* 78,2.

3. Cf. GS, n. 10.

4. Distinction and terminology from W. Cantwell Smith, *The Meaning and End of Religion* (New York: New American Library, 1964).

5. Cf. R. J. Werblowsky, *Beyond Tradition and Modernity: Changing Religions in a Changing World* (London: Athowe, 1976), chapter 6.

6. DH, nn. 1-3. The duty of seeking religious truth, the right to seek it freely and of not accepting inner constrictions in religious commitment and public profession was the subject of thorough reflection at the Second Vatican Council.

7. John Paul II, Encyclical *Redemptor Hominis,* n. 1.

8. NA, n. 2.

9. LG, n. 2.

10. John V. Taylor, "The Theological Basis of Interfaith Dialogue," *International Review of Mission,* October 1979, p. 379. Cf. the vigorous expressions on man's relation to Christ in *Redemptor Hominis,* n. 14.

11. "*Instinctus Dei invitantis,*" Thomas Aquinas, *Summa Theologiae,* II-II, q. 2, art. 9, ad 3.

12. J. V. Taylor, *op. cit.,* p. 376.

13. Cf. AG, n. 3; GS, n. 32.

14. Cf. A Feuillet, "Les martyrs de l'humanité et l'Agneau égorgé. Une interprétation nouvelle de la prière des égorgés en Ap. 6:9-11," *Nouvelle Revue Théologique* (March-April, 1977), pp. 183-207.

15. Origen had already interpreted this text as referring to the saints and wise men of the ancient world, *Contra Celsum,* IV 3.7.8.

16. F. Heiler, *Erscheinungsformen und Wesen der Religion* (Stuttgart: Kohlhammer, 1961), p. 155.

17. Cf. "proclaim," 1 Cor. 2:1; "announce," Eph. 3:8; "make known," Rom. 16:26; "manifest," Col. 4:3; "tell," Col. 4:4; "enlighten," Eph. 3:9; "teach," Col. 1:28.

18. *Redemptor Hominis, op. cit.,* n. 11.

19. Cf. LG, n. 17; AG, nn. 3, 9, and 11.

20. H. Bürkle, *Einführung in die Theologie der Religionen* (Darmstadt: Wissenschaftliche Buchgesellschaft, 1977), pp. 27-28.

The Economy of the Holy Spirit

Georges Khodr

Deeply imbued with the distinctive Eastern Christian understanding of the Holy Spirit, this Greek Orthodox bishop suggests that "within God's plan, the great religions constitute training schools of the Divine Mercy." Within this context he proposes "an ecclesiology and a missiology in which the Holy Spirit necessarily occupies a supreme place." He points out the dangers of maintaining those traditional defensive attitudes shaped by history, "a hostility to error which amounted almost to hatred." "The intolerance of Christians towards each other would be reflected in their attitude to non-Christian religions. It was a case of either saving the other person or killing him!" What is on trial, claims this Metropolitan of Mount Lebanon, near Beirut, is the theology of mission itself. "Contemporary theology must go beyond the notion of 'salvation history' to rediscover the meaning of *oikonomia*," the economy of Christ which "is unintelligible without the economy of the Spirit." Christ's coming has led the whole of humankind "to its true existence and brings about spiritual renewals, economies which can take charge of human souls until He comes." "The Church's mediatorial role remains unimpaired. But the freedom of God is such that He can raise up prophets outside the sociological confines of the New Israel just as He raised them up outside the confines of Old Israel." Such is the economy of the free-acting Spirit. Khodr concludes, "True mission laughs at missionary activity. Our task is simply to follow the tracks of Christ perceptible in the shadows of other religions." This article was an address at the 1971 meeting of the

Central Committee of the World Council of Churches in Addis Ababa. First published in *The Ecumenical Review* (April 1971), it was reprinted in *The Orthodox Church in the Ecumenical Movement,* edited by Constantin G. Patelos (Geneva: WCC, 1978).

The end of the First World War brought with it a keener sense of the unity of the world. Since the end of the Second World War we have experienced a process of planetization to which the heterogeneous nature of religious creeds is a major obstacle. The increasing need for unity makes dialogue imperative if we wish to avoid a *de facto* syncretism of resurgent religions all claiming universality. In face of this resurgence of religions and a plurality which shows no signs of yielding to the Gospel, the question arises as to whether Christianity is so inherently exclusive of other religions as has generally been proclaimed up to now.

The question is of importance not only for the Christian mission but also for world peace. But this is not primarily a practical problem. It is the nature of the truth itself which is at stake here. The spiritual life we live is one thing if Christ's truth is confined within the bounds of the historical Church; it is quite a different thing if it is unrestricted and scattered throughout the world. In practice and in content, love is one thing if Christianity is exclusive and a very different thing if it is inclusive. As we see it, the problem is not simply a theological problem. It embraces the phenomenology of the religions, their comparative study, their psychology and their sociology. These other disciplines undermine a certain legalistic dogmatism which has long prevailed in Christian countries and which was based on ignorance of other religions on the part of professional theologians. Above all it is the authenticity of the spiritual life of non-Christians which raises the whole problem of Christ's presence in them. It is therefore quite nonsensical for theologians to pronounce judgement on the relationship of Christianity to the other religions if they are unable to integrate the extra-Christian data creatively and critically into their theological reflections. Theology has to be a continual two-way commerce between the biblical revelation and life, if it is to avoid sterility. Moreover, if obedience to the Master means following Him wherever we find traces of His presence, we have an obligation to investigate the authentic spiritual life of non-Christians. This raises the question of Christ's presence outside Christian history. The strikingly evangelical quality of many non-Christians obliges us, moreover, to develop an ecclesiology and a missiology in which the Holy Spirit necessarily occupies a supreme place.

Dangers of the Traditional Attitude

We shall need to go back to the Acts of the Apostles, the first book of ecclesiology, to see what place is given there to the Gentiles. In the Cornelius narrative we learn that "in every nation the man who is god-fearing and does what is right is acceptable" to God (10:35). "In past ages God allowed all nations to go their own way" (14:16) "yet he has not left you without some clue to his nature" (14:17). There is among the Gentiles a yearning for the "unknown God" (17:23), a search for the God who "is not far from each one of us, for in him we live and move, in him we exist" (17:28). But this openness to the pagan world confers no theological status on it, for the "gods made by human hands are not gods at all" (19:26). Paul is quite categorical: "a false god has no existence in the real world" (I Cor. 8:4). In Revelation, a supremely ecclesiological book, paganism is identified as a lie (21:8) and as deceit (22:15). In this respect the New Testament is not innovating on the Old Testament, where paganism is regarded by the prophets as an abomination. Nevertheless, the view of the apostle as expressed in his Areopagus speech is that the Athenians worshipped the true God without recognizing Him as the Creator. His face had not been unveiled to them. In other words, they were Christians without knowing it. Paul gave their God a name. The Name, together with its attributes, is the revelation of God. We find here the germ of a positive attitude to paganism which goes hand in hand with its complete negation, inherited from Judaism. This explains why, from the beginning,

Christian apologetics would have two different attitudes. On the one hand, the gods are identified with images of wood or stone fashioned by human hands and are regarded as demons fighting against the Lord; on the other hand, a more positive and inclusive attitude is found. The defensive hostile approach of Christian apologetics increasingly became a fixed position as dogmatics crystallized into an official body of doctrine and as the Church and Christianity assumed an identity of their own in both East and West, and as the battle against heresy aroused in the minds of apologists of all periods a hostility to error which amounted almost to hatred. Furthermore, the intolerance of Christians towards each other would be reflected in their attitude to non-Christian religions. It was a case of either saving the other person or killing him or her! Strange notion of a truth divorced from love!

On the other hand, a different style of apologetics sought to continue the approach of Paul's Areopagus speech to the Athenians. We can trace this movement, starting from Justin with his famous notion of the *logos spermatikos* present even before Christ's coming. All who have lived according to the *Logos* are Christians. For this tradition of apologetics, there is no truth independent of the direct action of God. Clement of Alexandria, the leading representative of this line of thought, sees the whole of mankind as a unity and as beloved of God. On the basis of Hebrews (1:1) he asserts that it was to the whole of mankind and not only to Israel that "God spoke in former times in fragmentary and varied fashion." Mankind as a whole is subject to a process of education (a pedagogy: we should remember that, for Paul, the pedagogue was the Law and the pupil in his care was Israel). It is not a case here of a natural or a rational law, for "the *Logos* of God . . . ordered our world, and above all this microcosm man, through the Holy Spirit" (*Protreptikos,* 1:5). Within this divine visitation, philosophy enjoys a special privilege. Not only does the Alexandrine doctor not hesitate to see it as a steppingstone to Christian philosophy, he even teaches that it "was given to the Greeks as their Testament" (*Stromata* V, 8:3). Pagan and Greek philosophies are scattered fragments of a single whole which is the *Logos.*

Origen, too, stresses the importance of philosophy as knowledge of the true God. In his opinion, certain doctrines of Christianity are no different from the teaching of the Greeks, although the latter does not have the same impact or the same attraction. Origen's original contribution, however, was to see elements of the divine in the pagan religions and in Greek mythology.

The fathers of the Church continued to respect the wisdom of antiquity, although with a clearly apparent reserve. Gregory Nazianzus declared that a number of philosophers, like Plato and Aristotle "caught a glimpse of the Holy Spirit" (*Orat*. 31;5; *PG* 36, 137 3 c). Despite his sharp criticism of idolatry, he does not shrink from declaring that he sees in the religious life of mankind "the hand of God guiding men to the true God." In order not to unduly prolong this list of citations from the fathers, let me simply mention the view of St. Augustine in the West that since the dawn of human history, men were to be found, within Israel and outside Israel, who had partaken of the mystery of salvation, and that what was known to them was in fact the Christian religion, without it having been revealed to them as such. This entire trend in patristic thought could perhaps be summed up in the following sentences of Irenaeus: "there is only one God who from beginning to end, through various economies, comes to the help of mankind" (*Adv. Haer*. III, 12:13).

It is beyond the scope of this paper to outline, even briefly, the history of Christian thought concerning other religions. Suffice it to say that in the Greek-speaking Christian Byzantine East following John Damascene, the attitude towards Islam was somewhat negative. The West, too, was negative, with a few exceptions such as Abelard and Nicholas of Cusa.

The negative evaluation of other religions obviously rests on an ecclesiology which is bound up with a history which has been lived through and with a definite outlook on history. It is certain that a theology of the kind maintained by St. Thomas Aquinas, which advocated the death of infidels, and which had earlier been preached by St. Bernard of Clairveaux, went hand in hand with the Crusades which consolidated the brutal separation between Christianity and Islam as well as that between the Christian West and the Christian East. We should also take into account the extent to which the Arabo-Byzantine wars contributed to the identification of the *oikumene* with the Church in the East. In other words, because of the armed struggle in which mediaeval Christendom, Latin and Byzantine, became involved, ecclesiology was historicized, i.e. the Church took on the sociological shape of Christian nations. The Christian world, western and eastern, was the dwelling place of peace, light and knowledge. The non-Christian world was the dwelling place of war and darkness. This was a literal adoption of the Moslem distinction between *Dar el Islam* (the realm of Islam) and *Dar el Kufr* (the realm of the infidels). It was also a view of the Church as an *Umma*, a numerically and sociologically defined community. This area outside the Church had to be saved. Infidels, heretics and schismatics had to be brought into the Church by missionary activity, by proselytism, or by cultural colonialism if persecution and war became unacceptable, so that there might be "one flock and one shepherd." The established, institutional Church becomes the centre of the world. The history of the Christian Church becomes history itself. What occurs in the experience of the West fashions history. The rest of the world remains a-historical until it adopts Western experience which, moreover, by implacable logic and technological determinism, is destined to dominate the world. This philosophy of history will in its turn leave its stamp on theological thought, its basic outlook and methods. Thus the religions of the under-developed countries, which have not apparently been influenced by the dynamics of creative civilization, such as Hinduism, Buddhism, Islam, and even Orthodox Christianity, being still in a historically inferior era, will have to pass into a superior stage, to be historicized, by adopting the superior hierarchical type of Christianity. The rest of the world must come into the time-continuum of the Church through a salvation achieved by the universal extension of the Christian way of life founded on the authority of the West. This attitude rests on a view of the history of salvation imported into Protestantism in the last century and which has been adopted by the whole of western Christianity since the last war. Too much emphasis has been placed on the succession of salvation events, with the result that Christ appears as the end of the history of the Old Covenant and the end of human history. The eschatological dimension of the Church's faith and life thus tends to be blurred. God is indeed within history but we forget that the divine event is the unfolding of the mystery. I shall return to this later. What I should like to emphasize here is that this linear view of history is bound up with a monolithic ecclesiological approach which, while rightly rejecting the Graeco-Asian idea of eternally recurring cycles, turns its back on the idea of an eternity transcending history and based on a conception of the Church in which Christ is seen "not merely chronologically but also and above all ontologically."

Obviously this ecclesiology and linear concept of salvation impose a specific missionary approach. The Church is then geared either to good works of a charitable and humanitarian character or else to remedial confessional and sociological work among those who are not yet incorporated into the Church. Truth lies within the boundaries of the Church; outside them, error. The remedy for all this is certainly not the application of new methods, for example, the consecration of colored bishops or adaptation to the customs and traditions of a particular people. All this will still be felt to be just a more subtle form of spiritual imperialism. What is on trial here is the theology of mission itself. One example of a tradition entirely independent of this approach is the Nestorian Church's missionary tradition, which is almost unique in its effort to nurture the spiritual development of the religions it encountered by "improving" them from within (Buddhism in Tibet and China), while not "alienating" them. Mission in this way spiritually adopts the whole of creation. We find within the Persian Church in Mesopotamia the boldest attempt at an approach to Islam. The prophetic character of Muhammad is defined in Nestorian texts on the basis of a specific analysis of the Muhammadan message. But there is no blurring of the centrality and ontological uniqueness of Christ Jesus.

It comes down to this: contemporary theology must go beyond the notion of "salvation history" in order to rediscover the meaning of the *oikonomia*. The economy of Christ cannot be reduced to its historical manifestation but indicates the fact that we are made participants in the very life of God Himself. Hence the reference to eternity and to the work of the Holy Spirit. The very notion of economy is a notion of mystery. To say mystery is to point to the strength that is breathing in the event. It also points to the freedom of God who in His work of providence and redemption is not tied down to any event. The Church is the instrument of the mystery of the salvation of the nations. It is the sign of God's love for all people. It is not over against the world, separate from it; it is part of the world. The Church is the very breath of life for humanity, the image of the humanity to come, in virtue of the light it has received. It is the life of mankind itself, even if mankind does not realize this. It is, in Origen's words, the "cosmos of the cosmos." If, as Origen also says, the Son remains "the cosmos of the Church," then clearly the Church's function is, by means of the mystery of which it is the sign, to read all the other signs which God has placed in the various times in human history. Within the religions, its task is to reveal to the world of the religions the God who is hidden within it, in anticipation of the final concrete unfolding and manifestation of the Mystery.

This *oikonomia* is not new. It starts with creation as the manifestation of God's *kenosis*. The cosmos carries the mark of God just as Jacob did after wrestling with the Angel. In that world prior to the Law, God makes a covenant with Noah. This is the starting point of dialogue with all mankind, which continues the first dialogue of creation itself. We are confronted there with a cosmic covenant which continues independently of the Abrahamic covenant. Within this covenant live the peoples who have not known the Word addressed to the father of the faithful. Scripture tells us that angels watch over them. Speaking of these angels of the nations, Origen tells us that it was they who brought the shepherds the news of Christ's birth and in doing so completed their mission. Yes, indeed, but in this sense, that

Christ himself fulfils this Noachic covenant by giving it a salvation content and significance, having himself become the true covenant between God and the cosmos. The messianic prototype is already foretold in the Old Testament figure who is his "shadow cast before."

With Abraham's call, the election of the nations of the earth becomes clearer. In him they are already the object of his election. Abraham accomplishes the first exodus by departing from his own country. The second exodus will be accomplished by the people of Israel wandering through the wilderness to Canaan down to the day when Jesus is nailed to the cross like an outsider, a foreigner. In this second exodus, Israel lives figuratively the mystery of the *oikonomia*. Israel, saved from the waters on its way to the promised land, represents saved humanity. It is as such the image of the Church saved through Christ. The election is particular but from it the economy of the mystery is deployed for the whole of humanity. Israel is saved as the type and representative of the whole of mankind. It is furthermore manifest in the Old Testament that the saving events are the antitypes of the saving event of the exodus. The Hebrews saw here, not so much a linear sequence of saving events as rather a prototypical fact imitated in other facts, the sole continuity being God's fidelity to Himself. Israel as the scene of the revelation of the Word and as a people constituted by obedience to the Word is indissolubly linked with all other peoples who have received God's visitation "at sundry times and in diverse manners" and to whose fathers and prophets, considered by the Church fathers as the saints and just men of Gentile peoples, God spoke. What matters here is that the histories of Abraham, of Moses and of David, were rich with the divine presence. The sequence of the facts is of little importance. The Old Testament authors, like Matthew in his genealogy, were concerned only with spiritually significant facts which were relevant to the messianic hope or the messianic reality.

This significant relationship to Christ is also applicable outside Israel inasmuch as the other nations have had their own types of the reality of Christ, whether in the form of persons or teachings. It is of little importance whether the religion in question was historical in character or not. It is of little importance whether it considers itself incompatible with the Gospel. Christ is hidden everywhere in the mystery of his lowliness. Any reading of religions is a reading of Christ. It is Christ alone who is received as light when grace visits a Brahmin, a Buddhist or a Muhammadan reading his or her own scriptures. Every martyr for the truth, every person persecuted for what he believes to be right, dies in communion with Christ. The mystics of Islamic countries with their witness to suffering love lived the authentic Johannine *agape*. For if the tree is known by its fruits, there is no shadow of doubt that the poor and humble folk who live for and yearn for God in all nations already receive the peace which the Lord gives to all whom He loves (Lk. 2:14).

This work of salvation outside Israel "according to the flesh" and outside the historical Church, is the result of the resurrection which fills everything with the fulness of Christ. The coming of Christ, in whom "all things are held together" (Col. 1:17) has led the whole of mankind to its true existence and brings about spiritual renewals, economies which can take charge of human souls until He comes. The Church's mediatorial role remains unimpaired. But the freedom of God is such that He can raise up prophets outside the sociological confines of the New Israel just as He raised them up outside the confines of Old Israel. But these callings to prophecy and wisdom outside the sanctuary possess a secret bond with the power of the Risen One and in no way conflict with the uniqueness of Christ's economy. The plentitude of Christ may be veiled in history by human sin. People may fail to see the Church as the bearer of the power and glory of its Lord. What is visible is very often far from a pointer to the kingdom of God. But God can, if He pleases, send witnesses to those who have not been able to see the uplifting manifestation of Christ in the face which we have made bloody with our sins or in the seamless robe which we have torn by our divisions. Through these witnesses God can release a power far greater than the extra-biblical messages would themselves lead us to expect. True plentitude, however, is lived in the

second advent. The economy of salvation achieves its full
reality as the End, as the ultimate meaning of all things. The
economy of Christ is unintelligible without the economy of
the Spirit.

"God says, 'This will happen in the last days; I will pour
out upon everyone a portion of my spirit' " (Acts 2:17). This
must be taken to mean a Pentecost which is universal from
the very first. In fact we also read in the Acts of the Apostles
that "the gift of the Holy Spirit" had been "poured out even
on Gentiles" (10:45). The Spirit is present everywhere and
fills everything by virtue of an economy distinct from that of
the Son. Irenaeus calls the Word and the Spirit the "two
hands of the Father." This means that we must affirm not
only their hypostatic independence but also that the advent of
the Holy Spirit in the world is not subordinated to the Son, is
not simply a function of the Word. "Pentecost," says
Lossky, "is not a 'continuation' of the Incarnation, it is its
sequel, its consequence: . . . creation has become capable of
receiving the Holy Spirit" (Vladimir Lossky, *Théologie mys-
tique de l'Eglise d'Orient* [Paris: Aubier, 1944], p. 156). Between the two economies there is a reciprocity and a mutual
service. The Spirit is another Paraclete. It is He who fashions
Christ within us. And, since Pentecost, it is He who makes
Christ present. It is He who makes Christ an inner reality here
and now: as Irenaeus finely says: "Where the Spirit is, there
also is the Church" (*Adv. Haer*. III, 24, *PG* 7, 966 c). The
Spirit operates and applies His energies in accordance with
His own economy and we could, from this angle, regard the
non-Christian religions as points where His inspiration is at
work.

All who are visited by the Spirit are the people of God.
The Church represents the first fruits of the whole of mankind called to salvation. "In Christ all will be brought to
life" (I Cor. 15:22) because of this communion which is the
Church. At the present moment the Church is the sacrament
of this future unity, the unity of both "those whom the
Church will have baptized and those whom the Church's
bridegroom will have baptized," to use Nicholas Cabazilas's
wonderful expression. And when now we communicate in

the Body of Christ, we are united with all those whom the Lord embraces with His life-giving love. They are all within the eucharistic cup, awaiting the time of the Parousia when they will constitute the unique and glorious body of the Saviour and when all the signs will disappear before "the throne of God and of the Lamb" (Rev. 22:3).

If we accept the bases of this theology, how are we to define the Christian mission and the concrete approach of a Christian community to a non-Christian community?

1. The Christian who knows that, within God's plan, the great religions constitute training schools of the Divine mercy will have an attitude of profound peace and gentle patience. There will be an obedience to this plan being carried out by the Holy Spirit, an expectant hope of the Lord's coming, a longing to eat the eternal Paschal meal, and a secret form of communion with all men in the economy of the Mystery whereby we are being gradually led towards the final consummation, the recapitulation of all things in Christ.

2. There is a universal religious community which, if we are able to lay hold of what it offers, will enrich our Christian experience. What matters here is not so much that we should grasp the historical, literal, objective meaning of non-Christian scriptures, but that we should read these scriptures in the light of Christ. For just as the letter without the Holy Spirit can hide revelation from us in the case of the Old Testament Scriptures, Christ being the only key to them, so is it possible for us to approach other religions and their scriptures either in a purely critical frame of mind and as objective students of history and sociology, or else in order to discern the truth in them according to the breath of the Holy Spirit.

3. Within the context of these religions, certain gifted individuals penetrate beyond the signs of their own faiths just as the spiritual life goes beyond the Law, even though legalism does prevail in some cases. What we have to do is to penetrate beyond the symbols and historical forms and discover the profound intention of religious people and to relate their apprehension of divinity to the object of our Christian hope. This means that we must use the apophatic method in

speaking of God not only, among Christians, in the knowledge that all concepts of God are idols, but apply this method also to our ways of talking about God as He appears through the scriptures of the non-Christian religions. When we seek to understand the adherent of another religion, we should not be concerned to arrive at a descriptive account of him as an example of his particular faith, but we must rather treat him as someone who has something to teach us and something to manifest to us of God.

4. Communion is the *conditio sine qua non* of communication. This is why no dealings are possible from the Christian side without a conversion which banishes all confessional pride and all feelings of cultural or historical superiority. Such humility requires the Christ-like way of self-fulfilment through the other. A Christian community purified by the fire of the Spirit, holy unto God, poor for the sake of God, can in the weakness of the Gospel, take the risk of both giving and receiving with equal simplicity. It must accept the challenge as a brotherly admonition and be able to recognize, even in the guise of unbelief, a courageous rejection of lies which Christians have been long unwilling or unable to denounce.

5. With this attitude, communication will be possible. The presentation of Christ will be based on His self-humiliation, on His historical reality and His words. It is not so much a question of adding people to the Church. They will come in of their own accord once they begin to feel at home in it as in the Father's house. The supreme task is to identify all the Christic values in other religions, to show them Christ as the bond which unites them and His love as their fulfilment. True mission laughs at missionary activity. Our task is simply to follow the tracks of Christ perceptible in the shadows of other religions.

> "Night after night on my bed
> I have sought my true love;
> I have sought him but not found him,
> I have called him but he has not answered.
> I said, 'I will rise and go the rounds of the city,

through the streets and the squares, seeking my true
  love.'. . .
The watchmen, going the rounds of the city, met me,
and I asked, 'Have you seen my true love?'"

(Song of Songs, 3:1-3)

The task of the witness in a non-Christian context will be
to name Him whom others have already recognized as the
Beloved. Once they have become the friends of the Bridegroom it will be easy to name Him. The entire missionary
activity of the Church will be directed towards awakening the
Christ who sleeps in the night of the religions. It is the Lord
Himself who alone knows whether people will be able to cele-
brate an authentically glorious Paschal meal together before
the coming of the heavenly Jerusalem. But we already know
that the beauty of Christ shining in our faces is the promise of
our final reconciliation.

The Salvific Value of African Religions

Patrick Kalilombe

Are the African traditional religions authentic channels
of God's saving activity? Christian thinkers have traditionally supported their answers primarily from the
witness of Scripture, notes this Roman Catholic bishop
and biblical scholar from Malawi. But he also observes
that usually these scholars were *non-Africans*. However
"sympathetic and broadminded" they might be, they
still look at the problem "from the point of view of an
outsider who is not really personally involved in the religions at stake," and are conditioned by factors of which
an African "can normally hope to be free." Bishop
Kalilombe notices how foreign missionaries were most
struck by those biblical texts that "have overtones of
opposition against the 'gentiles' as enemies of God's
people and practitioners of idolatry and abominations,"
and normally ignored those which displayed God's positive, solicitous acts toward those who were not "special
choices (that of Israel and that of the Church)." The
African writer then offers "a contextualized Bible reading for Africa": what could happen if African traditional
religions were to be assessed by Africans themselves. He
concludes that "it is not fair to give a final judgment in
such important matters only from a partial standpoint, be
it Jewish or Christian, primitive or civilized, black or
white." This is an extract from the paper delivered to the
first Congress of African Biblists, held at Kinshasha,
December 1978. It first appeared in the June 1979 *African Ecclesial Review* (*AFER*), published by the
AMECEA Pastoral Institute, P.O. Box 908, Eldoret,
Kenya.

Are the African traditional religions salvific? Or to be more precise, were these traditional religious systems and practices effective means whereby in the past, before the coming of Christianity, their adherents in Africa were able to "seek the deity and, by feeling their way toward him, succeed in finding him (who) is not far from any of us, since it is in him that we live, and move, and exist" (Acts 17:27–28)? And for those who even today live sincerely by them, are these religions still authentic channels of God's saving activity, so that we could unequivocally assert that the practitioners of these traditional religions are saved through them, and not in spite of them?

Individual Salvation and Salvific Value of Religions: Distinct Questions

We need to distinguish two questions: one is the possibility of salvation for any individual who is not a member of Christ's visible Church. The second concerns the providential role of other religions, as historical, socially structured and outward expressions of human communities in their search for God.

As far as the first question is concerned, quite early in Church history the attempted answer took the form of the famous axiom: *Extra Ecclesiam nulla salus*. Such formulation, however, could never be taken in the absolute form that its wording suggests. As better, more comprehensive knowledge of human history and geography became available, it was necessary to start introducing more and more subtle distinctions, all amounting to the admission that, after all, salvation was possible outside the visible institutional Christian Church.[1] We can consider the question finally settled at least in its basic elements now that Vatican II has said in so many words that, "those also can attain to everlasting salvation who through no fault of their own do not know the gospel of Christ or His Church, yet sincerely seek God and, moved by grace, strive by their deeds to do His will as it is known to them through the dictates of conscience."[2]

But the problem of religions as such is a more difficult

one because it is not possible to bypass here far-reaching implications that touch the very center of the Church's self-understanding and the meaning and goal of its missionary outreach. What becomes of Christianity's uniqueness as God's final salvific self-revelation if it is conceded that other religions are also divinely ordained normal channels of God's salvific activity? Where is the urgency of the "Great Commission" (Matthew 28:19–20) if non-Christian communities can just as well find salvation in their own traditional religious systems? The Church has had to come to grips with these questions, for they are basic in determining what its own identity is in God's unfolding plan of salvation. They become all the more poignant as the historical Church becomes aware of the existence and dynamism of numerous civilizations, cultures and religious traditions that have developed outside the influence of Christianity. Given the divine command to go and make disciples of all the nations, what attitude should the Church have towards these social realities? Opposition or dialogue? Competition or cooperation? Respect or contempt? Fight or peaceful coexistence? Can these religions be seen positively and with respect, or should they be dismissed as of no theological importance. In other words, are these religions in some sort of lineal continuity with Christianity, or are they not?

Karl Rahner[3] asserted in 1961 that unfortunately it could not be said that Catholic theology, as practiced in recent times, had really paid sufficient attention to the question posed in this precise way. Indeed, judging from the normal practice of Christian missionary activity, it has to be admitted that until rather recently it was customary to deal heavy-handedly with what were called "pagan practices." Although some respect was often paid to elements found in these religions, the systems themselves were seen in a rather negative way as essentially aberrations, and little effort was made to explore the possibility of their providential role in the history of the peoples concerned. The good elements in them which could be respected as positive were accepted as such mainly because they happened to resemble what were taken as authentic Christian values. This did not affect the

negative judgment on the religions themselves. Only sporad-
ically, and mainly in recent times, has a serious attempt been
made to evaluate the religions themselves and to find out
what role they might have in God's plan of salvation for their
adherents. But even before Vatican II, theologians[4] finally
started discussing the question. Vatican II's *Declaration on
Relationship of the Church to Non-Christian Religions*
(*Nostra Aetate*) seems to allude to it in some way. It says:
"The Catholic Church rejects nothing which is true and holy
in these religions. She looks with sincere respect upon those
ways of conduct and of life, those rules and teachings which,
though differing in many particulars from what she holds and
sets forth, nevertheless often reflect a ray of that Truth which
enlightens all men."

The *Decree on the Church's Missionary Activity* has
more interesting reflections (n. 1, 1, 7, 9, 11) which, though
still rather timid and general, furnish avenues for a more
hopeful treatment of it by theologians. One such pregnant
reflection, and perhaps the most significant, is Vatican II's
favorite portrayal of the Church as "Universal Sacrament of
salvation" (*Ad Gentes*, 1). . . .

In discussing the question of non-Christian religions all
parties and opinions among Christian thinkers were starting
from the witness of the Scriptures and basing on it their
evaluation and judgment. What questions were being asked?
Were all the relevant elements of the evidence carefully taken
into account; or was there a tendency to highlight only certain
trends of thought appearing in the Scriptures while pushing
into the background other important trends which might have
modified the nature of the investigation? Were there certain
prior working assumptions and attitudes that commanded the
selection of the evidence and determined the relative weight
given to apparently conflicting lines of thought?

The reading of the Bible is never a totally neutral exercise. The reader who takes up the Bible comes with all sorts
of conditionings. Besides the more personal ones resulting
from the individual's own psychological and spiritual history,
he or she carries along also the effects of his/her belonging to
a specific class, family, culture, community or interest

group. The individual bears also the imprint of the epoch in history within which the investigation is being made. All this has an influence on how the Bible will be interrogated, what the expectations of the reader will be, what evidence will be readily selected and given importance, but also what "blind spots" will occur in the exercise.

I take as point of departure the fact that, as far as African traditional religions are concerned, the prevailing judgments and attitudes are the result of Bible study conducted *mainly by non-Africans*. These students, however sympathetic and broadminded, were still looking at the problem from the point of view of an outsider who is not really personally involved in the religions at stake. In a way, this was an advantage: it made for a type of objectivity and detachment that would have been impossible for an African. On the other hand, however, they could not claim to be totally impartial since they were in their turn conditioned by other factors of which an African can normally hope to be free. . . .

The main aim of this essay is to show what could happen if the enquiry were initiated from the point of view of an African Christian reader of the Scriptures. The contention is that a fresh vision could ensue in that former problems which used to dominate might be found to take a secondary place, while newer preoccupations might become more important and relevant. A slightly different way of posing the question could also result, demanding a new assessment of the testimony of Scripture. We might even hope to touch on some aspects of the Bible message that have remained "blind spots" until now because they were not really needed from the point of view of former preoccupations.

Examining the Context of Past Attitudes

Within the Christian tradition the problem of the encounter with other religious systems and traditions has not been a purely intellectual one, engaging people's minds on a calm theoretical level. It has always been first and foremost a practical, existential challenge, involving strong sentiments of a sacred duty to be accomplished, calling forth concrete tasks and programs and eliciting a lot of deep-seated emotions. It is necessary to start by examining the main aspects of the context that gave rise to the attitudes that people manifested in discussing this point.

One thing is sure. As far as African traditional religions are concerned, the discussions of professional theologians and biblists are only secondary. The main context within which the decisive attitudes towards these religions were formed is the missionary enterprise, especially in its more recent expressions starting with the mid-nineteenth century. Missionary work was seen as the Church's bounded duty to bring the true faith to pagans, or to save souls that were in darkness. The challenge attracted vigorous and enterprising people, ready for action and for suffering even up to death. It was like a military expedition: it thrived on an ethos of struggle and conquest. Understandably the enemy was Satan. But Satan was disguised and active through his network of false religions. He and his associates had to be encountered, unmasked in their perfidy, and then engaged in mortal battle. The missionary's encounter with the traditional African customs and religious practices was thus not a peaceful one. The missionary may have had sympathy and genuine love for the individual natives, for after all, they were the ones on behalf of whom the war was being waged. But towards their religious systems and practices, and towards those who were guardians and promotors of these practices, there could be no compromise.

And so when missionaries went to the Scriptures for guidance in their encounter with the traditional religions, the texts that struck them most were normally those that had overtones of opposition against the "gentiles" as enemies of God's People and practitioners of idolatry and abominations. It was so simple to see the Christian Church as the People of God, and the non-Christian religious systems as the expression of enmity against Yahweh and his plan of salvation.

The most natural selections were those passages where there are expressions of hostility towards the "pagans," for example, where there is abundant diatribe against the idols of the gentiles. Choice texts would be those in the ridicule style in which Deutero-Isaiah excells (Isaiah 44:9-20; 46:1-7), and those portions of the Old Testament which are tributary to this literary form (Psalm 115; Baruch 6; or even Daniel 14). These texts are a reinforcement of the affirmation of strict monotheism (rather than mere henotheism) so characteristic of exilic and post-exilic Judaism (cf. Isaiah 45:7-13, 18-25). It was a sort of apologetic style aiming at consoling and strengthening the chastened exiles or at restoring self-confidence to the struggling bands of the "Golah." This helped to develop the theme of the Holy People, separated from all that is impure and profane, a people privileged to have the Law of their God and the only true worship. It was at this time that the great synthesis of the Priestly Tradition was given its lasting form and became the commanding editorial framework of the Scriptures. But there was a dark side to this. From the notion of Holy People and the preoccupation to express this holiness and protect it, the tendency developed towards an exclusivist ghetto mentality. The Law ran the danger of legalism and intransigence as is witnessed by Ezra's fierce treatment of "mixed marriages" (Ezra 9-10). Later persecutions under the Seleucids and the Romans helped only to reinforce these tendencies. The Apocalyptic and allied literatures of these times do have admirable lessons. But they also betray a hardening of attitude towards the "gentiles." There is very little sympathy towards anything outside the "People of God."

These developments are to be seen mostly as prompted by a defensive spirit: the need of a socially and politically disadvantaged group to protect itself from corrosive outside forces and to compensate psychologically for its inferiority by exalting whatever redeeming aspects it believes it possesses. It is to be remembered that the New Testament dawned in the midst of this period. This will help us to put in proper context several texts which reflect attitudes of Christ's contemporaries (and those of the early Church) towards non-Jews. But here we must note that a current opposed to this narrow ghetto spirit and its negative attitude towards the gentiles had developed alongside the more intransigent one. We can only recall such obvious testimonies as the book of Ruth where we sense a subtle criticism of current "purist" ideas about who the "People of God" really are. The satirical novel of the Prophet Jonah is even more explicit in its castigation of Judaism's exclusive claim to God's favor. We have here a rather radical presentation of a theme which was dear to many prophets, as we shall see later on.

In the New Testament times, we have echoes of this more positive tradition. John the Baptist and Jesus himself are examples. The sayings about descent from Abraham are an important evidence. Both the Baptist (cf. Matthew 3:9–10; Luke 3:8) and Christ went out of their way to stigmatize the misplaced confidence in mere belonging to an ethnic group, albeit a divinely chosen one (cf. Matthew 3:11–12; John 8:37–41). The early Christian community, composed mainly of Jews, had the difficulty in ridding themselves of the ghetto mentality, as we can judge by the controversy about the requirements for the conversion of non-Jews (Acts 15). The book of Acts is quite clear in showing how hard it was even for Peter to widen his vision on this point (Acts 10). But the author of Romans feels the need to expound in a new way the theme about descent from Abraham (Romans 4, cf. also Galatians 3 and 4). These sayings of the Baptist, of Jesus, and of Paul are manifestly part of a tradition of protest against a hard-line attitude towards the "pagans."

There seems to have existed in the New Testament a current of thought which felt that the problem about those outside the visible membership of God's People was not as simple as the standard Jew might have wanted to make it. It was too simplistic to think that God loved his chosen people, but had no time for the others. In interpreting the message of the New Testament, this point is very crucial: it may help to give importance to some forgotten texts. Christian missionaries could have given more thought to this counter current in their assessment of the place of non-Christian religions in divine providence. It would seem strange, in fact, that missionaries would give relatively more importance to the contrary current, for they were interrogating the Scriptures in view of a commitment quite contrary to that of a ghetto community. Jewish religion, in spite of its late efforts at proselytism, remained basically a non-missionary community and tended to see its relation with outsiders mainly in terms of opposition and exclusion. The Christian Church, on the other hand, is institutionally outgoing: sent to go out to the whole world. There does not seem to be any necessary reason for the Christian Church to look at the encounter with non-Christian religions from a systematically negative viewpoint, and for thinking that the primary normative texts capable of guiding the Church in its missionary enterprise should be those that suggest an easy and blanket dismissal of other religions. The history of Christianity in Europe led to such a close link between the Christian faith and Western culture that it became difficult to distinguish between them, or between the expansion of religion and the expansion of Western civilization. This ambiguity becomes obvious especially starting with the Crusades. It will not have disappeared in the 16th and 17th centuries when the Christian nations of Spain and Portugal will be busy with their conquests in the New World. It certainly had not disappeared when colonial expansion came to its zenith in the second half of the 19th century and well into our own century. However much one hates to say this, it is not by pure coincidence that missionary work flourished most during the colonial period. In the atmosphere of the Western conquest, the meeting of Christianity with other religions was conceived of in the spirit typical of Christendom's crusading tradition. There is a streak of the Crusader in Western Christianity. It tends to identify its own interests and vision with those of God himself. We only have to think of the bitter sectarianism that has pitted Christian denominations against one another over the past generations. And yet they all claim to belong to one and the same Christ. It should not be surprising then that the same spirit of systematic opposition prevails whenever Christianity meets non-Christian traditions.

The source of this type of intransigence seems to be a tendency to simplify realities into an "either/or" pattern, whether it is a question of truths and beliefs or of life-styles and customs. It is as if anything that is different from what I believe to be true or good is a threat to my feeling of security and must be dismissed as bad or inferior. Variations then become oppositions; and it becomes difficult to think of such variations rather as complementary aspects which might create a richer reality by being combined rather than by excluding one another. Seeing variations and differences as complementary aspects first rather than oppositions has an advantage. It helps to discover many things that are valid and good in a position different from my own. And this is salutary when we are dealing with human realities, for such human realities can never claim to have the monopoly of goodness. The tendency to opposition has another side to it, a side we would do well to remember when we are dealing with the encounter of religions. The crusading mentality is usually accompanied by a highly motivated proselytism. When other religions and systems have been proven wrong their adherents are not simply left in peace: they must be persuaded to abandon those false religions and to adopt the true religion as presented by the crusader. This persuasion may be peaceful, relying on respectful dialogue and the power of moral attraction. Often, however, the crusader becomes impatient when conversions are not being realized fast enough for his liking. He may then resort to other methods of persuasion. It may not be outright physical force (although both Islam and Christianity have not always abstained from such methods), but it can be other ways that to a greater or lesser extent do not fully respect the religious freedom of the people. There have been instances where, for example, works of charity were used as mere instruments of proselytism. But in any case such a compulsive desire for converts can affect the modality of the encounter between the religions. It can push the crusader to falsify the picture in view of more immediate successes: the Christian religion will be presented only in its idealized form, while only the weaker and repulsive aspects of the other religions are highlighted.

What I am trying to say is that in the encounter of Christianity with other religions, the spirit that motivated the missionary was not always of a type to facilitate a more positive assessment of these religions. This may have impeded a fruitful study of the salvific nature of those religions. It also explains in part the choice of scriptural evidence adduced to account for Christianity's attitude towards them. As we have seen, the texts by which most store was laid were those which form part of a definite trend in the Old Testament: Israel's and Judaism's opposition to the gentiles, and the exclusive claims of God's Chosen People to divine favor.

Christianity claims to be the new People of God. It inherits that feeling of being a privileged people which Israel has had because of the Covenant (Exodus 19:4-6). But by the same token, Christianity has inherited also the danger that stalked Israel throughout its history: the danger of misunderstanding the real nature and aim of this choice by God, and of drawing false conclusions from it concerning God's relations with other peoples and nations. The covenant then, as a fulfilment of the promises made to Abraham and the ancestors, ran the risk of losing its *raison d'être* as a nationalistic privilege, independent from, or even cancelling, God's worldwide salvific interests. Israel's prophets were often obliged to rectify such misunderstandings. Amos (9:7-8) reminds the Israelites that the distant peoples are just as much objects of God's solicitude as they themselves. Yahweh is as concerned with what these foreign nations do to one another as with the way Israel and Judah are acting (Amos 1-2). The first chapters of Genesis (1-11) serve as the setting of the whole scene within which God's plan of salvation is to unfold: the whole of creation, the universe where the history of mankind takes place. Abraham's calling and the election of Israel would have no meaning except as part of this encompassing plan. So while he is dealing with the Chosen People, God's eyes are on the whole of mankind. The authentic traditions of Israel saw the covenant at Sinai as a covenant within a wider Covenant; for creation itself was the primordial Covenant; and God does not break his word. To him belong heaven and the heaven of heavens, the earth and all it contains, even when he makes special choice of Abraham's descendants. He is never partial or to be bribed (Deuteronomy 10:15-18). It is significant that the Wisdom literature which flourished especially among the Jews of the diaspora shows a broader view of God's active presence in the world. The reflections of the book of Wisdom on God's dealings with Israel's enemies are astounding in their insistence on divine forebearance. For indeed God "is merciful to all, because he can do all things and he overlooks men's sins so that they can repent . . . he loves all that exists and holds nothing of what he has made in abhorrence, for had he hated anything, he would not have formed it" (cf. Wisdom 11:26). We can feel here the same spirit as the one that prompted the author of the book of Jonah, and which refused to imagine God as partial or narrow (Wisdom 6, 8).

The Historical Visible Church and the Non-Christian Religions

There is, as we mentioned earlier, a current in the New Testament which carries on this open vision of God's dealings with the universe. The early Church was conscious of its task of proclaiming the Good News of Jesus up to the ends of the earth, because the Christ was the final revelation of the true God. The apostles and the early Christians were convinced that only through faith in Christ could the world be saved, "for all the names in the world given to men, this is the only one by which we can be saved" (Acts 4:12). But this conviction does not seem to have become an easy explanation of God's dealings with those who as yet did not know Christ explicitly. For the early Christians the problem was doubly complex. Those who did not know Christ were not only the ones called "gentiles" by the Jews, but also the Jews themselves in so far as they had rejected the Messiah. The pressing question then was to determine where this Chosen People now stood before their God in this new situation in which God's election is now through Christ. The state of the gentiles was only a subsequent problem. Were the Jews at any real advantage as compared with the non-Jews as far as faith in Christ was concerned? As we saw, this is basically the point at issue in the controversy about the conditions for conversion to Christ (Acts 15; Romans and Galatians). Although the resolution of the question at Jerusalem was rather a compromise as far as practical tactics were concerned, on the theoretical level a great step had been taken. It was now accepted that "in Christ Jesus, whether you are circumcised or not makes no difference—what matters is faith that makes its power felt through love" (Galatians 5:6). Or as the letter to the Romans would say: "A man is justified by faith and not by doing something the Law tells him to do. Is God the god of the Jews alone and not of the pagans too? Of the pagans too, most certainly, since there is only one God" (Romans 3:28–30). This was a radical statement: it says clearly that through Christ God has shown that he has no favorites: "Pain and suffering will come to every human being who employs himself in evil—Jews first, but Greeks as well; reknown, honor and peace will come to everyone who does good—Jews first, but Greeks as well. God has no favorites" (Romans 2:9–11). In this context Paul is able to turn to the "gentiles" and state that "pagans who never heard of the Law but are led by reason to do what the Law commands, may not actually 'possess' the Law, but they can be said to 'be' the Law. They can point to the substance of the Law engraved on their hearts—they can call a witness, that is, their own conscience—they have accusation and defense, that is, their own inner mental dialogue" (Romans 2:14–16).

This statement of humanity's basic equality before God is where the study of the salvific nature of non-Christian religions should start. It shows God present within the whole of mankind, in different ways perhaps, but really present nevertheless, whether through the agency of the Law among the Jews or through the working of conscience for the others. All peoples are subject to sin and God's wrath; but just so are they all open to the saving faith in Christ. Another way of putting it is to affirm that "God wants everyone to be saved and reach full knowledge of the truth. For there is only one God, and there is only one mediator between God and mankind, himself a man, Christ Jesus who sacrificed himself as a ransom for them all" (1 Timothy 2:4–6). It is possible to situate within proper context Paul's statement during his speech at Athens (Acts 17:26–28). It is a validation of the insights found in the first chapters of Genesis: there is a cosmic Covenant of love between God and mankind by the very fact of creation. Mankind may break this Covenant through sin and infidelity. But again and again God renews it and reaffirms his salvific intention. His special choices (that of Israel and that of the Church) are not an abolition of the cosmic Covenant. If anything, they are a hopeful sign or proof of what in less evident ways he is doing all along with the whole of mankind, and they are meant to serve this wider Covenant.

This does not answer all the questions. But if we start with it, then the answers to those other problems will follow a particular line where we do not have to come back on this important basis. For example, it will be necessary to find out what is meant by the affirmation that only faith in Christ brings salvation. The easy way out would be to say that those who do not know Christ explicitly cannot have faith in him: and cannot be saved. But our starting point will oblige us to return to the Scriptures and ask whether and how Christ can be really present even if his face is not explicitly revealed. This might help us to give fuller consideration, for example, to John's statement: "The Word was the true light that enlightens all men. . . . He was in the world that had its being through him, and the world did not know him" (John 1:9). We would return to the Wisdom literature in the Old Testament and meditate on the fuller meaning of the theme of God's Wisdom. And then we might take up the Captivity Letters. We would see that the Christ of God's plan of salvation (cf. Ephesians 1 and Colossians 1) is a cosmic presence that is not contained within the limits of the historical visible Church only.

Another problem would be to assess the role of this visible Church. Is God's intention to introduce every human being into this historical Church under pain of not being saved? The history of Israel would furnish us with food for thought. God did not call every person and nation in that special way by which he had called Israel. But as we have seen, this special election did not mean that God was neglecting the other nations in favor of Israel alone. On the contrary, although Israel often forgot this, the special election of the Chosen People was a call for service. Deutero- (and Trito-)

Isaiah makes this quite plain, especially in the Songs of the Suffering Servant of Yahweh (Isaiah 42:1-9; 49:1-6; 50:4-9; and esp. 52:13—53:12). In these texts the meaning of Israel's calling, history, suffering and final triumph is of worldwide validity. She lives, suffers, dies and rises again as an instrument of Yahweh's salvific designs for the whole world. Although the other nations are not racially or physically integrated into the Jewish nation, in a sense they are all brought into real association with her. In a way that is hard to explain in terms of experiential evidence, these nations can look up to Sion as to their "Mother, since each one of them was born in her, and all have their place in her" (Psalm 86:5-7). Not only are the explicit proselytes accepted (cf. Isaiah 56:1-8), but all the nations walk in her light (Isaiah 60) bringing in their riches into a worldwide commonwealth of the redeemed. Israel therefore is a sort of prototype, a light to enlighten the nations and make them realize their God-given destiny. The New Testament echoes this by comparing the New People of God to "Light," "Salt," "Leaven" of the earth, to a "City" up on the mountain whose presence assures the world that God is in the midst of his people (Matthew 5:13-16; also Philippians 2:14-16). This is the meaning of Vatican II's favorite description of the Church as "light of the nations" *(Lumen Gentium, 1)* and universal sacrament of salvation *(Ad Gentes, 1)*.

It would seem therefore that the Church's destiny is to be inserted into the heart of the world as a sacrament, i.e. visible and effective sign, of the coming Kingdom of God, pointing towards this Kingdom, and proving its efficacious working by acting as a privileged champion of the tenets of the Kingdom. By looking at the Church and by hearing its prophetic utterances, the rest of the world is challenged by the judgment of God on them, a judgment that, like light, reveals the dross and the good metal, and like fire burns the dross and refines the precious metal. If this is so, the Church's preoccupation should be less with mere recruitment of numbers, and more with authenticity and efficacy of its witness in the world. The other religions should be seen, not so much as an adversary or a threat, but as the field within which her witness makes the good grain grow and bear fruit a hundredfold, while the tares are being pulled out and burnt.

The Salvific Value of African Traditional Religions

What could happen if the problem of non-Christian religions were examined by people who are part of the societies among whom these religions have a validity? What would happen if African traditional religions were to be assessed by African Christians themselves? Perhaps the main lines of the enquiry would shift.

There would be a first basic change: it would be an enquiry from the inside rather than from the outside. I would have to return in spirit to where my people were. So we would not be talking anymore about the customs and beliefs of those "pagans" in the bush of Africa: I could not have the heart to speak of my own ancestors and religion in this contemptuous way. We are dealing with concrete people now: my father and mother, my uncles and aunts, my brothers and sisters, my relatives, friends and neighbors, a lot of people who mean a lot to me and whom I cannot handle as if they were mere objects of curiosity and detached study. And especially, I would remember that I am looking at a venerable and sacred tradition handed over by generations of ancestors. These beliefs and customs will command my respect and careful consideration, even when I may not share them. I cannot act as if these are childish superstitions or mere primitive mumbo-jumbo, for I feel with my whole person the seriousness of the problems, questionings, preoccupations, hopes, fears, desires and joys from which these religious attitudes spring. I have no right to look down on my father's culture or to offer simplistic solutions to questions I know to be very complex.

We can think here of Paul's case, when in the letter to the Romans (9–11) he had to meditate on the fact that the majority of his fellow Jews did not believe in Christ and were thus hostile to what was most precious in his own religious experience. His sorrow was so great, his mental anguish so endless, for these were his own flesh and blood. With them he shared a rich history of relations with God and the ancestors. So his questions take on a dramatic and deeply personal character. He sees difficulties and problems where perhaps a fellow Christian, but of a non-Jewish origin, might not have seen them. He finds himself unable to accept several easy answers that suggest themselves to his questioning mind. The problem of Jewish incredulity is not as simple to him as it might look to an outsider. It is not just a question of bad faith or blindness on the part of the Jews. The complicating factor is that God himself and his promises are all part of the question. And so Paul is forced to go back to the Scriptures and start a thorough-going midrash in order to find out the theological implications of the problem. In so doing he comes up with scriptural texts which take on a new meaning as approaches to the solution. We have an example of contextualized Bible investigation where the reading and interpretation are shaped by the personal involvement of the inquirer.

It is some such process that an African would have to initiate if he wanted to re-examine the problem of his ancestors' religious traditions. He would not start from a position of assumed righteousness and superiority as a member of an already Christianized culture might be tempted to do. He would therefore avoid selecting as guidance those texts of the Bible that represent doubtful tendencies of a superiority complex vis-à-vis the other cultures, or of an exclusivist mentality which would want to restrict God's favor and interest to one's own group as if God can be partisan and a respecter of persons.

But, above all, he would start from the conviction that God has been ever present among his own people, just as he has been in all peoples, cultures and religious tendencies of the world, not just as a condescension, but because this benevolent presence is in the logic of the cosmic Covenant of creation and re-creation. We must therefore assume that in all serious efforts of mankind to make sense of its own life and destiny, God has been in and with his peoples. The Spirit of God has indeed filled the whole world. There are enough serious trends of thought in the Scriptures to show that this feeling is not just sentimental, but is based on revelation. The

African Bible reader will thus not fear to state that the religious systems of his ancestors were not just tolerated by God. They were the results of the efforts of our cultures wherein the Spirit of God was an active agent. And therefore, there would be no fear in me to assert that, as long as these religions were the serious searchings of our cultures for the deity, they are to be respected as the normal divinely-given means for salvation, put by God in his will for the salvation of all the peoples.

This will not mean that everything in those religions is good or to be retained. Scripture will remind us strongly that human nature and its strivings are under the shadow of sin, and therefore constantly subjected to God's judgment whereby the evil is always condemned by him and by mankind's deepest level of conscience. But because God's Spirit is nevertheless actively present, it will be necessary to assume that there are also a lot of good and valid elements in this "grouping"; and these positive elements must be worthy of respect and survival since they are the results of God's activity which is never ultimately defeated by sin and death.

But I shall remember that, according to Scripture, this judgment is not reserved only to those nations that have been favored with a special election by God. For according to the Bible, the whole world lies under the wrath of God: "Jews and Gentile alike, because all have sinned and have fallen short of God's glory. God's wrath and condemnation tend to begin with his own household." And so I shall not be bothered by tendencious readings of the Bible which give an easy superiority to any special historical group and is taken as authorization to despise, reject, or condemn offhand whatever is different from, or looks strange to such a historical group.

Let us admit that this caution in assessing African non-Christian religions, and the systematic favorable prejudice in their regard, will come easy to me because I feel personally involved in these religions. But that does not need an apology: it simply shows that it is not fair to give a final judgment in such important matters only from a partial standpoint, be it Jewish or Christian, primitive or civilized, black or white. The problem of the salvific value of non-Christian religions should be tackled from a holistic standpoint in which full account is taken of the special choices or elections of God, but also of all the other elements in God's relations with the whole of mankind. Only thus can full justice be given to the witness of the Scriptures. For, indeed, "God has no favorites" (Romans 2:11).

NOTES

1. For a summary treatment of the fortunes of this axiom, cf. H. Küng, *The Church* (Garden City, N.Y.: Doubleday Image Book, 1967), pp. 313–19.

2. *Lumen Gentium,* n. 16.

3. K. Rahner, *Theological Investigations* (London: Darton, Longman & Todd, 1966), vol. 5, *Later Writings,* p. 117.

4. Like Danielou, Congar, and others. For a brief evaluation of these essays, cf. Schlette, *Towards a Theology of Religions* (New York: Herder & Herder, 1966), pp. 28–33.

The Uniqueness and Universality of Jesus Christ

Carl E. Braaten

This American Lutheran theologian probes the missiological significance of the question Jesus asked his earliest apostles or messengers, "Who do you say that I am?" How can we reconcile the uniqueness of Christ with his universality; his Lordship over all religions and our dialogue with people of other faiths? Carl E. Braaten, in describing various Roman Catholic and Protestant positions, clearly states and then defends his conviction: "My friends to the left who teach that there are many saviors to accommodate a pluralistic world and my friends to the right who teach that only those who share their faith will be saved in the end are both wrong. They do not have the truth of the gospel on their side." He notes that "Christology is not static." "The history of the religions once contributed all the Christological titles to the interpretation of the Jesus-event. . . . That process is still going on in the openness of world history, engendered by the universal missionary witness to Jesus as the Christ, the Lord and Savior of the world. . . . If the apostles and church fathers could find anticipations of Christ in the Old Testament, we have a right to expect a similar thing in the texts and traditions of other religions." Dr. Braaten is Professor of Systematic Theology, Lutheran School of Theology at Chicago, and author of *The Flaming Center: A Theology of the Christian Mission* (Philadelphia: Fortress Press, 1977). This article is the paper he read at the 1979 meeting of the American Society of Missiology, which was published simultaneously in January 1980 by the *Occasional Bulletin of Missionary Research* and by *Missiology*.

1. The Heritage of Exclusiveness

The true identity of Jesus Christ has been mediated to us today in texts and traditions which unanimously confess that he is the exclusive medium of eschatological salvation. Acts 4:12 is the classical locus of this Christological exclusiveness: "And there is salvation in no one else, for there is no other name under heaven given among men by which we must be saved." Christian exclusiveness has found several ways of manifesting itself. Traditionally, the Catholic type has focused on the church: "Outside the church there is no salvation." The statement first appeared in one of Cyprian's letters in the third century. It was reiterated in the papal bull *Unam sanctam* of Boniface VIII in 1302: "We believe that there is one holy catholic and apostolic church . . . outside of which there is no salvation. . . . We declare that it is necessary for salvation for every human creature to be subject to the Roman Pontiff."[1] Traditionally, the Protestant type has felt uncomfortable with the ecclesiocentric form of Roman Catholic exclusivism. It has focused instead on faith, quoting passages like John 3:18: "He who believes in him is not condemned; he who does not believe is condemned already, because he has not believed in the name of the only Son of God." Also Romans 10:17: "So faith comes from what is heard, and what is heard comes by the preaching of Christ."

The heritage of Christian exclusiveness runs deep into the New Testament and dominates the tradition from earliest times to the present. But from the beginning the very same tradition has created loopholes to provide people outside the Christian circle with the chance of salvation. Catholics of the most exclusive type conceded that people outside the church can be saved through the loopholes of "invincible ignorance" or "baptism by desire." Protestants in the older line of dogmatics appealed to 1 Peter 3:19, which states that Christ preached to the spirits in prison, as proof that people who did not encounter Christ and believe in this life would be given a "second chance" on the threshold of the future life. Sometimes they also talked about the invisible church whose limits are unknown, and thus presumably might also include some of the ''noble pagans.'' The judgment that reservations will be taken in heaven only for Christians, that only those who accept Christ by faith in this life or belong to his church, has seemed too harsh to be taken in a strictly literal sense.

Currently, there are voices being raised against every sort of Christian exclusivism, including all the loopholes that continue to reinforce the underlying premise. The focus now takes the form of the question whether there is full and equal salvation through the non-Christian religions. The loopholes only provided an exceptional way of salvation. What is needed now is a full acknowledgment of the other major religions as valid ways of salvation. We are living in one world with a plurality of cultures, religions, and ideologies. Either we acknowledge the legitimacy of this pluralism, or we threaten the possibility of living together in a peaceful world. We expect governments, corporations, and other agencies to do their part to cooperate in establishing conditions which drive toward the unity of the human world without diminishing the plurality of its forms. Why should not the religions of the world do their part? Christianity has begun to open up channels of dialogue with people of other religions. But many feel that the exclusivistic premise that it brings to the dialogue clogs the channels and makes a real exchange impossible.

Professor John Hick of Birmingham, England has taken the lead among Protestants in calling for a ''Copernican revolution,''[2] which aims to overturn the Christological dogma at the bottom of all Christian exclusivism. It is not enough to broaden the way of Christian salvation by speaking with Tillich of a ''latent church'' or with Rahner of ''anonymous Christianity.'' Those are the convenient modern loopholes. He calls them ''epicycles.'' So Hick goes deeper and lays the ax at the Christological roots of exclusivism. He says, ''For understood literally, the Son of God, God the Son, God-incarnate language implies that God can be adequately known and responded to *only* through Jesus; and the whole religious life of mankind, beyond the stream of Judaic-Christian faith is thus by implication excluded as lying outside the sphere of salvation.''[3] Pluralism is compatible with the unity of all humankind if we acknowledge that the various streams of religion in the world carry the same waters of salvation leading to eternal life with God. God is at the center of the universe of faiths; Jesus is only one of the many ways—the Christian way—that leads to God. He is not the one and only Son of God, Lord of the world, and Savior of humankind. Each religion has its own, and they do the job in their own way. In this way John Hick has successfully rooted out the last vestige of exclusivism.

On the Catholic side the left wing of Rahner's school has also abandoned the Christian claim that Jesus Christ is "different," "decisive," "unique," "normative," or "final," toppling the pillar on which the traditional claims to exclusiveness lean. For surely it makes no sense to argue that believing in Jesus Christ or belonging to his church are essential for salvation, if he is ultimately only one among many founders pointing the way to God. Paul Knitter has made the clearest case I know among Catholics for a revision of the traditional claim that Jesus Christ is the one and only Savior of humankind, that he is the once-for-all revelation of God's eschatological salvation in store for the whole world. In "A Critique of Hans Küng's *On Being a Christian,*"[4] Knitter like Hick lays his ax at the roots not only of the Christological dogma but of the apostolic kerygma as well. His motive is the same—to pave the way for dialogue with other religions that won't be "hamstrung"[5] by the exclusivist mindset. He writes, "Intellectually and psychologically is it not possible to give oneself over wholly to the meaning and message of Jesus and at the same time recognize the possibility that other 'saviors' have carried out the same function for other people?"[6] He answers "yes" and argues "that the claim for Jesus' exclusive uniqueness does not form part of the central assertions of Christian texts.'"[7] The claim that salvation takes place in Jesus only can be chalked up to "the historically conditioned world view and thought-patterns of the time.'"[8] Knitter concludes that there is no exclusive claim that belongs to the core of the Christian message. I think he would agree with Harnack that the exclusive element is not part of the kernel, but only the husk of the gospel. Reading Hick and Knitter is an experience of *déjà vu*.

Far to the right of this antiexclusivist position we find a new affirmation of the heritage of exclusiveness among the neo-evangelicals who are conducting a vigorous campaign against every form of universalism. The idea that there is salvation in the non-Christian religions is denied point-blank. At Lausanne the evangelicals declared dogmatically that "it is impossible to be a biblical Christian and a universalist simultaneously."[9] They now teach as dogmatic truth and as a criterion of being faithful to the gospel of Jesus Christ that all those who die or who have died without conscious faith in Jesus Christ are damned to eternal hell. If people have never heard the gospel and have never had a chance to believe, they are lost anyway. The logic of this position is that children who die in infancy are lost. The mentally retarded are lost. All those who have never heard of Christ are lost. Nevertheless, evangelicals cling to this view as the heart of the gospel and the incentive to mission.

I am convinced and I intend to argue that my friends to the left who teach that there are many saviors to accommodate a pluralistic world and my friends to the right who teach that only those who share their faith will be saved in the end are both wrong. They do not have the truth of the gospel on their side.

II. The Uniqueness of Jesus Christ

The tests and traditions that tell us about Jesus of Nazareth represent him as the expected Messiah of Israel, God's only Son, the Lord of creation, and the Savior of all humanity. We have no non-Christological picture of the historical Jesus.[10] Every recollection of his identity is penetrated by an identification that raises his significance to the highest possible power. If one should wish to subtract all the special titles of identification, one is not left with the identity of Jesus who is really Jesus.[11] One is, rather, left with the question whether or not Jesus of Nazareth ever existed or with an empty assertion of his naked historicity. But what of his meaning? What about his true identity?

When John the Baptist wondered about the true identity of Jesus, he asked, "Are you he who is to come, or shall we look for another?" (Mt. 11:3; Lk. 8:19). The answer of the early church was clear: Jesus is the One who was to come. He is the Messiah. Similarly, when Jesus asked his disciples on the way to Caesarea Philippi, "Who do men say that I am?" Peter answered, "You are the Christ, the Son of the living God" (Mk. 8:27; Mt. 16:16). The New Testament abounds with titles that serve to identify the uniqueness of Jesus. The historical Jesus most probably did not designate his true identity in terms of such titles of honor as Christ, Son of God, Lord, Savior, Logos, etc., but the early church did without any shadow of doubt.[12] These titles were conferred upon Jesus in the light of faith in the risen presence of Jesus. These are titles which in the same writings are bestowed upon God. Both God and Jesus are spoken of as Savior.[13] Both God and Jesus are spoken of as Lord. Jesus is the Savior because he will save his people from their sins. Jesus is the Lord because God has raised and exalted him above all others. Jesus is the subject of names that are above all other names because they are the names of God. They speak eloquently of the uniqueness of Jesus. New Testament theologians argue, of course, whether these titles of honor go back to the historical Jesus himself, or whether they have been written back into the Gospel texts from the post-Easter situation of faith. In one sense it doesn't matter which side is correct. For both must agree that the Jesus of history is represented to us in texts and traditions that describe his uniqueness. He is depicted not as *a* son of God, but as *the* only begotten Son of God, not as *a* savior, but as *the* Savior, not as *a* lord, but as *the* Lord, etc. These designations of Jesus as Lord and Savior identify him as the foundation of divine salvation. They are not name-tags loosely attached to the personal reality to which they refer. There is no nominalism intended in the transference of high titles of honor to Jesus of Nazareth. If we strip away the names which are above all the names that generally apply to other human beings, we have no way to speak of the meaning of Jesus. We can speak of him in the symbols of the texts and traditions, or we cannot speak of him at all, unless we fabricate our own image of Jesus and arbitrarily call him what we will. Nothing is more clear in the New Testament and the Christian tradition than the uniqueness of Jesus in whose name alone there is salvation, before whom every knee should bow and every tongue confess that he is Lord to the glory of God the Father (Phil. 2:10–11).

One of the earliest symbols of Christianity was the fish. In Greek the letters that spelled fish—IXTHUS—represented an ancient Christological confession: Jesus Christ Son of God Savior.[14] By what other names can Jesus be known? These are symbols that participate in the reality to which they refer, to use Tillich's definition of a symbol. Christian faith has no knowledge or interest in Jesus as Jesus, minus the names which symbolize his unique meaning. These symbols have a prehistory in the religions of that time, but when transferred to Jesus they crown him with a significance that underscores his uniqueness. They do not mean that Jesus is unique as every individual is unique. Although he is truly human, these titles place him in a class by himself. He is the one and only Christ, or he is not the Christ at all. He is the one and only Son of God, or he is not God's Son at all. He is the one and only Savior or he is no Savior at all. The exclusive claim is not a footnote to the gospel; it is the gospel itself. Not part of the husk, it is the kernel itself. The answer of the gospel to John the Baptist's question, "Are you the one who is to come?" is "Yes, and we shall not look for another" (Mt. 11:3).

All the Christological titles of the texts and traditions of historic biblical and catholic Christianity intend to lift up the uniqueness of Jesus as the living Christ, the risen Lord, and the eschatological Savior of the world. They alone can legitimate the role that Jesus came to assume as the cultic center in primitive Christian worship. Without these titles that acclaim the exclusive uniqueness of Jesus, he loses the vehicles of interpretation by which he is no mere dead hero of the past, buried in the ruins of his own time and place, but the living presence of God in the flesh. These titles—and they alone—tell us what the earliest believers in Jesus thought he was all about. They reveal the true identity of Jesus; at the core of this revelation is the exclusive uniqueness of Jesus in relation to God and his coming kingdom, in relation to the church, and in relation to the entire world of history and nature.

If we do not use these Christological titles as our linguistic access to the knowledge of Jesus' identity and meaning, then we shall have to find some other way of speaking about him, unless we are to remain silent. Who would we then say that he is, if he is not the one whom the earliest tests and traditions identify as the only true embodiment of God's word in history? Paul Knitter says that even though we strip away the Christological titles that declare the uniqueness of Jesus, he can still be vitally important to us Christians.[15] But so can Buddha, so can many things. When William Hamilton a decade ago was proclaiming the death of God, he was still clinging to Jesus. When asked, "Why Jesus?" he answered, "I have a hang-up on Jesus." Similarly, when the authors of the *Myth of God Incarnate* rejected the dogma of the incarnation as an unacceptable myth, they acknowledged that although they would have to abandon the ontological equation of Jesus with God, they would still go on speaking of Jesus Christ "as if he were God for us"[16] and use language that John Hick calls the "hyperbole of the heart."[17] But there is an old word for speaking of a creature "as if he were God"—idolatry. One of the "Myth of God Incarnate" theologians announces that Jesus will "always be the unique focus of my perception of and response to God."[18] But why Jesus? Who is he?

What is the essence of the uniqueness of Jesus? It does not lie in the fact that he was a historical individual who lived once upon a time in Palestine. Every one of us is a unique individual in the sense that none of us has a duplicate. I am the one who lives inside my skin at this time and place. But the uniqueness of Jesus is *sui generis*. He died as a unique historical individual at one time and place, under Pontius Pilate just outside the gate, but he was raised to be the living presence of God in every new age and every strange place. The issue of Jesus' uniqueness finally has to do with the resurrection. "God raised him to life again, setting him free from the pangs of death" (Acts 2:24).

When we confess the uniqueness of Jesus, we do not mean merely that he was a concrete individual man, which he was. We mean that he is the concrete embodiment of universal meaning. The true identity of Jesus was revealed to his disciples only after the resurrection, or at least only then could they begin to understand what he had been disclosing step by step along the way. If we could turn back the reel of history to the days before Easter, if we could only find some tapes or pictures of the man Jesus, if we could read the obituaries that appeared in the *Galilean Gazette*, I don't believe that we would gain a deeper insight into the true identity of Jesus. The true identity of Jesus is something which in the last analysis "flesh and blood" cannot reveal to us. More historical information will not solve the riddle of Jesus' personal identity. If a person looks into the abundant texts and traditions of the Christian past and concludes that Jesus is not the one they say he is, that person may invent other names and labels to transfer to Jesus, but in doing so the person is not adding to the fund of our knowledge about the historical Jesus, but only telling the world where he or she personally stands in relation to him. For the Christological titles that the apostles applied to Jesus were not broadcast on an objective screen of history. They were born in the struggles of following Jesus,[19] of preaching the kerygma of his cross and resurrection, and taking the gospel to the Gentiles. A Christological title is a dialectical statement that lives in the polar tension between subject and object. It says something about Jesus but also about the person making the confession. No one can call Jesus "Lord" except he has been grasped by the Holy Spirit (1 Cor. 12:3). The statement is not a product of objectifying analysis. Peter's confession, "You are the Christ, the Son of the living God," was an ecstatic statement—a miracle of the mind (Tillich).

The true identity of Jesus can be acknowledged only by faith in him as the risen Lord and the living Christ. We do not expect that anyone will confess the uniqueness of Jesus in the special sense implied by the sum of the Christological titles by means of a historiographical reconstruction of the historical Jesus. That Jesus is dead and buried and will always remain sealed in the tomb to people who do not believe that he now lives freely beyond the limits of his own earthly fate.

III. The Universality of Jesus Christ

The uniqueness of Jesus belongs to the core of the Christian gospel. What is unique about Jesus, however, is precisely his universal meaning. This particular and concrete man, Jesus of Nazareth, is unique because of his universal significance. His uniqueness lies in his universality. If Jesus is the Savior, he is the universal Savior. I cannot confine him to being my personal Savior, merely the focus of my own experience of God.

We are back to the beginning. If Jesus is the unique and universal Savior, how can there be a dialogue with other religions? Are not Christians bound to say that theirs is the only way of salvation, that non-Christians will be saved either by being evangelized here and now or by some loophole or other? We seem to be confronted with a dilemma. If Jesus is the unique and universal Savior, there is no salvation in the non-Christian religions. If there is salvation in the non-Christian religions, then Jesus is not the unique and universal Savior. Theology is facing this dilemma.

Christians should not be afraid of dialogue with other religions. The religions are part of the universal context in which the true identity of Jesus must find new expression. The Christological titles did not descend upon Jesus all at once and ready-made. There was a development in which new titles were discovered for Jesus in the hermeneutical process of transmitting the traditional texts within the horizon of new contexts. Every Christological title had to be born again in history in the process of encountering the story of Jesus in a new religious context. We do not yet fully know how we shall confess Jesus in the future of the dialogue with other religions. We shall continue to confess him in the language of our familiar texts and traditions. But the universality of Jesus means that he will live in the medium of symbols that may still seem strange to us. Churches and theologians are calling us to a new dialogue with the world religions. I do not have the benefit of personal involvement in any high-level, disciplined, and challenging dialogue with representatives of other religions. What we say now is part of our homework for a task that lies before us. Our churches and theologians are generally not prepared for such a dialogue. I do not want the church of which I am a part to be represented by a theology that has already abandoned the heart of the Christian gospel. We cannot accept the rules of a dialogue that require us to remain silent about what lies at the core of our movement. It is therefore very urgent that we know what we mean by the uniqueness and universality of Jesus Christ.

We have spoken about the uniqueness of Jesus, guided by the import of the major Christological titles applied to him after Easter. But how shall we understand the universality of Jesus?

Christians believe in the universality of salvation in Jesus' name. It is God's will that all people shall be saved and come to the knowledge of the truth (2 Tim. 2:4). Evangelicals generally accept universal salvation in this sense, as valid in principle for everyone. But they restrict salvation in the end to those who actually hear the gospel and put their faith in Christ.[20] Under this restriction the rift that has been opened up in the world through sin will widen to an eternal chasm, splitting the one world of God's creation into two unreconcilable halves, only God's half will be much smaller than the devil's, in fact, only a remnant of the whole. There is not much for the angels to sing about if the evangelicals get what they expect—a heaven sparsely filled with only card-carrying Christians.

Biblical universalism transcends the particularist eschatology of the evangelicals. There are stern warnings in the New Testament threatening eternal perdition. There are reservations; there are qualifications of the universal hope. But these are addressed more to those inside with apparently the right credentials than those outside. "This people honors me with their lips, but their heart is far from me" (Mt. 15:8; Mk. 7:6). "It is not those who say to me, 'Lord, Lord,' who will enter the kingdom of heaven" (Mt. 7:21). The New Testament warns of the spiritual danger of using the right evangelical words and ecclesiastical doctrines as the basis of trust and hope. There is spiritual danger in reducing the power and future of the universal Christ to the pinhole size of the believer's faith or the church's confession here and now.

New Testament universalism, however, is always a predicate of the uniqueness of Jesus Christ, not a metaphysical attribute of the world in process (as in the Origenistic doctrine of *apokatastasis ton panton*), or of a saving potential inherent in the world religions, or of an existential possibility universally available to every person in a moment of decision. The uniqueness Christians claim for Jesus as World-Savior lies in the revelation of his eschatological identity constituted by his resurrection victory over death as the "last enemy" of humankind. The uniqueness of Jesus is not a function of our Christian *blik*. It belongs to him by virtue of his enthronement as the Lord of the coming kingdom. A particularist eschatology can be constructed only by picking particular passages, and choosing to ignore others. What about the universalist thrust in the Pauline theology? "Just as all men die in Adam, so will all be brought to life in Christ" (1 Cor. 15:22). "For in him [Christ] all the fullness of God was pleased to dwell, and through him to reconcile to himself all things, whether on earth or in heaven, making peace by the blood of his cross" (Col. 1:19–20). "For he has made known to us in all wisdom and insight the mystery of his will, according to his purpose which he set forth in Christ as a plan for the fullness of time, to unite all things in him, things in heaven and things in earth" (Eph. 1:9–10). "That at the name of Jesus every knee should bow, in heaven and on earth and under the earth, and every tongue confess that Jesus Christ is Lord, to the glory of God the Father" (Phil. 2:10–11). "When all things are subjected to him, then the Son himself will also be subjected to him who put all things under him, that God may be everything to every one" (1 Cor. 15:28). Here we have the core of the kind of eschatological panentheism that has sparked the imagination of Wolfhart Pannenberg and others. ''And he is the expiation for our sins, and not for ours only but also for the sins of the whole world'' (1 John 2:2). We cannot take time for an exegesis of these passages. But I have piled verse upon verse to create a total impression of the universalizing tendencies in these passages.

The evangelicals ignore anything that smacks of a universal eschatology, preferring instead to hold a monopoly for Christians on the salvation which God in Christ has accomplished for the world, converting their believing in Christ or their belonging to the church into a meritorious thing that earns salvation and insures against damnation.[21] For a long time I was taught some version of this self-centered and vindictive eschatology, but I cannot remember ever literally believing the Christ-diminishing implication that in the end all the bad news piling up against the world would win out against the good news that dawned for the world on the morning of Easter.

In the strength of the Christian belief in the uniqueness and universality of Jesus Christ, it is imperative that Christians cheerfully enter into every arena of witness and dialogue with people of other faiths. ''For he who is not against us is on our side'' (Lk. 9:50). But what shall we expect to find in a dialogue with other religions? We have encountered the view of Knitter and Hick that there is salvation without Christ in the other religions, and therefore not only outside the church, not only apart from faith in Christ, but also apart from Christ altogether. The coming of Christ is not necessary for the salvation of humanity. They do not deny that there is salvation in Christ for Christians, but they do abandon the hope of the world's salvation in Christ alone as a chauvinistic doctrine, and along with it, of course, the Christological premise of the uniqueness and universality of Jesus which supports the hope.

The teaching that there is salvation in the other religions is spreading in the churches. No doubt, Rahner's influence is the major force on the Catholic side, and perhaps the process theologians are the dominant school on the Protestant side, since they operate with a purely representative view of salvation in Christ.[22] According to this view salvation does not happen for the world on account of Christ; it is only *represented* in a decisively clear way, although I have failed to find anything decisive or clear in Process Christology.

Christian theologians are debating the question whether or not there is salvation in other religions, and taking sides on the issue, without first making clear the model of salvation they have in mind. If a prospector says, "There is gold in those hills," he must know the difference between gold and the other metals. What is the salvation that theologians expect to find or not to find in other religions? Most of the debate so far has taken us nowhere, because vastly different things are meant by salvation. If salvation is whatever you call it, there is no reason for a Christian to deny that there is salvation in other religions. We may speak of salvation on two levels, phenomenologically and theologically. On a purely phenomenological level, there are numerous models of salvation and there are ways of delivering each of the models and making them work. When the nomads needed a land for their salvation, they were promised a land by their God, and they got it, and have suffered ever since. When the slaves in Egypt needed deliverance from oppression for their salvation, God called Moses to lead the exodus out of Egypt. When the wandering people of God needed food for their salvation from hunger, God supplied them with daily manna from above. And the history of salvation went on, creating different models for its expression, but always pointing forward to new dimensions generated by the experience of fundamental lack. Land is needed, but it's not enough. Freedom is needed, but it's not enough. Food is needed, but it's not enough.

If we are told there is salvation in the other religions, there is no a priori reason to deny it. It depends on what is meant by salvation. If salvation is the experience of illumination, then Buddha can save. I say this cautiously, because I stand on this side of the dialogue. If salvation is the experience of union with God, then Hinduism can save. If salvation is being true to the ancestors, then Shintoism can save. If salvation is revolution against the overlords and equality for the people, then Maoism can save. If salvation is liberation from poverty and oppression, then Marxism can save. If salvation is psychological health, there is salvation not only outside the church but outside the religions as well. If salvation is striving for humanization, for development, for wholeness, for justice, for peace, for freedom, for the whole earth, for what not, there is salvation in the other religions, in the quasi-religions, and in the secular ideologies. The reason Christians are confused and have appeared so smug about salvation is that they imagined they held a monopoly on salvation. Then when they have discovered virtues and values that match or excel what they find among Christians, they are prepared to accept the doctrine of salvation in non-Christian religions, perhaps even to the point of surrendering every version of the *sola Christi*. So we have moved from salvation available exclusively in a Christian specialty store to a veritable supermarket of salvation whose shelves are stacked with man-made substitutes at inflationary prices, packaged for cosmetic appeal and convenient consumption.

On a theological level salvation is not whatever you want to call it, the fulfillment of every need or the compensation for every lack. I do not deny that we may also speak of salvation in this extended phenomenological sense, with the warning that it has generated much of the confusion in which our topic languishes. Salvation in the Bible is a promise that God offers the world on the horizon of our expectation of personal and universal death. The gospel is the power of God unto salvation because it promises to break open the vicious cycle of death. Death is the power that draws every living thing into its circle. Here I cannot enter into the mystery of death. But if anyone denies the reality of death and its power to insinuate itself as the eschaton of all life, threatening the very conditions of the possibility of meaningful existence, I would take a patient "wait and see" attitude. It is just a question of time before death will punctuate everybody's personal story with its own annihilating force. We cannot derive a final meaning for life on this side of death. We can gain the partial salvation we are willing to pay for, but none of these techniques of salvation can succeed in buying off death.

Salvation in the New Testament is what God has done to death in the resurrection of Jesus. Salvation is what happens to you and me and the whole world in spite of death, if the resurrection of Jesus means what the apostolic kerygma and the catholic dogma have interpreted it to mean. The story of salvation is a drama of death and resurrection, whatever other human personal and social problems the word might take on. The gospel is the announcement that in one man's history death is no longer the eschaton, but was only the second to last thing. It has now become past history. Death lies behind Jesus, qualifying him to lead the procession from death unto new life. Since death is what separates the person from God in the end, only that power which transcends death can liberate the person for eternal life with God. This is the meaning of salvation in the biblical Christian sense. It is eschatological salvation, because the God who raised Jesus from the dead has overcome death as the final eschaton of life. Our final salvation lies in the eschatological future when our own death will be put behind us. This does not mean that there is no salvation in the present, no realized aspect of salvation. It means that the salvation we enjoy now is like borrowing from the future, living now as though our future could already be practiced in the present, because of our union with the risen Christ through faith and hope.

Theologians who speak of salvation in the non-Christian religions should tell us if it is the same salvation that God has promised the world by raising Jesus from the dead. The resurrection gospel is the criterion of the meaning of salvation in the New Testament sense. When Christians enter into dialogue with persons of other religions, they must do their utmost to communicate what they mean by the assertion that Jesus lives and explain how this gospel intersects the hopes and fears of every person whose fate is to anticipate death as the final eschaton. If the dialogue shows that other religions are not much moved by the problem of death, that the problem of death is limited to a particular way of viewing the human predicament, we would have to say that the encounter with Christianity itself becomes the occasion for everyone to see that the problem of death arises out of the structure of existence itself. The gospel falls upon the human situation and illuminates the universal existential problem. This is the hypothesis that Christians bring into an interreligious dialogue. A Christology that is silent about the resurrection of Jesus from the dead is not worthy of the Christian name and should not be called Christology at all.

The new challenge to Christology is to speak of the identity of Jesus Christ in the context of the world religions and secular culture. In the past, theology has dealt with the religions from afar, giving us a Christian interpretation of the non-Christian religions from a ready-made theological point of view. In a sense this is all we can do prior to the event of dialogue. But if we really believe that the uniqueness of Jesus lies in his universality, that his identity is always being mediated through the concrete events of history, then we should be open to exploring what the non-Christian religions can contribute to our understanding of the universal identity of Jesus Christ. The history of the religions once contributed all the Christological titles to the interpretation of the Jesus-event. Some of them were rooted in the ancient Hebrew traditions, others not, but all of them were transformed in the process of being assimilated into the traditions about Jesus. That process is still going on in the openness of world history, engendered by the universal missionary witness to Jesus as the Christ, the Lord and Savior of the world.

I asked one of my African graduate students, "If you were to appropriate a religious symbol of highest significance from the framework of traditional African religious experience, what would you call Jesus?"

His answer was "The ancestor."

I responded, "In the past the missionary told you what you should or should not say, repeating the texts and traditions of his own religious context. But now you must decide for yourself whether it is appropriate to call Jesus the ancestor, whether that would be faithful to the biblical text and relevant to the African context. I don't know." Then I muttered something about, "Before Abraham was, I am," not really knowing what it might mean today.

The identity of Jesus cannot be limited to the particular

contexts of our past. Christology is not static. New contexts have made it possible for new meanings to blossom on old texts. They relate to the concrete struggles of people for life, health, wholeness, fulfillment, salvation. In India Jesus is pictured by some as the Avatar. To us this means practically nothing, but in India possibly a great deal. In many parts of the Third World, Jesus is the liberator. Liberation has become the focal image of a whole new Christology. To us it may also mean something, but not exactly the same as to people suffering the conditions of poverty, exploitation, and oppression. In the patristic era Jesus was called the Logos, and that carried a metaphysical meaning quite different from the same word in the Gospel of John. In Nazi Germany, Martin Niemöller preached about Jesus as the true *Führer*. In the context of Western atheism and the trend to depersonalization in technological society, Dorothy Sölle has animated the theme of Jesus as the "representative." Similar titles, such as "advocate," "delegate," and "deputy," have been used to speak of the meaning of Jesus for modern people, and perhaps soon, if not already, someone in the Far East will suggest "chairman." Every culture has to ask of Jesus in its own way, "Are you the One who is to come, or do we look for another?" Every people will have to answer, "Who do you say that I am?" in a language they can understand. The crucifix of Jesus as a tortured Peruvian Indian on the cover of Gustavo Gutiérrez's book *Theology of Liberation* could not have been sculpted in another part of the world.

The point we have been making is that the exclusive uniqueness of Jesus, mediated by the texts and traditions that announce his resurrection as the living Lord, drives us to discover his universal significance, not in another world after this one, but in the real contexts of ongoing history. His true identity is still being disclosed in the encounter of the gospel with the world religions. It is not a case of the gospel meeting the world religions down a one-way street, laying on them the traditional symbols of Christology and receiving nothing back. The dialogue will be a two-way street, in which the condition of openness to the other religions will be motivated by a knowledge that they also somehow speak of Jesus Christ. The Old Testament is the paradigm case of how one religion of another time and place can speak of Jesus Christ in a proleptic way. If the apostles and the church fathers could find anticipations of Christ in the Old Testament, we have a right to expect a similar thing in the texts and traditions of other religions. For God has not left himself without a witness in these religions.

We have steered a course between the Scylla of evangelicalism without the universality of Jesus Christ and the Charybdis of universalism without the uniqueness of Jesus Christ. But ours is not essentially a middle position combining elements at random from the right and the left. Rather, the right and the left are splinters of a holistic vision of the eschatological Christ whose uniqueness lies in his concrete universality.[23] This universality is being worked out in the world mission of the church. The ultimate horizon of this historically mediated universality is hope for an eternal restitution of all things in God. We have a universal hope in Christ, not a universal gnosis. It is a hope that engenders the actions of witness and mission in history, not a knowledge that pretends to know the final outcome of things in advance. It is a hope that the Lord of the church will also finally rule as the Lord of the world, inclusive of all its religions.[24] Meanwhile, we can witness and work as though God is at work behind the backs of the plurality of world religions, pushing them forward into a final unity that has become proleptically incarnate for all in Jesus Christ. There are not two ways of salvation.[25] There is one salvation, one way of salvation, one Savior of the world, and that is the eschatological salvation valid for all through the one who came that all might find life, who died that the world might be reconciled, who was raised that hope might live for the victory of God and the restitution of all things in him.

NOTES

1. Quoted in Robert L. Wilken, "The Making of a Phrase," *Dialog, A Journal of Theology* 12 (Summer 1973): 174.

2. John Hick, *God and the Universe of Faiths* (New York: Macmillan, 1973), pp. 121ff.

3. John Hick, "Jesus and the World Religions," in *The Myth of God Incarnate*, ed. John Hick (Philadelphia: Westminster Press, 1977), p. 179.

4. Paul F. Knitter, "A Critique of Hans Küng's *On Being a Christian*," *Horizons* 5, no. 2 (1978): 151-64.

5. *Ibid.*, p. 156.

6. *Ibid.*, p. 153.

7. *Ibid.*

8. *Ibid.*, p. 154.

9. J. D. Douglas, ed., *Let the Earth Hear His Voice*, (Minneapolis: World Wide Publications, 1975), p. 76.

10. See C. F. D. Moule, *The Origin of Christology* (London: Cambridge Univ. Press, 1977), and Willi Marxsen, *The Beginnings of Christology: A Study in Its Problems* (Philadelphia: Fortress Press, 1969). These two writings represent the right and the left in current New Testament scholarship dealing with the relation between the historical Jesus and Christology. Both lead us to the same conclusion: that attempt to construct a totally non-Christological interpretation of the historical Jesus proves itself to be a failure.

11. This was the judgment that Martin Kahler reached as early as 1892 in his book, *The So-Called Historical Jesus and the Historic Biblical Christ*, ed. Carl E. Bratten (Philadelphia: Fortress Press, 1964).

12. For an excellent summary of the current state of New Testament scholarship regarding the Christological titles, see Christoph Demke, *Die Einzigartigkeit Jesu* (Berlin: Evangelische Verlagsanstalt, 1976).

13. See Oscar Cullmann, *The Christology of the New Testament* (Philadelphia: Westminster Press, 1959), pp. 239-47.

14. *Ibid.*, p. 245.

15. Paul Knitter, *op. cit.*, pp. 153, 155.

16. Frances Young, "A Cloud of Witnesses," in *The Myth of God Incarnate*, *op. cit.*, p. 39.

17. John Hick, "Jesus and the World Religions," p. 183.

18. Frances Young, "A Cloud of Witnesses," p. 38.

19. The role of "following Jesus" in Christology has been recently stressed by Jon Sobrino in *Christology at the Crossroads* (Maryknoll, N.Y.: Orbis Books, 1978).

20. See Harold Lindsell, "Universalism," in *Let the Earth Hear His Voice*, *op. cit.*, pp. 1206-13.

21. Of course, no one holding such a view would acknowledge that granting such a causal role to faith and/or membership in the church could be regarded as "a meritorious thing that earns salvation."

22. See Schubert M. Ogden, "The Point of Christology," *Journal of Religion* 55, no. 4 (October 1975): 375-95; David Griffin, *A Process Christology* (Philadelphia: Westminster Press, 1973); John Cobb, *Christ in a Pluralistic Age* (Philadelphia: Westminster Press, 1975).

23. Our point is that evangelical particularity and catholic universality are both inherent in the biblical picture of the historical Jesus of Nazareth as the resurrected Christ of God.

24. A Christocentric evangelical universalism is epistemologically a vision of hope generated by a living faith in an unconditionally loving God

who showed his invincible power by raising Jesus from the dead. See Robert William Jenson, *The Knowledge of Things Hoped For* (London: Oxford Univ. Press, 1971).

25. The notion of two ways of salvation has been clearly proposed by H. R. Schlette, *Colloquium salutis—Christen und Nichtchristen heute* (Cologne, 1965); also "Einige Thesen zum Selbstverstandnis der Theologie angesichts der Religionen," in *Gott in Welt II*, ed. J. B. Metz (Freiburg: Herder, 1964), pp. 306–16.

II: Dialogue on Dialogue

The Theological Basis of Interfaith Dialogue

John V. Taylor

In any dialogue, states the Anglican Bishop of Winchester, England, appreciation must precede the reconciliation of ideas, especially if past isolations have bred ignorance and suspicion. Yet "Christians ought not to imagine that there is anything particularly new or radical in this open attitude to the other great faiths." The Bible and church history show otherwise. John V. Taylor's experiences as a former missionary in Africa and as the past general secretary of the Church Missionary Society help him to illustrate what he calls the "jealousies" of different faiths, "those points in every religion concerning which the believers are inwardly compelled to claim a universal significance and finality." Yet the Christian claim on the absolute centrality of Jesus Christ, if correctly understood, "ought logically to relieve [one] of anxiety and argument about the salvation and future destiny of those whose lives are lived out within other traditions of response." And if through dialogue we honestly expose our experiences to one another's questioning, Christians will be helped to reappraise their own tradition and reformulate their own fidelities. "A genuine openness to the questions that another faith poses can mean, for the believer of any religion, a deeper entry into one's own faith." This essay was the first Lambeth Interfaith Lecture in November 1977; it appeared in *The Crucible* (January–March, 1978), the quarterly journal of the Board for Social Responsibility of the General Synod of the Church of England, and in the *International Review of Mission*, October 1979.

Dialogue, as I understand it, means a sustained conversation between parties who are not saying the same thing and who recognize and respect the differences, the contradictions, and the mutual exclusions between their various ways of thinking. The object of this dialogue is understanding and appreciation, leading to further reflection upon the implication for one's own position of the convictions and sensitivities of the other traditions.

Appreciation must precede reconciliation of ideas. This is a more exacting exercise than any of us would wish for, because every human being finds it difficult to sustain contradictions and live with them. Instinctively we either try to destroy what is opposed to our understanding of truth or we pretend that the antithesis is unreal. The reason for this is, I believe, that we are all naturally frightened by the unsolved opposites in ourselves and find it very painful to include and accept the dark self alongside the light, the destroyer as well as the creator in us, both the male and the female element in our personality, both the child and the parent which we are. We want to be a simple unity but in fact we are a structure of contradictions. It takes a high degree of maturity to let the opposites co-exist without pretending that they can be made compatible.

It takes the same maturity to respect an opinion that conflicts with one's own without itching to bring about a premature and naive accommodation. I suppose this is what is entailed in loving one's enemies. One has to appreciate the reason for their opposition, grant its integrity, and deal honestly with its challenges, without surrendering any of one's own integrity or diminishing the content of one's examined convictions. And there will generally have to be a great deal of that kind of loving before we can expect any genuine reconciliation of ideas and beliefs. The loving which is expressed through the attempt to listen and understand and honor, through the frank recognition and appreciation of convictions that deny one's own, through the opening of one's imagination to the real otherness of the other, is, in my view, the function of interfaith dialogue.

Past Isolation Has Bred Ignorance and Suspicion

We have a lot of leeway to make up, for we have all suffered from hundreds of years of religious isolation. During the first few centuries of the Church's history Christians took it as a matter of course that they were surrounded by people with different religions from their own. They had to face questions about their own practice and belief posed by their Jewish environment first of all and soon after, by the Graeco-Roman culture or the religions of Parthia and further east. They had to learn how to keep themselves separate for survival, but they also had to learn how to reconcile their undeniable spiritual experience with the framework of ideas that supported these other faiths and philosophies. Religious pluralism was the milieu of the first Christians.

But the society of Western Christendom, in which the thought and tradition of our Church was developed and fixed, was very different. It was hemmed in by the encircling power and superior culture of Islam and confined to the western corner of the vast Euro-Asian continent. Had the Church of those centuries been so minded it might have developed a positive and open relationship with the Jewish communities in its midst. Unhappily this was not its mood and, in any case, the greatest flowering of Jewish culture and teaching took place in Islamic Spain, cut off from contact with Christendom.

As a counter aggression the Church developed a crusading ethos that became a fundamental feature of its tradition, an ethos which even today is second nature to many Christians. That stirring poem of heroic war, the Song of Roland, reflects the utter ignorance of Islam which was typical of Christian thought in the 11th century. Muslims are regarded as pagans and polytheists worshipping three great idols called Mahmoud, Termagent, and Appolyon! My guess is, though I do not have access to the evidence, that the popular notions of Christianity among Muslims or even Jews of those days were equally ignorant.

One of the bitter fruits of this long history of non-communication is the tendency in every religious culture to read deliberate hostility into the quite innocent attitudes of people of another faith. I recall a fairly typical experience at Rawalpindi in 1968 when I was invited to meet the staff of the Islamic Research Institute. A very liberal and remarkably open discussion was traumatically upset by the intervention of a young historian from North Africa who protested that the contemporary Church was as relentlessly hostile to Islam as it had ever been, and he instanced missionary sympathy with the Southern Sudanese revolt, widespread Christian rejoicing over Israel's capture of the Old City of Jerusalem, and the churches' support of Biafra. I would place in the same category the widespread Jewish conviction that the hesitancy of Christian leaders to endorse every advance of the Jewish State is evidence of their immutable antagonism, and the tendency of many African Christians to see behind the atrocities of [Uganda's] Amin, for instance, a pan-Islamic policy of expansion. Dialogue, as I understand it, means overcoming the immediate urge to dismiss these suspicions as untrue, accepting the fact that, true or not, the suspicions are part of the data of our relationships, and facing the possibility that perhaps the other person has more reason to be suspicious of me than I have hitherto admitted. If we all made that effort of imagination it might make us humbler and gentler.

Each Religion is a Tradition of Response by Ordinary People

We come to the dialogue, therefore, lumbered with our past histories and the fears they have engendered in us. But if we are to go forward history must be forgotten, or at least forgiven. For dialogue is between the living, the people of here and now. Dialogue seeks a new beginning. Dialogue also has to take account mainly of the normal adherents of the different faiths, not the great saints nor the great sinners, for in a sense they prove very little. I was reminded of this a month ago in Assisi where two Franciscan stories were retold to me one after the other. The first concerns Saint Francis' strange meeting with Sala'din. They had no common language, so little dialogue can have taken place. Yet near the end of the encounter Sala'din is reported to have said "If ever I meet a second Christian like you I would be willing to be baptized. But that will not happen."

And less than 300 years later a king in Peru said something very similar, yet horribly different, to a Franciscan friar. This friar, accompanying an expedition of the Conquistadores, was offering the vanquished Incas the choice of conversion or death. When their king demurred, his hands were cut off and the appeal was then repeated: "Be baptized and you will go to heaven." "No," said the king, "for if I went to heaven I might meet a second Christian like you." Those two incidents may show the terrible liability to decline which is inherent in any great spiritual movement. But they also warn us against focusing our dialogue upon the exceptionally good or bad in the history of any religion.

For I believe we should think of every religion as a people's particular tradition of response to the reality which the Holy Spirit of God has set before their eyes. I am deliberately not saying that any religion is the truth which the Spirit has disclosed, nor even that it contains that truth. I think it may often be misleading to speak of the various religions as revelations of God, for that suggests that God disclosed part of himself to one people and a different part to others. Is that how a compassionate father loves the various children of his family? It is surely truer to believe that God's self-revelation and self-giving is consistent for all, but that different peoples have responded differently. All we can say without presumption is that this is how people in a particular culture have responded and taught others to respond to what the Spirit of God through the events of their history and the vision of their prophets made them aware of.

By putting it this way we do justice both to the God-given element and to the man-made element in every religion. We also leave room for the recognition that every religious tradition includes the response of disobedience as well as the response of obedience. For human beings can use religion against God or as an escape from him just as much as they use religion for God and as an approach to him. And both the obedience and the disobedience gets built into the tradition and passed on to later generations. And they, in their turn, may respond more readily to the unceasing calls and disclosures of the Spirit, and so be moved to reform some part of the tradition. So every living faith is found to be in a continual process of renewal and purification while at the same time it conserves the tradition and transmits it as something recognizably the same. In every religion, therefore, we shall find the same tension between conservatism and development, and it must be so if past fidelity and present response are both to be seen as an answer to him who is beyond all religion.

But since every religion is a historically determined tradition of response to what the Spirit of God has forever been setting before men's eyes, we must expect to find that each religion has become a self-consistent and almost closed system of culture and language. Communication between one such system and another is fraught with difficulty which must not be underestimated.

As dialogue begins, therefore, we shall frequently find that the same word carries an entirely different cluster of meanings in the different traditions; we may also discover with surprise that quite different words are used to mean the same thing. I recall a very well-known and respected participant in the dialogue between Christians and Hindus exclaiming in the course of a conversation—"What makes this so painful is that again and again, when my Hindu brother and I seem to be drawing closer than ever before, and at a deeper level, at that very moment the immense gulf between us opens up again."

This is to a considerable extent a problem of hermeneutics, the structure of meanings in communication. Different cultures develop different horizons of understanding, as they are called. And therein lies some degree of hopefulness. Professor Heinrich Ott of Basel University, speaking at the World Council of Churches consultation at Chiang Mai in Thailand last April [1977], said: "We can look for a partial convergence of the horizons of understanding on the two sides. There arises a new common horizon for the partners in the dialogue, a new world, so to speak, with new possibilities and understanding and speech—and therefore the disclosure of new theological dimensions.''

The Open, Inclusive View in Christian Theology

Christians ought not to imagine that there is anything particularly new or radical in this open attitude to the other great faiths. In spite of the long isolation of the Middle Ages and the theology of exclusive salvation which is familiar to us, there has always been in the Jewish-Christian tradition another more inclusive view of the wideness of God's grace and redemption.

The exclusive Covenant with Israel is not the only one in the Old Testament. The Covenant with Noah embracing all the sons of men and, indeed, all creation, reverberates through the words of much later prophets and psalmists. God has shown his particular favor in more than one exodus deliverance. ''Have I not brought up Israel out of the land of Egypt, and the Philistines from Caphtor, and the Syrians from Kir?'' (Amos 9:7) More than one nation, therefore, enjoys the experience of being chosen for blessing and for bringing blessing to the world. ''In that day shall Israel be the third with Egypt and Assyria, a blessing in the midst of the earth: for the Lord of Hosts has blessed them, saying: Blessed be Egypt my people, and Assyria the work of my hands, and Israel mine inheritance'' (Isaiah 19:25).

Therefore any sense of exclusive privilege on the part of a particular religion, including the Church, lays it open to a stringent judgment in comparison to the other faiths of men. ''From the rising of the sun to the going down of the same my name is great among the Gentiles, and in every place incense is offered in my name and a pure offering. But you have profaned it'' (Malachi 1:11). Does it not seem likely that this haunting reference to the rising and going down of the sun was in the mind of Jesus when he pointed to the faith of the Roman centurion, saying: ''Many shall come from the East and from the West and shall sit down with Abraham and Isaac and Jacob in the Kingdom of heaven, but the sons of the

Kingdom shall be cast into outer darkness'' (Matthew 8:11–12). The Church cannot read those words today without applying them to itself, and, indeed, they strike at the heart of all exclusive religious claims.

Following up this element in the Gospel, Paul also refers more than once to God's universal disclosure of himself, and this is not only in the Book of the Acts but in the Epistles as well. "For all that may be known of God by men lies plain before their eyes, indeed God has disclosed it to them himself" (Romans 1:19). He goes on, of course, to show how universally men have closed their eyes against the truth made known to them, but that is a theme I have already touched upon in calling religions traditions of response.

When we examine the later teaching of the Church we find that the stark statement, "No salvation outside the Church," was never allowed to go unmodified. Justin Martyr, for example, wrote: "Christ is the firstborn of God and we have declared that he is the Word of whom every race of men were partakers; and those who lived according to the Logos are Christians even though they have been thought atheists, as, among the Greeks, Socrates and Heraclitus." And Augustine writing as an old man in his *Retractions* made this startling statement: "The reality itself, which we now call the Christian religion, was present among the early people and up to the time of the coming of Christ was never absent from the beginning of the human race: so that the true religions which already existed now began to be called Christian." I am very sensitive of the arrogance that such a statement must seem to convey to adherents of other great faiths today, and I shall deal with that problem in a moment. At this point my concern is to show the presence of an inclusive as well as an exclusive theology of the world religions in the Christian tradition.

But what about St Peter's often quoted and clear claim that "there is no other name given among men by which we may be saved"? Wait a minute. What was the context of that affirmation? He was referring to the cure of the crippled beggar at the Beautiful Gate of the Temple. He was saying that Jesus of Nazareth is the source of every act of healing and salvation that has ever happened. He knew perfectly well that vast numbers of people had been healed without any knowledge of Jesus, yet he made the astounding claim that Jesus was the hidden author of all healing. He was the totally unique savior because he was totally universal.

Now I am not addicted to proof-texts, and if I were I would be beset by a species of gadfly that attacks all teachers of Christianity in these days, insisting that any text that seems to prove something is ipso facto suspect. But even if Peter did not himself make quite such a categorical or far-reaching assertion, it is clear that almost from the start Christians have claimed some kind of identity between Jesus of Nazareth and the life-giving forces of the creation, between the historic man and the universal principle. Jesus, they say, is central to what St Paul called "The predeterminate purpose of God."

Christians Claim an Absolute Centrality for Jesus Christ

We should remember, in passing, that this kind of claim is not peculiar to the Christian religion. The Muslim would say, I believe, that the Holy Qu'ran is central to the predeterminate purpose of God. For the Jew, God's covenant with Israel and her settlement in the Holy Land is central to the divine purpose for all mankind. For the Buddhist the concept of the Buddha in one form or another is central to the purpose behind human existence. It is the nature of religious experience to put into the believer's hands a key which is absolute and irreducible. But when one considers the indifferent things that are claimed as the key, comparisons crumble.

For the Christian, this belief that Jesus is central to God's purpose for mankind ought logically to relieve him of anxiety and argument about the salvation and future destiny of those whose lives are lived out within other traditions of response. This should not be the major issue in our theological reflection about the significance of the world religions. The phrase "before the foundation of the world" occurs in two significant New Testament texts: the well-known Revelation that describes the Lamb slain before the foundation of the world, and Ephesians 1:4 which says that "in Christ he chose us before the world was founded." Both texts tell us something about the constitution of the universe we inhabit. Both texts employ a startling metaphor of a time before time began. If we first accept this metaphor or image without unravelling it into non-mythical terms it says that, from the beginning, the world was held in existence by the Redeemer who was to die. This is a pre-forgiven universe. God has chosen in eternity to take upon himself the risk and the cost of creating this kind of world. As a pre-condition of creation he took upon himself the judgment and death of the sinner. Being forgiven is therefore a more primary condition of man than being in ignorance of Christ. So any and every movement of man's mind and will that can properly be called a response of faith is truly faith in Christ to some degree even though Christ is still only the invisible magnetic pole that draws us on.

But perhaps it makes more sense to our modern minds if we unravel this time metaphor. Its meaning must have something to do with the connection between God's being and God's doing—what God is eternally in himself and what God does which is necessarily within time. Now the peculiar insight of the Bible, which has recently been strongly endorsed by at least one school of Western philosophy, is this: there is no such thing as merely being, not even in God. One is only what one has done, or what one is inwardly and irrevocably committed to doing. This concept often eludes us because of the influence of Greek abstraction upon our thought. To say that a person is loving or just is actually meaningless until that person is committed in particular acts of love and justice. It is by acting truly and consistently at moments when the opposite is a real alternative that one comes to be truthful and reliable. Action creates being—not the other way round.

No person and not even God can be merciful and forgiving in the abstract or in a timeless vacuum where there is nothing and no one to forgive. So we might truly say that in order to be the Father whose property it is always to have mercy it is necessary for God to have committed himself to a concrete act of bearing the death of the sinner. This is not to say that God's existence is contingent on the events of history. He is contingent only upon his own sovereign commitment to be what he will be. But that itself is a commitment to action in time. So, with our minds open to recognize the reality of the experience of divine grace and salvation within all the faiths of mankind, we can say that what God did through Jesus Christ is the one act which it was always necessary that he should accomplish in time and at the right time if he was to be the God who throughout time is accessible and present to every human being in judgment and mercy, grace and truth. Or, in other words, whenever we see people enjoying a living relationship with God and experiencing his grace we are seeing the fruits of Calvary though this may neither be acknowledged nor known. It still makes a vast difference to people when they have seen the Cross of Jesus as the indicator of the inner nature of God, and that remains the theme of the Christian witness. But in bearing that witness we do not have to deny the reality of the experiences of grace and salvation that are found in all the faiths of mankind.

Every Religion Has Its "Jealousies"

You will realize, of course, that in what I have just said I have been talking as a Christian to Christians and wrestling with a theological problem in Christian terms. I recognize that the claims I have made for the person of Jesus are quite unacceptable to friends whose religion is different from mine. Yet I profoundly believe that this *kind* of statement should be welcomed from any of the parties in interfaith dialogue.

It is not enough to limit our search to the areas of common ground, though these will always give us deep satisfaction when we find them. For there is something else which is in fact common to us all and that is what I would call the "jealousies" of the different faiths. I mean those points in every religion concerning which the believers are inwardly compelled to claim a universal significance and finality. I have already referred to some of them—the Muslim conviction that the Holy Qu'ran is not just another revelation but is God's last word; the Jewish conviction that Israel's covenant and her attachment to the Holy Land has a central significance in the determinate purpose of God; the Christian conviction that in the life and death and resurrection of Jesus God

acted decisively for all mankind. The great faiths of Southern
Asia may be inclined to argue that such absolute claims are
typical of the semitic religions only, yet after many conversations I begin to wonder whether Hindu relativism is not itself
another of those absolutes of a particular faith which cannot
be surrendered without destroying the essential identity of
that faith.

All such convictions are strictly irreducible. I call them
the "jealousies" of the different faiths, deliberately using
that ambiguous word, because, seen from outside a particular
household of faith, such claims are bound to seem narrowly
possessive; but within the household they reflect an experience
which cannot be gainsaid. Every profoundly convincing encounter with God is with a jealous God. This simply means
that having experienced God in that way, no other God will
do. It is totally unhelpful to condemn such responses as arrogant. The meaning of things conveyed by such an experience is of such moment that it must be seen to have universal
relevance, and to deny this is to be false to the experience
itself.

So my Muslim brother says "Every child is born a Muslim," and I know what he means precisely because I have to
say "Every child is born in Christ." It is too facile to say
simply that we mean the same thing. Each of us can recognize the contradiction between our views. But, given a deep
mutual respect for one another's irreducible conviction, this
does not bring our discourse to a standstill. As Professor
Heinrich Ott put it during the World Council of Churches
consultation at Chiang Mai, "Genuine dialogue will not then
be prevented by the belief of each partner that the ultimate
and deepest insight into the truth nevertheless lies on his
side." Nor, I would add, will it be prevented by the longing
in each of the partners that the other shall come in his own
way to see that truth as he sees it. If we sustain our dialogue
undaunted by the emergence of these rock-like contradictions
and exclusions we shall, in fact, find what Father Yves Raguin of the Society of Jesus called at that same consultation
"the paradox that there is no dialogue possible unless we

realize the magnitude of the differences and try *from this* to find a common ground.''

In other words, one of the most significant things we have in common on which to build our mutual understanding is the experience of having a conviction that by definition precludes the other person's belief, and being unable to accommodate it with integrity. One recalls the underlying truth of Kipling's hackneyed verse:

> Oh, East is East and West is West, and never the twain
> shall meet,
> Till Earth and Sky stand presently at God's great judge-
> ment seat;
> But there is neither East nor West, Border nor Breed nor
> Birth,
> When two strong men stand face to face, though they
> come from the ends of the earth.

So I would again plead with those who want to make all the intractable convictions relative and level them down for the sake of a quick reconciliation: Leave us at least our capacity for categorical assertion, for that is what we have in common.

So let us not deceive one another about these absolute claims. They cannot be relativized, and the idea that the great faiths can be harmonized by doing that is too shallow. In our discourse with adherents of other faiths we may put our particular "jealousies" in parenthesis, as it were, and have our private reservations, but we must not expect one another to abandon them. We may learn to reformulate these irreducible convictions in the light of our dialogue. But we know that the reformulation may never reduce or dilute the content of the experience which it interprets.

Some Experiences Have to be Absolute and Universalized

Let me explain that with reference again to the Christian position. I take an example that is currently in the forefront of our Christian debate, the doctrine of the Incarnation. We need to distinguish three stages of development:

a) The impact which Jesus of Nazareth made upon those who knew him and those who heard about him which compelled them to make extraordinary claims about his authority and his identity;

b) The resurrection experience which vindicated and enlarged those claims;

c) The Church's recognition of the implications of these claims and her attempts to fit them into the ideas about God which already existed.

It seems pretty clear that the question "Whom do ye say that I am?" was not only put into the mouth of Jesus by the later teachers of the Christian Church, but was thrust upon people during the ministry of Jesus of Nazareth by the authority of his words and actions and personality. Even before the resurrection, certain titles were being given to him, though we may argue whether they originated in his own thought or in his followers' response to him. But in whatever way we argue these points, we must hold to the fact that the Christian belief in the divinity of Jesus grew out of the overwhelming impact which he made upon people then, and still continues to make.

What makes the first apostolic witnesses so remarkable is that, as they thought out the implications of the response they had been compelled to make to Jesus, they refused to retract any part of that response or diminish the claims they were making for him, even when it began to appear that their response and their claims were in conflict with all the accepted ideas about God. The first Christians were astonishingly fearless in pursuing the implications of the response to him which Jesus had compelled. It was not a case of gathering new ideas from the mystery religions or from Greek philosophy, nor even from the Old Testament, and building them into a theology about Jesus which moved beyond the original experience. On the contrary, what we see during the first four centuries of the Christian Church is a logical following-out of the implications of an original experience which they were not prepared to deny. One might say that they were according Jesus the lordship of their universe long before they dared to say, in so many words, that he was their Kurios. They were worshipping God in him long before they ventured to speak of his divinity. They had been saved by him long before they had worked out any theory of salvation. And what we see in St Paul, and in all the later Christian teachers, is a bold experimenting with one metaphor after another to describe their experience and fit it into their understanding of God and the universe.

If the theologians of the early centuries failed—and I think we have to admit that in some of their formulations they did fail—it was because they stuck too rigidly to their previous ideas about God which owed more to a philosophical system than to a living experience. Through most of its history, the Church has gone on trying to maintain belief in the God who can undergo neither change nor suffering; yet, for those who have seen the glory of God in the face of Jesus Christ, that old axiom has had to be abandoned. What we say about Jesus Christ is that, if our idea of God differs in any respect from what we see in him and in his life, death, and resurrection, then it is our idea of God that has to be changed; and not because of any prescribed dogma, but because, once we have seen him, we could not find it in us to worship a God who was different. Or, as someone has recently said, the impact of Jesus is such that, thereafter, only a wounded God will do.

We Must Expose Our Experience to One Another's Questioning

I have again been talking as a Christian to Christians, aware that others have been overhearing our debate on a central theme of our faith. But I make no apology for that because I believe that, if interfaith dialogue is to become sincere and deep, we have got to expose to one another the ways in which, within our separate households of faith, we wrestle with the questions that other religions put to us. To be overheard as we face up to these disconcerting questions will make us very vulnerable to one another. But if we are not ready to lower our defenses, if in fact we are most interested in scoring points than in knowing one another we may as well give up dialogue altogether.

So, besides letting one another know the absolutes in their own faith that may not be surrendered, the partners in the dialogue must also give serious reflection to the critique which each inevitably brings to bear upon the convictions of the other, however painful and disturbing this may be. If, as I have said, our irreducible loyalties belong to our experiences, and only secondarily to the doctrines that enshrine them, we must be prepared to have the experiences questioned. Christians, for example, must allow their discourse with Jews to re-open a question which has troubled us from the earliest days: How can Jesus be Messiah and agent of the eschatological kingdom, when it is so patent that things are not made new and the End is still awaited? Defensiveness ought not to make us unwilling to admit that this constitutes a real problem for us. Jewish experience through history may have a lot of light to throw upon the mystery of non-fulfilment in the covenants of God, and the hiddenness of God's victories. The Jewish-Christian dialogue, if pursued with mutual compassion, might blossom into a new theological understanding of the meaning of hope.

Or again, the questions that Hinduism asks about the true definition of Christ's relation to God—asked in unaffected concern as often as in dispute—should send the Christians back not to abandon their claims but to a fresh exploration of terms and metaphors, just as the challenge of Greek philosophy did in the early centuries. After some years of intensive dialogue with Hindu friends Klaus Klostermeier wrote: "It will never be possible to contain Christ's mystery and the essence of Christianity completely and adequately in terms and ideas. . . . If we start to ponder over the terms used by Greek Christologists and think them out to their logical extremes, then we fall into absurdities and heresies. The first Christologists were so aware of the newness of Christ and of the inadequacy of all known terms, that they preferred to talk about Christ paradoxically. . . . A seeming contradiction, it is, however, the only means that compels our thinking to excel itself.... Christ is neither the incarnation of the Jewish idea of God nor the apotheosis of the Greek idea of man. In India, too, we will have to make use of paradoxes in order to lay open the mystery of Christ: the paradox evokes an existential cognition because it compels man to surpass the purely terminological, to advance into the essence, into the one reality where no contradiction subsists.''

To reformulate involves risking the loss of the original truth, yet it is also the only way in which that truth can live and grow into fuller comprehension. Re-appraisal of one's own tradition and reformulation of one's own fidelities calls for an extraordinary mixture of humility and boldness. I have to put the question, ''Do all the partners in the interfaith dialogue come with an equal degree of self-questioning?'' I sometimes wonder, from what I have seen, whether Christians, for all our past aggressiveness, are not now exhibiting a greater share of self-criticism and mobility than those who meet us in the debate. However that may be—and I could be wrong about it—a genuine openness to the questions that another faith poses can mean, for the believer of any religion, a deeper entry into one's own faith. ''If,'' said Father Yves Raguin at Chiang Mai, ''we have this humble attitude of one who is seeking for the real meaning of what he believes, and for the real face of the one in whom he believes, dialogue will be easy with the faithful of other religions.''

The Things We Have in Common

I have said, paradoxically, that the primary common ground that we share in the dialogue is the sense of an absolute fidelity demanded of us towards certain convictions, even though the convictions themselves are irreconcilable. But besides that uncomfortable common factor there are a few other things which we do indubitably share.

We believe now that the Ultimate Reality upon which the faith of all believers is focused in every religion is the same, though our interpretations of his essential nature are still at variance.

The new interchange between people of different faiths has established the fact that all religions express an awareness of human alienation, enslavement, and need for healing and deliverance, and in all religions people experience an inward liberation, a sense of being accepted and made new.

Though the rituals of corporate and individual prayer differ widely, as does the degree of personalized encounter in the actual experience of prayer, yet the sense of oneness and communication with a gracious Divinity is common to them all, as is the hunger of the heart for such communion.

To be able to acknowledge this modest list of shared experiences is great gain, though the recognition of it raises as many questions as it answers. We are a long way from agreeing upon the meaning we may give to this common ground. And all the time the shadow of misapprehensions falls between us. So I end, as I began, with my plea for patient persistence. We are, after all, only at the beginning of a new kind of exploration. And when, as will often happen, we feel we are in the dark, we should not be ashamed to stand still rather than rush wildly forward.

> . . . Wait without hope,
> For hope would be hope for the wrong thing. Wait without love,
> For love would be love of the wrong thing. There is yet faith,
> But the faith and the hope and the love are all in the waiting. . . .

The Rules of the Game

Raimundo Panikkar

Born into two major religious traditions, Roman Catholic and Hindu, Raimundo Panikkar has concerned himself since his early years in India with the harmony of a pluralistic religious world. From this Catholic priest's reflection on a variety of dialogue experiences in Asia, North America, and Europe, he offers here the consequences or "rules of the game" of his insistent principle: "the religious encounter must truly be a religious one," not "history of religions" or "comparative religions," not a "congress of philosophy" or "theological symposium" or "a mere ecclesiastical endeavor." Panikkar is presently Professor of Religious Studies at the University of California at Santa Barbara. He is the author of some thirty books, including *Myth, Faith and Hermeneutics* (New York: Paulist Press, 1979). This article is reprinted from chapter three of his *The Intrareligious Dialogue* (Paulist Press, 1978).

One principle that should govern the meeting of religions, and a few corollary consequences, is this: *The Religious encounter must be a truly religious one.* Anything short of this simply will not do.

Some consequences are the following:

I. It Must Be Free from Particular Apologetics

If the Christian or Buddhist or believer in whatever religion approaches another religious person with the a priori idea of defending his own religion by all (obviously honest) means, we shall have perhaps a valuable defense of that religion and undoubtedly exciting discussions, but no religious dialogue, no encounter, must less a mutual enrichment and fecundation. One need not give up one's beliefs and convictions—surely not, but we must eliminate any apologetics if we really want to meet a person from another religious tradition. By apologetics I understand that part of the science of a particular religion that tends to prove the truth and value of that religion. Apologetics has its function and its proper place, but not here in the meeting of religions.

II. It Must Be Free from General Apologetics

I understand very well the anguish of the modern religious person seeing the wave of "unreligion" and even "irreligion" in our times, and yet I would consider it misguided to fall prey to such a fear by founding a kind of religious league—not to say crusade—of the "pious," of religious people of all confessions, defenders of the "sacred rights" of religion.

If to forget the first corollary would indicate a lack of confidence in our partner and imply that he is wrong and that I must "convert" him, to neglect this second point would betray a lack of confidence in the truth of religion itself and represent an indiscriminate accusation against "modern" Man. The attitude proposing a common front for religion or against unbelief may be understandable, but it is not a religious attitude—not according to the present degree of religious consciousness.

III. One Must Face the Challenge of Conversion

If the encounter is to be an authentically religious one, it must be totally loyal to truth and open to reality. The genuinely religious spirit is not loyal only to the past, it also keeps faith with the present. A religious Man is neither a fanatic nor someone who already has all the answers. He also is a seeker, a pilgrim making his own uncharted way; the track ahead is yet virgin, inviolate. The religious Man finds each moment new and is but the more pleased to see in this both the beauty of a personal discovery and the depth of a perennial treasure that his ancestors in the faith have handed down.

And yet, to enter the new field of the religious encounter is a challenge and a risk. The religious person enters this arena without prejudices and preconceived solutions, knowing full well he may in fact have to lose a particular belief or particular religion altogether. He trusts in truth. He enters unarmed and ready to be converted himself. He may lose his life—he may also be born again.

IV. The Historical Dimension is Necessary but Not Sufficient

Religion is not just *Privatsache,* nor just a vertical "link" with the Absolute, but it is also a connection with mankind; it has a tradition, a historical dimension. The religious encounter is not merely the meeting of two or more people in their capacity as strictly private individuals, severed from their respective religious traditions. A truly religious Man bears at once the burden of tradition and the riches of his ancestors. But he is not an official representative, as it were, speaking only on behalf of others or from sheer hearsay: He is a living member of a community, a believer in a living religious tradition.

The religious encounter must deal with the historical dimension, not stop with it. It is not an encounter of historians, still less of archeologists; but a living dialogue, a place for creative thinking and imaginative new ways that do not break with the past but continue and extend it.

This is hardly to disparage historical considerations; quite the contrary, I would insist on an understanding of the traditions in question that is at once deep and broad. The first implies not only that we be familiar with the age-old tradition, but also with the present state of that particular religion. Taking as our example that bundle of religions which goes under the name of "Hinduism," I would contend that a profound understanding of this tradition cannot ignore its evolution up to the present day, unless we are ready to accept an arbitrary and skewed interpretation. A scholar may indeed limit himself to Vedic studies, for example, but someone engaged in a truly religious encounter can scarcely justify basing his understanding of Hinduism solely on Sāyana's interpretation of the Vedas while completely ignoring that of, say, Dayānānda or Aurobindo (the relative merits of various interpretations is not our concern here). Similarly no modern Christian can be satisfied with Jerome's interpretation of the Bible, or with the mediaeval understanding of it.

Our point is that no study of an idea, cultural pattern or religious tradition is adequate unless we consider all its possibilities, just as no botanist can claim to know a seed until he knows the plant that grows up from that seed. Moreover, in this case, the movement of understanding is dynamic and reciprocal. Thus I would contend not only that any study of the nature of *dharma*, for instance, is incomplete if it does not consider the present-day understanding of that concept, but also that the ancient notion is likely to be only partially understood if its development up to modern times is left aside. This also implies that someone who tries to understand the notion of *dharma*, whether in ancient or modern India, cannot do so *in vacuo*: the very words he uses are already culturally charged with meanings and values.

Further, the traditions must also be understood in a broader perspective, one that oversteps the provincial boundaries of geography and culture. To understand the Hindu tradition—staying with our example—we cannot limit ourselves to the Indian subcontinent. The impact of Buddhism on eastern and central Asia is so well known that I need only mention it; the Ramāyāna and the Mahābhārata have been shaping forces in many countries south of Burma; Śiva is worshiped in Indonesia. Pursuing these avenues of research is not a mere academic tangent, but serves to complete the picture we begin to see through indigenous sources. Even more, we cannot limit our attention to past cross-cultural contacts, and ignore the multitude of contemporary instances. Many an Indian value asserts itself today on the shores of California and in universities throughout Europe. Whether the change in climate distorts or enhances the original values is a separate question; the influence is unmistakable. In return, Western values have, for better or for worse, deeply penetrated not only the great cities but also the most remote villages of India. Given such developments, can our understanding of Indian religions remain imprisoned in a scholarly ivory tower whose drawbridge was raised when the Muslims arrived? The phenomenon of feedback does not refer only to the diffusion of gadgets and other technological paraphernalia throughout the world; popularized ideas from every continent now travel literally at the speed of light to the farthest corners of the planet and the deepest recesses of the human psyche.

The importance of the historical dimension notwithstanding, what is at stake in the religious encounter is not "History of Religions" or even "Comparative Religion," but a living and demanding faith. Faith is life and life cannot be reduced to imitating the past or merely reinterpreting it. The religious encounter is a religious event.

V. It Is Not Just a Congress of Philosophy

Needless to say, without a certain degree of philosophy no encounter is possible, and yet the religious dialogue is not just a meeting of philosophers to discuss intellectual problems. Religions are much more than doctrines. Within one religion there may even be a pluralism of doctrines. To pin down a religion to a certain definite doctrinal set is to kill that religion. No particular doctrine *as such* can be considered the unique and irreplaceable expression of a religion. Indeed, *denying* a particular doctrine without overcoming it or substituting another for it may be heresy, but no religion is satisfied to be *only* orthodoxy, ignoring orthopraxis. To be sure, creation, God, *nirvāna* and the like are important concepts, but the real religious issue lies elsewhere: in the real "thing" meant by these and other notions. I may share with my Muslim colleague the same idea of the transcendence of God and he may be of the same opinion as his Buddhist partner regarding the law of *karma* and yet none of us may feel compelled to change his religion.

Clearly, I need to understand what the other is saying, that is, what he means to say, and this involves a new understanding of interpretation itself. Now the golden rule of any hermeneutic is that the interpreted thing can recognize itself in the interpretation. In other words, any interpretation from outside a tradition has to coincide, at least phenomenologically, with an interpretation from within, i.e., with the believer's viewpoint. To label a *mūrtipūjaka* an idol worshiper, for instance, using idol as it is commonly understood in the Judeo-Christian-Muslim context rather than beginning with what the worshiper affirms of himself, is to transgress this rule. An entire philosophical and religious context underpins the notion of *mūrti;* we cannot simply impose alien categories on it. Although the problem remains formidable, one of the most positive achievements of our times is that we have come to realize that there are no immutable categories that can serve as absolute criteria for judging everything under the sun.

Briefly then, I would like to consider two principles that govern any sound hermeneutical method and the way in which they may be critically coordinated.

The *principle of homogeneity:* An ancient conviction, held in both East and West, has it that only like can know like. In other words, a concept can be properly understood and evaluated only from within a homogeneous context. Every cultural value has a definite sphere where it is valid and meaningful; any unwarranted extrapolation can only lead to confusion and misunderstanding. Nothing is more harmful than hurried syntheses or superficial parallelisms. Here is the place and the great value of traditional theology, which provides the internal understanding of a religion, the self-understanding of that religion as it is lived. Without this previous work, fruitful interreligious encounters would not be possible.

The *dialogical principle:* Applying the principle of homogeneity with strict rigor or exclusivity would paralyze a critical approach and halt any progress toward mutual understanding. I may understand the world-view that underlies the religious practice of another—human sacrifice, for instance—yet I may still consider it immature, wrong, even barbaric. Why is this? It may be that I have developed another form of awareness or discovered another principle of understanding that leads me to see the inadequacy of a certain notion (here that which upholds human sacrifice). I may have acquired a perspective under which I am able to criticize another point of view; perhaps I can now detect incongruencies or assumptions that are no longer tenable. In this sort of activity, the dialogical principle is at work. Only through an internal or external dialogue can we become aware of uncritical or unwarranted assumptions. This dialogue does not merely look for new sources of information, but leads to a deeper understanding of the other and of oneself. We are all learning to welcome light and criticism, even when it comes from foreign shores.

Coordination: By themselves, each of these principles is barren and unsatisfying; together they provide a means of cross-cultural understanding that is both valid and critical. Those concerned with Indian traditions, whatever their background, are convinced that they cannot disregard the methodological principles of modern critical scholarship. At the same time, they are quite aware that neither science nor Western categories constitute an absolute standard, nor do they have universal applicability. These two insights give rise to the coordination of the two principles. Here we cannot elaborate the guidelines for such a coordination. It is enough to say that the effort must be truly interdisciplinary and interpersonal, involving not only the traditional fields of "academia," but also the people whose religions we are considering. No statement is valid and meaningful if it cannot be heard, understood and, in a way, verified by all those concerned, and not merely bandied about by the *literati*.

Indeed, philosophical clarification is today extremely important since by and large religions have lived in restricted areas and closed circles, and have tended to identify a particular set of philosophical doctrines—because they were useful to convey the religious message—with the core of the religion. The mutual enrichment of real encounter and the consequent liberation may be enormous.

VI. It Is Not Only a Theological Symposium

As an authentic venture, the true religious encounter is filled with a sort of prophetic charisma; it is not just an effort to make the outsider understand my point. Indeed, at least according to more than one school, true theology also claims to be a charismatic deepening in meaning of a particular revelation or religion. Generally, however, theologians are more concerned with explaining given data than with exploring tasks ahead. Obviously hermeneutics is indispensable; but still more important is to *grasp* what is to be interpreted prior to any (more or less plausible) explanation. Theology may furnish the tools for mutual understanding but must remember that the religious encounter imperative today is a new problem, and that the tools furnished by the theologies are not fit to master the new task unless purified, chiseled and perhaps forged anew in the very encounter.

As an example of what is needed, we may use the notion of homology, which does not connote a mere comparison of concepts from one tradition with those of another. I want to suggest this notion as the correlation between points of two different systems so that a point in one system corresponds to a point in the other. The method does not imply that one system is better (logically, morally or whatever) than the other, nor that the two points are interchangeable: You cannot, as it were, transplant a point from one system to the other. The method only discovers homologous correlations.

Now a homology is not identical to an analogy, although they are related. Homology does not mean that two notions are analogous, i.e., partially the same and partially different, since this implies that both share in a "tertium quid" that provides the basis for the analogy. Homology means rather that the notions play equivalent roles, that they occupy homologous places within their respective systems. Homology is perhaps a kind of existential-functional analogy.

An example may clarify what I mean.

It is quite clearly false, for instance, to equate the Upanishadic concept of *Brahman* with the biblical notion of *Yahweh*. Nevertheless it is equally unsatisfactory to say that these concepts have nothing whatever in common. True, their context and contents are utterly different, they are not mutually translatable, nor do they have a direct relationship. But they are homologous, each plays a similar role, albeit in different cultural settings. They both refer to a highest value and an absolute term. On the other hand, we cannot say that *Brahman* is provident and even transcendent, or that *Yahweh* is all-pervading, without attributes, etc. Nevertheless we can assert that both function homologously within their own cultures.

Or, to give another example, an examination of the traditional Indian notion of *karma* and the modern Western understanding of historicity under the aegis of this principle could reveal a common homologous role: Each one stands for that temporal ingredient of the human being which transcends individuality.[1] Even more intriguing, perhaps, would be a consideration that homologizes the Indian notion of Īśvara (Lord) and the Western idea of Christ.[2]

Whatever shape it will take, whatever contents it will carry, I am convinced that a new theology (though this very name means nothing to a Buddhist) will emerge precisely out of these encounters between sincere and enlightened believers of the various religious traditions.

Yet the religious encounter is not a mere theological reflection. Theologies—in the widest sense of the word—have a given basis: They are efforts at intelligibility of a given religious tradition and generally within that tradition itself (*fides quaerens intellectum*). But here we do not have such a belief or such a basis. There is neither a common given nor accepted basis, revelation, event or even tradition. Both the very subject matter and the method are to be determined in the encounter itself. There is no common language at the outset. Short of this radical understanding the encounter of religions becomes a mere cultural entertainment.

VII. It Is Not Merely an Ecclesiastical Endeavor

To be sure, the dialogue among religions may take place at different levels and on each level it has its peculiarities.

Official encounter among representatives of the world's organized religious groups is today an inescapable duty. Yet the issues in such meetings are not the same as those in a dialogue that tries to reach the deepest possible level. Ecclesiastical dignitaries are bound to preserve tradition; they must consider the multitude of believers who follow that religion, for and to whom they are responsible. They are faced with practical and immediate problems, they must discover ways to tolerate, to collaborate, to understand. But in general they cannot risk new solutions. They have to approve and put into practice already proven fruitful ways. But where are those proofs to come from? The religious encounter we have in mind will certainly pave the way for ecclesiastical meetings and vice versa, but must be differentiated and separated from them.

VIII. It Is a Religious Encounter in Faith, Hope and Love

I apologize for the Christian overtones of this terminology and yet I think its meaning is universal.

By *faith* I mean an attitude that transcends the simple data, and the dogmatic formulations of the different confessions as well; that attitude which reaches an understanding even when words and concepts differ, because it pierces them, as it were, goes deep down to that realm which is the religious realm par excellence. We do not discuss systems but realities, and the way in which these realities manifest themselves so that they also make sense for our partner.

By *hope* I understand that attitude which, hoping against all hope, is able to leap over not only the initial human obstacles, our weakness and unconscious adherences, but also over all kinds of purely profane views and into the heart of the dialogue, as if urged from above to perform a sacred duty.

By *love*, finally, I mean that impulse, that force impelling us to our fellow-beings and leading us to discover in them what is lacking in us. To be sure, real love does not aim for victory in the encounter. It longs for common recognition of the truth, without blotting out the differences or muting the various melodies in the single polyphonic symphony.

IX. Appendix

A. Some Practical Lessons

What do these rules mean in practice? The chief lessons gleaned from my experience could be summarized as follows:

There must be *equal preparation* for the encounter on both sides, and this means cultural as well as theological preparation. Any dialogue—including the religious one— depends on the cultural settings of the partners. To overlook the cultural differences that give rise to different religious beliefs is to court unavoidable misunderstandings. The first function of the dialogue is to discover the ground where the dialogue may properly take place.

There must be real *mutual trust* between those involved in the encounter, something that is possible only when all the cards are on the table, i.e., when neither partner "brackets" his personal beliefs.

The *different issues* (theological, practical, institutional, etc.) have to be carefully distinguished; otherwise there is going to be confusion.

B. A Christian Example

Christ is the Lord, but the Lord is neither only Jesus nor does my understanding exhaust the meaning of the word.

Church, as the sociological dimension of religion, is the organism of salvation (by definition); but the Church is not coextensive with the visible Christian Church.

Christendom is the socio-religious structure of Christianity and as such is a religion like any other. It must be judged on its own merits without any special privileges.

God wills that all Men should reach salvation. Here salvation is that which is considered to be the end, goal destination or destiny of Man, however this may be conceived.

There is no salvation without faith, but this is not the privilege of Christians, nor of any special group.

The means of salvation are to be found in any authentic religion (old or new), since a Man follows a particular religion because in it he believes he finds the ultimate fulfillment of his life.

Christ is the only mediator, but he is not the monopoly of Christians and, in fact, he is present and effective in any authentic religion, whatever the form or the name. Christ is the symbol, which Christians call by this name, of the ever-transcending but equally ever-humanly immanent Mystery. Now these principles should be confronted with parallel Humanist, Buddhist and other principles, and then one should be able to detect points of convergence and of discrepancy with all the required qualifications. Further, the Christian principles have no a priori paradigmatic value, so that it is not a question of just searching for possible equivalents elsewhere. The fair procedure is to start from all possible starting points and witness to the actual encounters taking place along the way.

C. Summing Up

The religious encounter is a religious, and hence sacred, act through which we are taken up by the truth and by loyalty to the "three worlds" with no further aim or intention. In this creative religious act the very vitality of religion manifests itself.

NOTES

1. Cf. R. Panikkar, *Myth, Faith and Hermeneutics* (New York: Paulist Press, 1979), chapter XIV.

2. Cf. R. Panikkar, *The Unknown Christ of Hinduism* (London: Darton, Longman & Todd, 1964), pp. 119-31.

Evangelicals and Interreligious Dialogue

David J. Hesselgrave

Evangelical Protestants should not risk locking themselves up "in a closet of monologue," insists David Hesselgrave. "Now is the time for evangelicals to review their attitude of disinterest and nonparticipation in dialogue." But what kinds of interreligious dialogue are recommended for evangelical participation? The author suggests five types: dialogue on dialogue; on freedom of worship and witness; on meeting human need; on breaking down barriers of distrust and hatred in the religious world; and on "the mutual comprehension of conflicting truth claims." David J. Hesselgrave is Director of the School of World Mission and Evangelism, Trinity Evangelical Divinity School, in Deerfield, Illinois. This extract is from a larger paper he gave in a consultation at Trinity in March 1976. All the papers and responses are published in *Theology and Mission,* edited by Hesselgrave (Grand Rapids, Mich.: Baker Book House, 1978).

Evangelicals are being challenged to demonstrate a new kind of bravery today. If the Christian messenger is to be taken seriously, he or she must demonstrate an interest in those great human concerns which are the topics of contemporary discussion. If the Christian messenger is to be heard, he or she must not be too timid to enter the forums of world opinion. If the Christian message is to be understood it must be framed with reference to the context of competing world views and faiths in which it is to be preached. If the Christian mission is to progress, its advocates must be prepared to advance in a new world of resurgent non-Christian religions.

Unless as evangelicals we are willing to risk locking ourselves up in a closet of monologue where we speak primarily to one another, the question for us is not, "Shall we engage in dialogue?" but, "In what kinds of dialogue shall we engage?" *Scriptural precedent clearly enjoins—and the Christian mission entails—interreligious dialogue that answers the questions and objections of unbelievers, proclaims the good news of Jesus Christ, and beseeches men to repent and believe.* Scriptural principle clearly precludes—and the Christian conscience condemns—any dialogue that compromises the gospel or countermands the great commission. Within these boundaries there are various types of dialogue which merit consideration by evangelicals.

Type 1: Dialogue on the nature of interreligious dialogue. It is to be deplored that the evangelical point of view has not been adequately represented in dialogues on dialogue. That lack of participation is due to several factors. First, for reasons of conscience evangelicals do not often hold membership in communions and organizations sponsoring such dialogues. Second, ecumenists are often predisposed not to include evangelicals in such dialogues lest predetermined purposes be jeopardized. Third, evangelicals are suspicious that little or no good can come from their participation. Fourth, because of lack of exposure to this kind of forum, evangelicals sometimes feel ill-prepared to engage in it. One could wish, therefore, that ecumenists would exhibit the same irenic spirit toward evangelicals that they do toward non-Christians. But one could also wish that, when the conditions are right, evangelicals thought it as important to faithfully expound their understanding of biblical teachings within the forums of Christendom as to faithfully proclaim those teachings in the contexts of heathendom.

Type 2: Interreligious dialogue that promotes freedom of worship and witness. There can be no question but that religious freedom is being challenged in one way or another among vast populations of people today. To accede quietly to totalitarian repression of religious faith, or to claim freedoms and privileges for one's own faith that are refused to others—such approaches are tacit denials of the most basic of men's inalienable rights. By what means will we implore the world's rulers and remind ourselves to respect those rights? The pursuit of that question may well merit interreligious conversation and even action.

Type 3: Interreligious dialogue concerned with meeting human need. This is similar to Sharpe's "secular dialogue," but it is not necessarily the same. In the first place, "secular dialogue" may not be the best nomenclature. Though definition of the term resolves some problems, it raises others. In the second place, from a Christian point of view it may be necessary that this dialogue stop short of complete cooperative action because it is incumbent upon the Christian that all he does in word and deed be done in the name of his Lord Christ (Col. 3:16). Nevertheless, discussion of ways and means may be invaluable in view of overwhelming and increasing human need.

Type 4: Interreligious dialogue designed to break down barriers of distrust and hatred in the religious world. If hatred is enjoined by any religion at all, it is certainly not enjoined by Christianity. Christians are admonished to love not only one another but all men. Canon Max Warren seems to imply that interreligious dialogue is basically of this type (or of Type 5, below).[1] It will be apparent that I have some difficulty with this understanding, but my disagreement is not with the idea that this kind of dialogue indeed can be profitable in breaking down barriers. There are excellent examples—too few, to be sure—that dialogue of this type can be used to dissolve distrust and break up log jams that have deterred the conversion of large groups of non-Christians.

Type 5: Interreligious dialogue that has as its objective the mutual comprehension of conflicting truth claims. This is close to Sharpe's "discursive dialogue" (especially as he has elaborated in one context),[2] but in contrast to discursive dialogue it is not committed to dialectic and the proposition that reason alone is a sufficient guide to truth. Its objective is to arrive at a common meaning, not necessarily a common faith. Evangelicals should give serious consideration to proposing and participating in this kind of dialogue because apart from it (in *some* form—so why not face-to-face?) real communication of the Christian faith becomes exceedingly difficult. It is apparent that our Lord and Paul understood the religious systems of their respondents and adapted to them. For altogether too long evangelical missionary communication has been monological because of lack of this understanding.

Conclusion

The Christian mission in the closing decades of the twentieth century challenges both the ecumenist and the evangelical to make a reappraisal of their attitudes toward, and participation in, interreligious dialogue.

Now is the time for ecumenists to review the direction that dialogue has taken and subject it to the standards of the revealed will of God in the Scriptures. Any form of dialogue that compromises the uniqueness of the Christian gospel and the necessity that the adherents of other faiths repent and believe it should be rejected and supplanted by forms of dialogue that enjoin conversion to Christ.

Now is the time for evangelicals to review their attitude of disinterest and nonparticipation in dialogue. To insist upon the uniqueness of the Christian gospel and the need of all people for salvation in Christ is not tantamount to engaging in biblical dialogue. Something new is needed. While it may be in the interest of the Christian mission to participate in those types of dialogue that have positive benefits and do not require abandonment or obfuscation of the Christian message, it definitely would be in the interest of the Christian mission to participate in those types of dialogue that enable evangelicals to enter the forums of the world with the understanding, commitment, and courage that characterized the apostolic era.

In a world of religous pluralism evangelical witness, preaching, and teaching should become increasingly dialogical—answering those questions and objections raised by non-Christian respondents rather than simply answering questions of the evangelical's own devising. In the words of my colleague and friend, Carl F. H. Henry, "The only adequate alternative to dialogue that deletes the evangelical view is dialogue that expounds it. The late twentieth century is no time to shirk that dialogue."[3]

NOTES

1. Cf. Max Warren, "Pre-Evangelism and Evangelism," *Milligan Missiogram* 2, no. 3, 3 (Fall 1975): 1. Warren says, "Dialogue . . . insofar as it is a genuine, humble, receptive listening to the other man's testimony to his own religious experience, and a courteous answering to ours, is certainly a form of Pre-Evangelism. It must not be confused with Evangelism."

2. Eric J. Sharpe, "The Goals of Inter-Religious Dialogue," in *Truth and Dialogue in World Religions: Conflicting Truth Claims,* ed. John Hick (Philadelphia: Westminster Press, 1974), pp. 89-90. After discussing the various types of dialogue, Sharpe says, "In only one case is there a fair measure of clarity. The goal of discursive dialogue is usually taken to be a better understanding of the other person's religious stance, possibly in order to facilitate the communication of the Christian message. It has been repeatedly pointed out this century that it is useless for the Christian missionary to embark upon a programme of evangelization without a thorough prior knowledge of the people to whom his message is addressed—their language, their culture, their modes of thought, religious and secular, and so on. And for those whose Christian faith involves an imperative missionary dimension, and who are still prepared to make use of the terminology of dialogue, the attempt to enter into a sympathetic understanding of the non-Christian must take some such form as that which I have called discursive dialogue."

3. Carl F. H. Henry, "Confronting Other Religions," *Christianity Today* 13, no. 22 (August 1, 1969):31.

Guidelines on Dialogue

World Council of Churches, with an introduction by Stanley J. Samartha

During the 1970s the World Council of Churches initiated a major study on the meaning and practice of dialogue with people of other faiths and ideologies. What is the theological basis and purpose of such dialogue? Does dialogue lead to syncretism? Does it "blunt the cutting edge of mission" and "substitute for Christian proclamation"? How does the Christian community within the human community become one of service and witness without compromising commitment to the Triune God? Such questions generated enthusiasm, difficulties, and controversies in the ecumenical discussions, as the director of the WCC dialogue program, Dr. Stanley J. Samartha, describes the process. Combining the results of the 1977 Chiang Mai (Thailand) consultation on "Dialogue in Community" and consequent recommendations, the WCC Central Committee in 1979 commended to member churches *Guidelines on Dialogue*. Part I reflects on the nature of the human community, the communities of our neighbor and the Christian community. Part II then gives reasons for dialogue having a rightful place within Christian life, points out the dangers of syncretism, and formulates questions on the theological significance of people of other faiths and ideologies. Finally, Part III offers practical recommendations. Dr. Samartha, a minister of the Church of South India and former professor of history of religions at Serampore Theological College in West Bengal, has been on the WCC staff since 1968. See also his "Dialogue as a Continuing Christian Concern" in *Mission Trends No. 1,* and "Mission and Movements of Innovation" in *Mission*

Trends No. 3. This introduction is a substantial abridgement of his article in *The Ecumenical Review* for April 1979. The *Guidelines* are published in a separate booklet by the World Council of Churches, 150 route de Ferney, 1211 Geneva 20, Switzerland.

In January 1979, the Central Committee of the World Council of Churches (WCC) at its meeting in Kingston, Jamaica, adopted a set of *guidelines* on dialogue with people of living faiths and ideologies. The decision marks an important stage in the relation of Christian communities to their neighbours of other faiths and ideological convictions. Depending on the extent to which the churches will engage in dialogue, this might indicate a historic turn in the relations between Christian communities and communities of other faiths and ideological convictions.

I. Chiang Mai Statement: A Landmark

Christian interest in neighbours of other faiths is not new. World conferences on mission and evangelism have discussed the significance of other religions many times, but invariably in connection with mission. In fact, dialogue emerged out of the womb of mission and it has never been easy for missions to cut the umbilical cord and to recognize the independence of the growing child without denying the relationship. In the World Council of Churches it was only in 1971 that a major debate on dialogue took place, at the Central Committee meeting in Addis Ababa. In the years that followed, the debate on the subject in the churches was marked by enthusiasm and expectation on the one hand, hesitation, doubts and fears on the other. Quite often, ecumenical discussions on dialogue became difficult and controversial, indicating both the complexity and importance of the issues involved. Perhaps the most difficult one was at the WCC Assembly at Nairobi (1975) where the debate in Section III on "*Seeking Community*—the Common Search of People of Various Faiths, Cultures and Ideologies" was unsatisfactory and inconclusive.[1]

In retrospect, however, the Nairobi controversy proved to be more an opportunity than a setback. Instead of leading to a premature demise of dialogue, it helped to strengthen it as an ecumenical concern by drawing pointed attention to serious issues that are important in the life of churches, not just in Asia, but in other parts of the world as well. Thus, what could have remained a parochial interest gained recognition in the Assembly as an ecumenical concern which could no more be politely ignored. Nairobi also emphasized the inescapable need for careful theological reflection on some of the unresolved questions. The issues were mainly three.

First, there was the need to be clear about the nature and purpose of dialogue, particularly its theological basis. What exactly is the purpose of dialogue with neighbours of other faiths? To join them? To eliminate differences? To shape a world religion?

This led to a second question: Does dialogue lead to syncretism? Perhaps no other word in the ecumenical vocabulary has aroused more fears, created more unnecessary controversy, and, more often than not, succeeded in sidetracking urgent issues in the life of the churches in pluralistic situations than the term syncretism. One reason for this is the negative connotation the term has acquired in the context of mission. Another reason may be that particular cultural contexts and historic situations where the Gospel is preached and Christian faith expressed are so different that it is extremely difficult to make an acceptable statement in the ecumenical context. The belated attempts to give it a more positive content are unlikely to produce any fresh insights, at least till the muddy waters surrounding the debate settle down a little.

The third question was obviously related to the other two: Does dialogue blunt the cutting edge of mission? Is it a substitute for proclamation? What is the relation between dialogue, witness and mission?

In this connection it is necessary to draw attention to the Chiang Mai Consultation 1977 which, through careful biblical studies and theological discussions, considered these and other issues under the title "Dialogue in Community."[2] The

Chiang Mai statement may rightly be regarded as a landmark in the development of the dialogue debate in the ecumenical context. It helped to overcome the difficulties caused by the Nairobi debate, resolved some of the tensions, and produced a theological basis widely accepted as providing common ground for the churches to move forward. Some of the reasons why the Chiang Mai statement was widely accepted are as follows:

—it recognizes dialogue as "a means of living out our faith in Christ in service of community with our neighbours"; "it has a distinctive and rightful place within Christian life"; "the engagement in dialogue testifies to the love we have experienced in Christ." "It is the Christian faith which sets us free to be open to the faiths of others, to risk, to trust and to be vulnerable."[3]

—the description of communities and the community of humankind helps to clear the earlier misunderstandings about the term "world community" and indicates the distinctiveness of the Christian community in the world.

—it does "not see dialogue and witness as standing in any contradiction to one another"; dialogue is not seen as an alternative to mission but as "one of the ways in which Jesus Christ can be confessed in the world today."

—the observations on syncretism take into account the warnings of Nairobi; the statement draws attention both to the dangers involved in "translating" the Christian message and the necessity of taking risks; it also emphasizes "the need to give one another space and time" as Christians explore the richness of the Gospel in different cultural settings.

—on the theological significance of people of other faiths and ideologies, although some of the issues remain, there is a perceptible change in the framework in which theological questions are formulated and the mood in which Christians approach people of other faiths and ideologies. The process of reflection has to be continued by Christians as they share life in the community with their neighbours.

II. Partners in the Quest for Community

Thus during the years between Addis Ababa, 1971 and Kingston, Jamaica 1979, much water has flown under, and sometimes over, the dialogue bridge. These Guidelines are based on difficulties confronted, insights gained, and lessons learned in the experience of actual dialogues. This experience is not limited to meetings organized by the WCC but includes the experience of churches in many different parts of the world. Churches, study centers, groups and individuals, and friends of other faiths deeply concerned with this matter, have discussed these questions and shared their comments with us. Moreover, although Christians have taken the initiative in many meetings, it should not be forgotten that Christians have also responded to initiatives taken by neighbours of other faiths. Thus, the basis for reflection and preparation of Guidelines has been considerably widened and deepened over that of previous years. The Working Group on Dialogue appointed by the Fifth Assembly has constantly kept in touch with developments, scrutinized the responses from the churches, revised formulations where necessary and prepared the draft of Guidelines that came before the Central Committee. In view of all this, the criticism sometimes made that this is one of the "elitist" enterprises of the WCC, seems to be born out of prejudice and ignorance rather than an informed understanding of the long process that goes on in the churches before a policy statement is officially accepted by the Central Committee.

Two critical observations may be made here. The first is that the influence of ideologies, particularly institutionalized ideologies, that shape the lives of large communities of people is not sufficiently reflected in the Guidelines. The second is that the power factor, particularly political power, in the relation between religious communities on the one hand and between religious communities and ideologies on the other does not receive the attention it deserves. One reason for this state of affairs is that the experience of the dialogue sub-unit and its related groups in different parts of the world was very largely with partners of religious communities. There are historical reasons for this. It seemed natural and more justifiable to build on actual experiences than try to do justice to an area where experience was rather limited. Some reflection on ideologies did take place in the World Council of Churches and there is a growing awareness of the ideological assumptions in some of the programmes. But before any guidelines can be formulated, more careful reflection is necessary, taking into account the experience of churches in those countries where certain ideologies are institutionalized in state structures. The absence of any extended reflection on ideologies is therefore a conscious self-limitation. The power factor in the relation between communities of people is also important because it is now becoming increasingly clear that difficulties in relations between religious communities are not just because of the theological distance between them but also because of a serious disproportion in the possession and use of power—money, technology, communication media and political tools. The political climate in which Christian communities live in different parts of the world is so varied, and the relation between state and religions so different, that before any serious reflection can take place ecumenically, more attention should be given to local and regional situations.

Furthermore, it is obvious that even as these Guidelines are being commended to the churches for "testing and evaluation," it is necessary for the churches and the ecumenical movement to be sensitive to *new factors* that have entered the scene. As the ecumenical movement moves on to the next decade, the consequences of these new factors for the life and witness of the churches in the world need to be carefully assessed. The manner in which these Guidelines are interpreted and acted upon may well depend on the interplay of these factors in various countries, not least in multi-religious societies. Some of these factors are the following:

—the political implications of dialogue, particularly as they touch power relations between communities of faith or of ideologies. The emerging trends in the world of Islam and the connection between political aspirations and religious revival in some other religions as well are important.

—the intensity and the acceleration of speed in the struggle for a just, participatory and sustainable society. Christians are not alone in the struggle. Neither are they the only community who connect the struggle for a just society with the imperatives of faith. Therefore, the contributions of neighbours of living faiths and ideologies need to be seriously taken into account.

—the emergence of world inter-religious organizations seeking peace and justice in world community has implications which the churches cannot ignore. These are no more ponderous "parliaments of religion" called to hear long speeches about "spiritual matters," but seek to bring religious resources to the struggle for justice and peace.

—the pressure of science and technology relentlessly pushing people towards a technological society. This calls for new ways of understanding the relation between nature, humanity and God on the one hand and new forms of community life to sustain personal values on the other.

—the search for new forms of spirituality to sustain personal and community life, particularly by youth. If spirituality is the attempt to nourish our life in God in order to be alive in the world, and if freedom and spontaneity are marks of the Spirit, reaching across human barriers should become more an adventure than a risk.

With all this in mind, the following statement and Guidelines were commended by the Central Committee "to member churches for their consideration and discussion, testing and evaluation, and for their elaboration in each specific situation."

PART I

ON COMMUNITY

A. Communities and the Community of Humankind

1. Christians begin their reflection on community from the acknowledgement that God as they believe Him to have come in Jesus Christ is the Creator of all things and of all humankind; that from the beginning He willed relationship with Himself and between all that He has brought to life; that to that end He has enabled the formation of communities, judges them and renews them. When Christians confess Him as one Holy Trinity, when they rejoice in His new creation in the resurrection of Christ, they perceive and experience new dimensions of the given humanity which God has given. Yet, the very nature and content of our Christian confession draws Christians to pay the closest attention to the realities of the world as it has developed under God's creative, disciplinary and redemptive rule. So they are led to attempt a description of communities and the community of humankind in the light of a basic Christian confession but in terms which may also find understanding and even agreement among many of other faiths and ideologies.

2. Men and women are all born into relationships with other people. Most immediately there are the members of their families, but quickly they have to explore wider relationships as they go to school or begin work. This may take place in the complexity of relationships within a village society, or within the modern urban centres of town and city which attract ever larger populations. They experience still wider associations within nation, race, religion, and at the same time they may belong to different social classes or castes which condition their ideological outlooks. Then the newspapers they read, the radio and T.V. programmes they hear and see give them an awareness of the multitude of ways in which the lives they live are dependent on people in other parts of the world, where ways of life are amazingly varied.

From these, and many related contexts, they derive their sense of being part of some communities and apart from others. The sense of identity with some communities and of alienation from others is something never completely understood but it remains reality for us all at the many levels of our existence.

3. Within each particular community to which people may belong they are held together with others by the values they share in common. At the deepest level these have to do with their identity, which gives them a sense of being "at home" in the groups to which they belong. Identity may be formed with a long historical experience, or in the face of problems newly encountered; it may express itself in communal traditions and rituals shaped through centuries, or in newer forms sometimes less coherent and sometimes more rigid. Religions and ideologies have formative influence on communities; but religions and ideologies have themselves been shaped by other elements of the culture of which they are part—language, ethnic loyalty, social strata, caste. Some communities may tend to uniformity in this regard, while others have long traditions of pluralism, and it is not infrequent that individual families may share more than one set of beliefs.

4. Human communities are many and varied. They are involved in a constant process of change which evokes their comparison with flowing rivers rather than stable monuments. But if change is always present, there can be no doubt that it has been accelerated in the present times, especially by scientific technology, economic forces and the mass media. Some changes are so rapid and dramatic as to give the experience of the loss of community and of the human isolation which follows. In other instances communities are structured and reshaped: once closed communities being thrown into relationship with others with which they find themselves engaged in the task of nation building; communities formerly of a single cultural identity being opened to a cultural pluralism and plurality of religious systems; communities in which traditional religious systems may undergo far-reaching

change, and, revitalized, provide renewed identity and continuity with the past. Amidst these changes many people are alienated from all community and have either given up the quest for community or are seeking it from many sources.

5. An important aspect of this accelerated change has been brought about by the complex network of relationships which has been created between human communities in recent times. More urgently today than ever in the past, the traditions of our individual communities are being drawn towards one another, sometimes into a new harmony, sometimes into a destructive whirlpool in the flowing rivers. The inter-relatedness of human communities brings with it many new challenges to mutual concern and pastoral care, the response to which, both individually and collectively as communities, will determine the character of the reality of "the community of humankind."

6. The response is often given in the form of ideologies. In fact the accelerated change has made people more sensitively aware of the need for conscious social and political action, because they find themselves in the midst of many ideological projects which attempt in various ways to shape or reshape society. Traditional communities do not escape the impact of ideological thinking and action and their varied responses may bring conflict as well as renewal.

7. There are dangers inherent in this situation, but experience of human inter-relatedness in different local situations deepens awareness of the richness of the diversity of the community of humankind which Christians believe to be created and sustained by God in His love for all people. They marvel and give thanks for this richness, acknowledging that to have experienced it has given many of them an enriched appreciation of the deeper values in their own traditions—and in some cases has enabled them to rediscover them. But at the same time they feel sharply conscious of the way in which diversity can be, and too often has been, abused: the temptation to regard one's own community as the best; to attribute to one's own religious and cultural identity an absolute authority; the temptation to exclude from it, and to isolate it from

others. In such temptations Christians recognize that they are liable to spurn and despoil the riches which God has, with such generosity, invested in His human creation . . . that they are liable to impoverish, divide and despoil.

8. Because of the divisive role to which all religions and ideologies are so easily prone, they are each called to look upon themselves anew, so as to contribute from their resources to the good of the community of humankind in its wholeness. Thinking of the challenge to the Christian faith Christians are reminded both of the danger of saying "peace, peace" where there is no peace and of Jesus' words in the Sermon on the Mount: "Happy are those who work for peace: God will call them His children" (Matt. 5:9). As workers for peace, liberation and justice, the way to which often makes conflict necessary and reconciliation costly, they feel themselves called to share with others in the community of humankind in search for new experiences in the evolution of communities, where people may affirm their interdependence as much as respect for their distinctive identities. Such a vision may be helpful in the search for community in a pluralistic world; it is not one of homogeneous unity or totalitarian uniformity, nor does it envisage self-contained communities, simply co-existing. Rather it emphasizes the positive part which existing communities may play in developing the community of humankind (cf. para. 6). For Christians the thought of a community of communities is further related to the kingly rule of God over all human communities.

B. The Christian Community: The Churches and the Church

9. Scattered within the world of human communities, we as Christians look for signs of God's kingly rule and truly believe in our community with Christians everywhere in the Church, the Body of Christ. Being fully in the world, the Christian community shares in the many distinctions and divisions within and between the communities of humankind. It manifests immense cultural variety within itself, which we

are bound to acknowledge as affecting not only the practice but also the interpretation of the faith by different groups of Christians. This is exemplified in South Asia by Christians who speak of their struggle, within cultures moulded by Hinduism, Buddhism and Islam, to express their Christian faith in a spirit at once obedient to the Gospel and related to the cultural context. In Europe and North America the understanding and practice of the Christian faith has been deeply influenced by western culture.

10. Our experience as Christians in this widely scattered community is very varied. There are churches who live in situations of social, cultural and national suppression, where their identity is threatened and their freedom restricted. There are times and places where Christians may have to stand apart from others in loyalty to Christ but this does not absolve Christians who have indulged in the temptations of cultural arrogance and communal exclusiveness, both consciously and unconsciously. Thus they have contributed to the divisions within the community of humankind, and have created antagonisms between different groups within the Christian community itself. Christians, therefore, must stand under the judgment of God. We believe that there is a real sense in which our unity with all peoples lies in our common participation in all that has so tragically created divisions within the world. It is in this way that we relate to our theme the experience of the empirical churches that they constantly need God's forgiveness.

11. But amidst this complex, confusing and humbling situation we believe that the Gospel of our Lord Jesus Christ retains its divine given-ness. The Gospel cannot be limited to any particular culture, but through the inspiration of the Holy Spirit sheds its light in them all and upon them all. Nor is the truth of the Gospel distorted by the sinfulness of its Christian adherents. Rather, the Gospel calls them individually and in community to repentance and confession, and invites them into newness of life in the risen Christ. This reality of renewed Christian community pertains to our very deepest experience as Christians. There are many ways of speaking of this experience. For example:

—our communion in the Church as sacrament of the reconciliation and unity of humankind recreated through the saving activity of God in Jesus Christ;

—our communion with God who, in the fullness of His Trinity calls humankind into unity with Him in His eternal communion with His entire creation;

—our communion in fellowship with all members of the Body of Christ through history, across distinction of race, sex, caste and culture;

—a conviction that God in Christ has set us free for communion with all peoples and everything which is made holy by the work of God.

Though we may express our conviction of the reality of this community in different ways, we hold fast to God in Christ who nourishes His church by Word and Sacraments.

12. We must acknowledge the close relation between our concern for dialogue and our work for visible Church unity. It is not only that the different confessional traditions have been an influence on the different approaches to dialogue and that questions concerning dialogue are seriously discussed within and between churches, but also the contribution of Christians to dialogue is distorted by division among them.

13. In the WCC we experience both the possibility for common confession of faith and worship together and also the obstacles to Christian unity. We are agreed in giving a vital place in our thinking to Bible study and worship; we are able to worship our one Lord in the very different ways of the churches represented among us. Yet we are also aware of problems concerning the authority of the Bible remaining unsolved among us and of the fact that we are not yet part of one eucharistic fellowship. It is not surprising therefore that there is controversy among Christians about the meditative use (rather than simply the intellectual study) of the holy books of other faiths and about the question of common worship between those of different faiths. There is need for further careful and sensitive study of these issues.

14. As Christians we are conscious of a tension between

the Christian community as we experience it to be in the world of human communities, and as we believe it in essence to be in the promise of God. The tension is fundamental to our Christian identity. We cannot resolve it, nor should we seek to avoid it. In the heart of this tension we discover the character of the Christian Church as a sign at once of people's need for fuller and deeper community, and of God's promise of a restored human community in Christ. Our consciousness of the tension must preclude any trace of triumphalism in the life of the Christian Church in the communities of human-kind. It must also preclude any trace of condescension to-wards our fellow human beings. Rather it should evoke in us an attitude of real humility towards all peoples since we know that we together with all our brothers and sisters have fallen short of the community which God intends.

15. We understand our calling as Christians to be that of participating fully in the mission of God (missio Dei) with the courage of conviction to enable us to be adventurous and take risks. To this end we could humbly share with all our fellow human beings in a compelling pilgrimage. We are specifi-cally disciples of Christ, but we refuse to limit Him to the dimensions of our human understanding. In our relationships within the many human communities we believe that we come to know Christ more fully through faith as Son of God and Saviour of the world; we grow in His service within the world; and we rejoice in the hope which He gives.

PART II

ON DIALOGUE

C. Reasons for Dialogue

16. The term "dialogue in community" is useful in that it gives concreteness to Christian reflection on dialogue. Moreover it focuses attention on the reasons for being in dialogue, which can be identified in two related categories.

Most Christians today live out their lives in actual community with people who may be committed to faiths and ideologies other than their own. They live in families sometimes of mixed faiths and ideologies; they live as neighbours in the same towns and villages; they need to build up their relationships expressing mutual human care and searching for mutual understanding. This sort of dialogue is very practical, concerned with the problems of modern life—the social, political, ecological, and, above all, the ordinary and familiar.

But there are concerns beyond the local which require Christians to engage in dialogue towards the realization of a wider community in which peace and justice may be more fully realized. This leads in turn to a dialogue between communities, in which issues of national and international concern are tackled.

17. No more than "community" can "dialogue" be precisely defined. Rather it has to be described, experienced and developed as a lifestyle. As human beings we have learned to speak; we talk, chatter, give and receive information, have discussions—all this is not yet dialogue. Now and then it happens that out of our talking and our relationships arises a deeper encounter, an opening up, in more than intellectual terms, of each to the concerns of the other. This is experienced by families and friends, and by those who share the same faiths, or ideology; but we are particularly concerned with the dialogue which reaches across differences of faith, ideology and culture, even where the partners in dialogue do not agree on important central aspects of human life. Dialogue can be recognized as a welcome way of obedience to the commandment of the Decalogue: "You shall not bear false witness against your neighbour." Dialogue helps us not to disfigure the image of our neighbours of different faiths and ideologies. It has been the experience of many Christians that this dialogue is indeed possible on the basis of a mutual trust and a respect for the integrity of each participant's identity.

18. Dialogue, therefore, is a fundamental part of Christian service within community. In dialogue Christians actively respond to the command to "love God and your

neighbour as yourself.'' As an expression of love, engagement in dialogue testifies to the love experienced in Christ. It is a joyful affirmation of life against chaos, and a participation with all who are allies of life in seeking the provisional goals of a better human community. Thus ''dialogue in community'' is not a secret weapon in the armoury of an aggressive Christian militancy. Rather it is a means of living one's faith in Christ in service of community with one's neighbours.

19. In this sense dialogue has a distinctive and rightful place within Christian life, in a manner directly comparable to other forms of service. But ''distinctive'' does not mean totally different or separate. In dialogue Christians seek ''to speak the truth in a spirit of love,'' not naively ''to be tossed to and fro, and be carried about with every wind of doctrine'' (Eph. 4:14–15). In giving their witness they recognize that in most circumstances today the spirit of dialogue is necessary. For this reason we do not see dialogue and the giving of witness as standing in any contradiction to one another. Indeed, as Christians enter dialogue with their commitment to Jesus Christ, time and again the relationship of dialogue gives opportunity for authentic witness. Thus, to the member churches of the WCC we feel able with integrity to commend the way of dialogue as one in which Jesus Christ can be confessed in the world today; at the same time we feel able with integrity to assure our partners in dialogue that we come not as manipulators but as genuine fellow-pilgrims, to speak with them of what we believe God to have done in Jesus Christ who has gone before us, but whom we seek to meet anew in dialogue.

D. The Theological Significance of People of Other Faiths and Ideologies

20. Christians engaged in faithful ''dialogue in community'' with people of other faiths and ideologies cannot avoid asking themselves penetrating questions about the place of these people in the activity of God in history. They ask these questions not in theory, but in terms of what God may be

doing in the lives of hundreds of millions of men and women who live in and seek community together with Christians, but along different ways. So dialogue should proceed in terms of people of other faiths and ideologies rather than of theoretical, impersonal systems. This is not to deny the importance of religious traditions and their inter-relationships but it is vital to examine how faiths and ideologies have given direction to the daily living of individuals and groups and actually affect dialogue on both sides.

21. Approaching the theological questions in this spirit Christians should proceed...

—with repentance, because they know how easily they misconstrue God's revelation in Jesus Christ, betraying it in their actions and posturing as the owners of God's truth rather than, as in fact they are, the undeserving recipients of grace;

—with humility, because they so often perceive in people of other faiths and ideologies a spirituality, dedication, compassion and a wisdom which should forbid them making judgments about others as though from a position of superiority; in particular they should avoid using ideas such as "anonymous Christians," "the Christian presence," "the unknown Christ," in ways not intended by those who proposed them for theological purposes or in ways prejudicial to the self-understanding of Christians and others;

—with joy, because it is not themselves they preach; it is Jesus Christ, perceived by many people of living faiths and ideologies as prophet, holy one, teacher, example; but confessed by Christians as Lord and Saviour, Himself the faithful witness and the coming one (Rev. 1:5-7);

—with integrity, because they do not enter into dialogue with others except in this penitent and humble joyfulness in the Lord Jesus Christ, making clear to others their own experience and witness, even as they seek to hear from others their expressions of deepest conviction and insight. All these would mean an openness and exposure, the capacity to be wounded which we see in the example of our Lord Jesus Christ and which we sum up in the word vulnerability.

22. Only in this spirit can Christians hope to address themselves creatively to the theological questions posed by other faiths and by ideologies. Christians from different backgrounds are growing in understanding in the following areas in particular:

—that renewed attention must be given to the doctrine of creation, particularly as they may see it illuminated by the Christian understanding of God as one Holy Trinity and by the resurrection and glorification of Christ;

—that fundamental questions about the nature and activity of God and the doctrine of the Spirit arise in dialogue, and the christological discussion must take place with this comprehensive reference;

—that the Bible, with all the aids to its understanding and appropriation from the churches' tradition and scholarship, is to be used creatively as the basis for Christian reflection on the issues that arise, giving both encouragement and warning, though it cannot be assumed as a reference point for partners in dialogue;

—that the theological problems of church unity also need to be viewed in relation to the concern for dialogue;

—that the aim of dialogue is not reduction of living faiths and ideologies to a lowest common denominator, not only a comparison and discussion of symbols and concepts, but the enabling of a true encounter between those spiritual insights and experiences which are only found at the deepest levels of human life.

23. We look forward to further fruitful discussions of these issues (among many others) within our Christian circles but also in situations of dialogue. There are other questions, where agreement is more difficult and sometimes impossible, but these also we commend for further theological attention:

—What is the relation between the universal creative/redemptive activity of God towards all humankind and the particular creative/redemptive activity of God in the history of Israel and in the person and work of Jesus Christ?

—Are Christians to speak of God's work in the lives of all men and women only in tentative terms of hope that they may experience something of Him, or more positively in terms of God's self-disclosure to people of living faiths and ideologies and in the struggle of human life?

—How are Christians to find from the Bible criteria in their approach to people of other faiths and ideologies, recognizing, as they must, the authority accorded to the Bible by Christians of all centuries, particular questions concerning the authority of the Old Testament for the Christian Church, and the fact that the partners in dialogue have other starting points and resources, both in holy books and traditions of teaching?

—What is the biblical view and Christian experience of the operation of the Holy Spirit, and is it right and helpful to understand the work of God outside the Church in terms of the doctrine of the Holy Spirit?

E. Syncretism

24. In dialogue Christians are called to be adventurous, and they must be ready to take risks; but also to be watchful and wide awake for God. Is syncretism a danger for which Christians must be alert?

25. There is a positive need for a genuine "translation" of the Christian message in every time and place. This need is recognized as soon as the Bible translators begin their work in a particular language and have to weigh the cultural and philosophical overtones and undertones of its words. But there is also a wider "translation" of the message by expressing it in artistic, dramatic, liturgical and above all in relational terms which are appropriate to convey the authenticity of the message in ways authentically indigenous, often

through the theologically tested use of the symbols and concepts of a particular community.

26. Despite attempts to rescue the word "syncretism" it now conveys, after its previous uses in Christian debate, a negative evaluation. This is clearly the case if it means, as the Nairobi Assembly used the word, "conscious or unconscious human attempts to create a new religion composed of elements taken from different religions." In this sense syncretism is also rejected by the dialogue partners, although there may be some who in their alienation are seeking help from many sources and do not regard syncretism negatively.

27. The word "syncretism" is, however, more widely used than at Nairobi and particularly to warn against two other dangers.

The first danger is that in attempting to "translate" the Christian message for a cultural setting or in approach to faiths and ideologies with which Christians are in dialogue partnership, they may go too far and compromise the authenticity of Christian faith and life. They have the Bible to guide them but there is always risk in seeking to express the Gospel in a new setting: for instance, the early Christian struggle against heresy in the debate with Gnosticism; or the compromising of the Gospel in the so-called "civil religions" of the West. It is salutary to examine such examples lest it be supposed that syncretism is a risk endemic only in certain continents.

A second danger is that of interpreting a living faith not in its own terms but in terms of another faith or ideology. This is illegitimate on the principles of both scholarship and dialogue. In this way Christianity may be "syncretized" by seeing it as only a variant of some other approach to God, or another faith may be wrongly "syncretized" by seeing it only as partial understanding of what Christians believe that they know in full. There is a particular need for further study of the way in which this kind of syncretism can take place between a faith and an ideology.

28. Both these are real dangers and there will be differences of judgment among Christians and between churches as to when these dangers are threatening, or have

actually overtaken particular Christian enterprises. Despite the recognized dangers Christians should welcome and gladly engage in the venture of exploratory faith. The particular risks of syncretism in the modern world should not lead Christians to refrain from dialogue, but are an additional reason for engaging in dialogue so that the issues may be clarified.

29. Within the ecumenical movement the practice of dialogue and the giving of witness have sometimes evoked mutual suspicion. God is very patient with the Church, giving it space and time for discovery of His way and its riches (cf. II Pet. 3:9). There is need within the ecumenical fellowship to give one another space and time—space and time, for instance, in India or Ghana to explore the richness of the Gospel in a setting very different from that of "Hellenized" Europe; space and time, for instance, in Korea to develop the present striking evangelistic work of the churches; space and time, for instance, in Europe to adjust to a new situation in which secularity is now being changed by new religious interest not expressed in traditional terms. The diversity of dialogue itself must be recognized in its particular content and in its relation to specific context.

PART III

Guidelines Recommended to the Churches for Study and Action

It is Christian faith in the Triune God—Creator of all humankind, Redeemer in Jesus Christ, revealing and renewing Spirit—which calls us Christians to human relationship with our many neighbours. Such relationship includes dialogue: witnessing to our deepest convictions and listening to those of our neighbours. It is Christian faith which sets us free to be open to the faiths of others, to risk, to trust and to be vulnerable. In dialogue, conviction and openness are held in balance.

In a world in which Christians have many neighbours, dialogue is not only an activity of meetings and conferences, it is also a way of living out Christian faith in relationship and commitment to those neighbours with whom Christians share towns, cities, nations and the earth as a whole. Dialogue is a style of living in relationship with neighbours. This in no way replaces or limits our Christian obligation to witness, as partners enter into dialogue with their respective commitments.

These guidelines are offered to member churches of the WCC and to individual congregations in awareness of the great diversity of situations in which they find themselves. The neighbours with whom Christians enter into relationship in dialogue may be partners in common social, economic and political crises and quests; companions in scholarly work or intellectual and spiritual exploration; or, literally, the people next door. In some places, Christians and the church as an institution are in positions of power and influence, and their neighbours are without power. In other places it is the Christians who are powerless. There are also situations of tension and conflict where dialogue may not be possible or opportunities very limited. In many places people of different living faiths interact not only with each other, but also with people of various ideologies, though sometimes it is difficult to make a clear-cut distinction between religions and ideologies, for there are religious dimensions of ideologies and ideological dimensions of religions, Christianity included. The emergence of new religious groups in many countries has brought new dimensions and tensions to inter-religious relationships. With all this diversity in mind, the following guidelines are commended to member churches for their consideration and discussion, testing and evaluation, and for their elaboration in each specific situation.

Learning and Understanding in Dialogue

1. *Churches should seek ways in which Christian communities can enter into dialogue with their neighbours of different faiths and ideologies.*

They should also discover ways of responding to similar initiatives by their neighbours in the community.

2. *Dialogues should normally be planned together.*

When planned together with partners of other living faiths or ideological convictions they may well focus on particular issues: theological or religious, political or social.

3. *Partners in dialogue should take stock of the religious, cultural and ideological diversity of their local situation.*

Only by being alert both to the particular areas of tension and discrimination and to the particular opportunities for conversation and cooperation in their own context will Christians and their neighbours be able to create the conditions for dialogue. They should be especially alert to infringements of the basic human rights of religious, cultural or ideological minority groups.

4. *Partners in dialogue should be free to "define themselves."*

One of the functions of dialogue is to allow participants to describe and witness to their faith in their own terms. This is of primary importance since self-serving descriptions of other peoples' faith are one of the roots of prejudice, stereotyping and condescension. Listening carefully to the neighbours' self-understanding enables Christians better to obey the commandment not to bear false witness against their neighbours, whether those neighbours be of long established religious, cultural or ideological traditions or members of new religious groups. It should be recognized by partners in dialogue that any religion or ideology claiming universality, apart from having an understanding of itself, will also have its own interpretations of other religions and ideologies as part of its own self-understanding. Dialogue gives an opportunity for a mutual questioning of the understanding partners have about themselves and others. It is out of a reciprocal willingness to listen and learn that significant dialogue grows.

5. *Dialogue should generate educational efforts in the community.*

In many cases Christians, utilizing the experience of dialogue, must take the initiative in education in order to restore the distorted image of the neighbours that may already exist in their communities and to advance Christian understanding of people of other living faiths and ideologies.

Even in those situations where Christians do not live in close contact with people of the various religious, cultural and ideological traditions, they should take seriously the responsibility to study and to learn about these other traditions.

Member churches should consider what action they can take in the following educational areas:

(i) Teaching programmes in schools, colleges and adult education systems to enhance the understanding of the cultural, religious and ideological traditions of humankind; such programmes should, wherever possible, invite adherents of those traditions to make their contribution.

(ii) Teaching programmes in theological seminaries and colleges to prepare Christian ministers with the training and sensitivity necessary for inter-religious dialogue.

(iii) Positive relationships with programmes in university departments and other institutes of higher learning which are concerned with the academic study of religion.

(iv) The review of material used and teachings customarily given in courses of instruction at all levels in the churches, including at theological colleges and seminaries, with a view to eliminating anything which encourages fanaticism and insensitivity to people of other faiths and ideologies.

(v) The development of church school materials for the study of people of other faiths and ideologies.

(vi) The provision of courses for people who may be sent to serve in other cultures or who may travel as tourists in such cultures to promote their greater understanding and sensitivity.

(vii) Responsible reaction to school text books and media presentations which may prejudice the image of the neighbour.

(viii) The creative use of the media, radio, television etc., wherever possible in order to reach a wider audience in efforts to expand understanding of people of other faiths and ideologies.

Sharing and Living Together in Dialogue

6. *Dialogue is most vital when its participants actually share their lives together.*

It is in existing communities where families meet as neighbours and children play together that spontaneous dialogue develops. Where people of different faiths and ideologies share common activities, intellectual interests and spiritual quests, dialogue can be related to the whole of life and can become a style of living-in-relationship. The person who asks a neighbour of another faith to explain the meaning of a custom or festival has actually taken the first step in dialogue

Of course, dialogue between long-term neighbours may be frustrated by deeply engrained suspicions, and men and women will have to reckon not only with the communities they seek but also with the barriers between their present communities.

7. *Dialogue should be pursued by sharing in common enterprises in community.*

Common activities and experiences are the most fruitful setting for dialogue on issues of faith, ideology and action. It is in the search for a just community of humankind that Christians and their neighbours will be able to help each other break out of cultural, educational, political and social isolation in order to realize a more participatory society It may well be that in particular settings such common enterprises will generate interreligious committees or organizations to facilitate this kind of dialogue-in-action.

8. *Partners in dialogue should be aware of their ideological commitments.*

Dialogue should help to reveal and to understand the ideological components of religions in particular situations. When

Christians find themselves in communities with neighbours of other living faiths they may have common or diverse ideological convictions.

In such situations partners need to be sensitive to both religious and ideological dimensions of the ongoing dialogue. Where Christians find themselves in communities with people of secular ideological convictions, the dialogue will at least expose shared contributions in a common search for the provisional goals of a better human community. Here dialogue may begin as a kind of "internal dialogue" seeking to bring to explicit reflection and discussion issues in the encounter of the Gospel both with ideological factors in various communities where Christians find themselves, and with the ideological assumptions of Christians themselves.

9. *Partners in dialogue should be aware of cultural loyalties.*

Dialogue and sensitivity to neighbours need to be developed in the area of relating Christian faith to cultures. This applies especially to those places where traditional and popular culture has been unduly despised and rejected by the churches. A culture should not be romanticized or made into a false absolute but it may often challenge and enrich the expression of the Christian faith. After careful interpretation and discrimination local cultures may make meaningful contributions in symbols and liturgy, social structures, relations, patterns of healing, art, architecture and music, dance and drama, poetry and literature.

10. *Dialogue will raise the question of sharing in celebrations, rituals, worship and meditation.*

Human communities draw together, express, and renew themselves in ritual and worship, and dialogue presumes an attitude of respect for the ritual expressions of the neighbour's community. Dialogue at times includes extending and accepting invitations to visit each other as guests and observers in family and community rituals, ceremonies and festivals. Such occasions provide excellent opportunities to enhance the mutual understanding of neighbours.

Working together in common projects and activities or

visiting in homes and at festivals will eventually raise the very difficult and important question of fuller sharing in common prayer, worship or meditation. This is one of the areas of dialogue which is most controversial and most in need of further exploration.

Whether or not any such activities are undertaken, dialogue partners will want to face squarely the issues raised, sensitive to one another's integrity and fully realizing the assumptions and implications of what is done or not done.

Planning for Dialogue

11. *Dialogue should be planned and undertaken ecumenically, wherever possible.*

Member churches should move forward in planning for dialogue in cooperation with one another. This may well mean that regional and local councils of churches will have a separate commission on dialogue.

12. *Planning for dialogue will necessitate regional and local guidelines.*

As the member churches of the WCC consider, test and evaluate these guidelines they will need to work out for themselves and with their specific partners in dialogue statements and guidelines for their own use in particular situations. The WCC can best assist the member churches in their specific dialogues by itself concentrating upon the worldwide features of the Christian dialogue with people of particular religions and ideologies. For this purpose, the WCC will arrange appropriate consultations at the world level.

13. *Dialogue can be helped by selective participation in world interreligious meetings and organizations.*

There are now many organizations linking world religions and seeking to enable them to cooperate for various purposes, such as the struggle for peace and justice in the community and among the nations. Christians involved in dialogue need to be selective in their participation in the meetings arranged by such organizations. Christian representatives should guard the mutual recognition of and respect for the integrity of each faith. On occasion it may be necessary for Christians to make clear that their participation does not necessarily signify acceptance of the underlying assumptions of a particular meeting or organization. Christians will normally avoid being identified with alliances against other religions or against ideologies as such. The WCC will be willing to provide consultant-observers for selected meetings of this kind but will not at present take a direct official part in the organizational structure of world interreligious organizations.

To enter into dialogue requires an opening of the mind and heart to others. It is an undertaking which requires risk as well as a deep sense of vocation. It is impossible without sensitivity to the richly varied life of humankind. This opening, this risk, this vocation, this sensitivity are at the heart of the ecumenical movement and in the deepest currents of the life of the churches. It is therefore with a commitment to the importance of dialogue for the member churches of the WCC that the Central Committee offers this Statement and these Guidelines to the churches.

NOTES TO INTRODUCTION

1. See *Breaking Barriers: Nairobi 1975,* ed. David M. Paton (Grand Rapids: Eerdmans, 1976), pp. 70-85. Also my "Courage for Dialogue: An Interpretation of the Nairobi Debate," *Religion and Society* 23, no. 3 (Bangalore, September 1976):22-35.

2. This consultation brought together in Chiang Mai, Thailand, 85 people—Protestant, Orthodox and Roman Catholic—to discuss the theological implications of the theme: Dialogue in Community. The full text, together with group reports, was published in *Dialogue in Community,* 2nd ed. (Geneva: WCC, 1978). The statement was widely circulated among churches and comments called for. Responses were received from the following countries: Australia, Ghana, India, Japan, Indonesia, Sri Lanka, USA, Canada, Iran, Britain, France, Federal Republic of Germany, German Democratic Republic, Italy, The Netherlands, Norway and Switzerland.

3. All quotations in this article, unless otherwise indicated, are from the *Guidelines* document

Dialogue, Encounter, Even Confrontation

John R. Stott

Evangelical Protestants have had sharp, negative reactions against some expositions of dialogue with people of other faiths. An acknowledged evangelical leader, one of the framers of the 1974 Lausanne Covenant, presents here a biblical basis for "true dialogue," as well as the historical background for the "conservative Christian's argument against dialogue" which considers it as "bordering on treason against Jesus Christ." John R. Stott, a minister in the Church of England, argues that "true dialogue" is a mark of Christian authenticity, humility, integrity, and sensitivity. But there is need also for encounter, even confrontation (what he calls "elenctics"), "in which we seek both to disclose the inadequacies and falsities of non-Christian religion and to demonstrate the adequacy and truth, absoluteness and finality of the Lord Jesus Christ." This article, from chapter three ("Dialogue") in Stott's *Christian Mission in the Modern World*, published in 1975 by InterVarsity Press, Downers Grove, IL 60515, is reprinted with permission.

"Mission" denotes the self-giving service which God sends his people into the world to render, and includes both evangelism and socio-political action. Within this broadly conceived mission a certain urgency attaches to evangelism, and priority must be given to it; "evangelism" means announcing or proclaiming the good news of Jesus. . . . Is there any room for "dialogue" in the proclamation of the good news? It is well known that during the past decade or two the concept of "dialogue with people of other faiths" has become the ecumenical fashion, and that evangelicals have tended to react rather sharply against it. Is our negative reaction justified? And what are the issues anyway?

Extreme views

Extreme positions have been taken on both sides of this debate. Evangelical Christians have always—and in my judgment rightly—emphasized the indispensable necessity of preaching the gospel, for God has appointed his church to be the herald of the good news. An eloquent summons to proclamation has been issued by Dr. Martyn Lloyd-Jones in his book *Preaching and Preachers* (Hodder and Stoughton, 1971). His first chapter is entitled "The Primacy of Preaching" and on its first page he writes: "to me the work of preaching is the highest and the greatest and the most glorious calling to which anyone can ever be called. If you want something in addition to that I would say without any hesitation that the most urgent need in the Christian Church today is true preaching, and as it is the greatest and most urgent need in the Church, it is obviously the greatest need for the world also" (p. 9). Indeed, because man's essential trouble is his rebellion against God and his need of salvation, therefore "preaching is the primary task of the Church" (p. 25). To his passionate advocacy of preaching Dr. Lloyd-Jones has sometimes added his distaste for the concept of dialogue: "God is not to be discussed or debated. . . . Believing what we do about God, we cannot in any circumstances allow Him to become a subject for discussion or debate or investigation . . . as if He were but a philosophical proposition" (pp. 46, 47).

And the same goes for the gospel: the gospel is suitable for proclamation, not for amiable discussion. Now if by "discussion" we have in mind the work of clever diplomats at the conference table, whose objective is to satisfy (even appease) everybody, and whose method is to reach consensus by compromise, I find myself in whole-hearted agreement with Dr. Lloyd-Jones. The gospel is a non-negotiable revelation from God. We may certainly discuss its meaning and its interpretation, so long as our purpose is to grasp it more firmly ourselves and commend it more acceptably to others. But we have no liberty to sit in judgment on it, or to tamper with its substance. For it is God's gospel not ours, and its truth is to be received not criticized, declared not discussed. Having said this, however, it is necessary to add that, properly understood, "dialogue" and "discussion" are two different things.

At the other extreme there is a growing dislike for preaching, or at least for preaching of an authoritative or dogmatic kind. Proclamation is said to be arrogant; the humble way of communication is the way of dialogue. It would be difficult to find a more articulate exponent of this view than Professor J. G. Davies of Birmingham. In his small book *Dialogue with the World* (SCM 1967) he writes: "Monologue is entirely lacking in humility: it assumes that we know all and that we merely have to declare it, to pass it on to the ignorant, whereas we need to seek truth together, that our truth may be corrected and deepened as it encounters the truths of those with whom we are in dialogue" (p. 31). Further, "monologue ... is deficient in openness" (p. 31), whereas "dialogue involves complete openness" (p. 55). Professor Davies goes on:

> To enter into dialogue in this way is not only difficult, it is dangerous. Complete openness means that every time we enter into dialogue our faith is at stake. If I engage in dialogue with a Buddhist and do so with openness I must recognize that the outcome cannot be predetermined either for him or for me. The Buddhist may come to accept Jesus as Lord, but I may come to accept the authority of the Buddha, or even both of us may end up as agnostics. Unless these are *real* possibilities, neither of us is being fully open to the other.... To live dialogically is to life dangerously. (p. 55)

For myself I regard this as an intemperate overstatement. It is true that good Christian preaching is always dialogical, in the sense that it engages the minds of the listeners and speaks to them with relevance. But it is not true to say that all monologue is proud. The evangelist who proclaims the gospel is not claiming to "know all," but only to have been put in trust with the gospel. We should also, as I believe and shall soon argue, be willing to enter into dialogue. In doing so we shall learn from the other person both about his beliefs and also (by listening to his critical reaction to Christianity) about certain aspects of our own. But we should not cultivate a total "openness" in which we suspend even our convictions concerning the truth of the gospel and our personal commitment to Jesus Christ. To attempt to do this would be to destroy our own integrity as Christians.

Dialogue in the Bible

In this dialogue about dialogue, perhaps the place to begin is with definition. A more simple and straightforward definition I have not found than that framed at the National Evangelical Anglican Congress held at Keele in 1967: "Dialogue is a conversation in which each party is serious in his approach both to the subject and to the other person, and desires to listen and learn as well as to speak and instruct" (para. 83).

After this definition it is important to note that the living God of the biblical revelation himself enters into a dialogue with man. He not only speaks but listens. He asks questions and waits for the answers. Ever since his question went echoing among the trees of the garden of Eden, "Where are you?" God has been seeking his fallen creature, and addressing questions to him. Of course the approach of the Infinite to the finite, of the Creator to the creature, of the Holy to the sinful has always been one of gracious self-disclosure. Nevertheless, the form his revelation has taken has often been dialogical. "Gird up your loins like a man," he said to Job. "I will question you, and you shall declare to me" (Job 38:3; 40:7). And his address to Israel through the prophets was full of questions.

'Come now, let us reason together, says the Lord.' . . .
'What wrong did your fathers find in me that they went far from me . . . ?'
'Why do you complain against me?' . . .

Have you not known? Have you not heard?
Has it not been told you from the beginning?
Have you not understood from the foundations of the
   earth? . . .
How can I give you up, O Ephraim!
How can I hand you over, O Israel!
(Isaiah 1:18; Jeremiah 2:5, 29; Isaiah 40:21; Hosea 11:8)

Jesus too, who himself as a boy was found in the temple
"sitting among the teachers listening to them and asking
them questions" (Luke 2:46), during his public ministry entered into serious conversations with individuals like
Nicodemus, the Samaritan woman and the crowds. He sel-
dom if ever spoke in a declamatory, take-it-or-leave-it style.
Instead, whether explicitly or implicitly, he was constantly
addressing questions to his hearers' minds and consciences.
For example, "When . . . the owner of the vineyard comes,
what will he do to those tenants?" (Matthew 21:40). Again,
"Which of these three, do you think, proved neighbour to the
man who fell among the robbers?" (Luke 10:36). Even after
the Ascension when he revealed himself to Saul of Tarsus on
the Damascus Road, and the prostrate and blinded Pharisee
appeared at first to have been crushed by the vision, Jesus
addressed him a rational question: "Why do you persecute
me?" and provoked the counterquestions "Who are you,
Lord?" and "What shall I do, Lord?" (Acts 9:4, 5; 22:10).
   It is instructive to notice that later when Saul began his
great missionary journeys as Paul the apostle, he used some
form of dialogue as an integral part of his method. At least Luke
not infrequently uses the verb *dialegomai* to describe an aspect
of his evangelism, especially during the second and third expe-
ditions. True, there is some uncertainty about the precise
meaning of the verb. In classical Greek it meant to "con-
verse" or "discuss" and was particularly associated with the
so-called "dialectic" as a means of instruction and persuasion developed in different ways by Socrates, Plato and Aristotle. In the Gospels it is once used of the apostles' argumen-
tative discussion with each other [of] who was the greatest
(Mark 9:34). In reference to Paul's ministry Gottlob Schrenk

in Kittel's *Theological Dictionary* (Eerdmans) says that it refers to the "delivering of religious lectures or sermons" but has no reference to "disputation." The Arndt-Gingrich lexicon, on the other hand, though conceding that it sometimes means "simply to speak or preach" (*e.g.* Hebrews 12:5), maintains that it is used "of lectures which were likely to end in disputations." The context certainly suggests this too.

Thus in the synagogue at Thessalonica for three weeks "Paul ... argued with them from the Scriptures, explaining and proving that it was necessary for the Christ to suffer and to rise from the dead, and saying 'This Jesus, whom I proclaim to you, is the Christ.'" Luke then adds: "some of them were persuaded" (Acts 17:1–4). Here five words are brought together—arguing, explaining, proving, proclaiming and persuading—which suggest that Paul was actually debating with the Jews, hearing and answering their objections to his message. In Athens we are told that he "argued" both "in the synagogue with the Jews and the devout persons, and in the market place every day with those who chanced to be there" (17:17). This is an important addition because it shows that his reasoning approach was with casual Gentile passers-by as well as with Jews in the synagogue. In Corinth he "argued in the synagogue every sabbath and persuaded Jews and Greeks" (18:4), while at Ephesus he first "entered the synagogue and for three months spoke boldly, arguing and pleading about the kingdom of God" and then for two years "argued daily in the hall of Tyrannus" possibly for as long as five hours a day (19:8–10; cf. 18:19).

Paul also used the same method in Christian preaching, for during the famous "breaking of bread" at Troas, during which the young man Eutychus fell asleep with nearly disastrous consequences, *dialegomai* is again used to describe Paul's address (Acts 20:7, 9). The last example is also interesting, because we find Paul having a dialogue with the procurator Festus, arguing with him in private about "justice, self-control and future judgment" until Festus grew alarmed and terminated the conversation (24:25). In summary, then, we may say that Paul included some degree of dialogue in most if not all his preaching, to Christians and non-

Christians, to Jews and Gentiles, to crowds and individuals, on formal and informal occasions. Indeed, to add a final text, Paul seems to have expected all the disciples of Jesus to be involved in continuous dialogue with the world, for he urged the Colossians: "Let your speech always be gracious, seasoned with salt, so that you may know how you ought to answer every one" (Colossians 4:6). Here are Christians in such close contact with "outsiders" (v. 5) that they are able both to speak to them (with gracious and salty speech) and to answer their questions.

The kind of "dialogue" which was included in Paul's ministry was, however, very different from what is often meant by the word today. For Paul's dialogue was clearly a part of his proclamation and subordinate to his proclamation. Moreover, the subject of his dialogue with the world was one which he always chose himself, namely Jesus Christ, and its object was always conversion to Jesus Christ. If this was still the position few who hesitate about dialogue would disagree with it. But often the modern dialogue of Christians with non-Christians seems to savour rather of unbelief than of faith, of compromise than of proclamation. It is time now to investigate this argument against dialogue. Afterwards I will seek to marshal some arguments in favour of true dialogue. . . .

The Argument Against Dialogue

The conservative Christian's argument against dialogue as bordering on treason against Jesus Christ can best be understood historically. The World Missionary Conference at Edinburgh in 1910 took place in an atmosphere of great confidence. I do not call it "self-confidence," because certainly their confidence was in God. Nevertheless, they confidently predicted the imminent collapse of the non-Christian religions. Temple Gairdner in his official account of the conference could write: "The spectacle of the advance of the Christian Church along many lines of action to the conquest of the five great religions of the modern world is one of singular interest and grandeur" (*Edinburgh 1910,* p. 135). This mood was rudely shaken by the outbreak of the First World War four years later. And at the second missionary conference at Jerusalem in 1928 the atmosphere was already different. Delegates were aware of the growth of secularism, and even suggested that against this universal enemy a common religious front was necessary.

Ten years later, in 1938, the third ecumenical missionary conference was held at Tambaram near Madras. Its key figure was the Dutchman Hendrik Kraemer, whose book *The Christian Message in a non-Christian World* had been written and published shortly before the conference assembled. Partly under the influence of Karl Barth's dialectic, in which he opposed religion to revelation as man's religiosity over against God's word, Kraemer stressed that there was a fundamental "discontinuity" between the religions of man and the revelation of God. He rejected both aggressive Christian missions on the one hand and on the other the notion that Christ was the fulfilment of non-Christian religions (popularized by J. N. Farquhar's *The Crown of Hinduism*, OUP 1913), and in their place he urged the uncompromising announcement of the gospel, although "in a persuasive and winning manner" (p. 302). He called the church to repossess its faith "in all its uniqueness and adequacy and power," and added: "We are bold enough to call men out from these [other religions] to the feet of Christ. We do so because we believe that in him alone is the full salvation which man needs" (quoted by James A. Scherer in his contribution to *Protestant Cross-Currents in Mission*, Abingdon 1968, p. 34).

As the Tambaram Conference closed, the black storm clouds of the Second World War, and of the new paganism it threatened to unleash, were already darkening the horizon, and when the war ended and ecumenical activity began again, "the coming dialogue between east and west" which Kraemer had foretold was already being canvassed by other voices. Both Protestant and Roman Catholic theologians began to formulate very differently from Hendrik Kraemer the relation between Christianity and other religions. In 1963 H. R. Schlette could write that "anyone who determines his ethical and actual individual way of life on the basis of an authentic desire to live a human life according to an order founded on truth, attains salvation'' (quoted by Carl F. Hallencreutz in *New Approaches to Men of Other Faiths*, WCC 1969, p. 78). Similarly, Karl Rahner in his *Theological Investigations V* (Darton, Longman & Todd), began to popularize the idea that the sincere non-Christian should rather be thought of as an ''anonymous Christian'': ''Christianity does not simply confront the member of an extra-Christian religion as a mere non-Christian but as someone who can and must already be regarded in this or that respect as an anonymous Christian.'' In consequence, ''the proclamation of the gospel does not simply turn someone absolutely abandoned by God and Christ into a Christian, but turns an anonymous Christian into someone who also knows about his Christian belief in the depths of his grace-endowed being by objective reflection and by the profession of faith. . . .'' It is in line with this thinking that Raymond Pannikar has written his book *The Unknown Christ of Hinduism* (Darton, Longman & Todd) and that Professor John Macquarrie has urged the replacement of competitive missions (adherents of different religions trying to convert each other) with a common mission undertaken by all the great religions together ''to the loveless and unloved masses of humanity.''

One of the fundamental beliefs of ecumenical scholars who think and write like this today is that Christ is already present everywhere, including other religions. This being so, it is in their view presumptuous of the Christian missionary to talk of ''bringing'' Christ with him into a situation; what he does is first to ''find'' Christ already there and then maybe to ''unveil'' him. Some go further still. They not only deny that missionaries take Christ with them, or can be the media of Christ's self-revelation to the non-Christian; they even suggest that it is the non-Christian who is the bearer of Christ's message to the Christian. For example, during the discussions on dialogue in Section II at Uppsala [General Assembly, 1968] one of the World Council's secretariat proposed the following wording: ''In this dialogue Christ speaks through the brother, correcting our limited and distorted understanding of the truth.'' If this wording had been agreed, not only would the non-Christian have been acclaimed as ''the brother,'' but the only reference to Christ speaking in the dialogue would have been of his speech to the Christian through the non-Christian. This would have turned evangelism upside down and presented dialogue as the proclamation of the gospel to the Christian by the non-Christian! Fortunately, as a result of pressure from evangelical Christians, the wording was changed to read: ''Christ speaks in this dialogue, revealing himself to those who do not know him and correcting the limited and distorted knowledge of those who do.'' I do not think we should object to this formulation.

But is Christ present in the non-Christian world? In our increasingly pluralistic society and syncretistic age this is the basic theological question which we cannot dodge. It would be facile to reply with a bare ''yes'' or ''no.'' We need rather to ask ourselves what Christ's apostles taught on this crucial issue. We will look in turn at statements of Peter, Paul and John.

Peter began his sermon to Cornelius: ''Truly I perceive that God shows no partiality, but in every nation any one who fears him and does what is right is acceptable to him'' (Acts 10:34, 35). Some have argued from this assertion that sincere religious and righteous people are saved, especially because the story begins with an angel's statement to Cornelius that ''your prayers and your alms have ascended as a memorial before God'' (v. 4). But such a deduction is inadmissible. To declare that a man who fears God and practices righteousness is ''acceptable'' to him cannot mean that he is ''accepted'' in the sense of being ''justified.'' The rest of the story makes this plain. This sincere, godfearing and righteous man still needed to hear the gospel. Indeed, when Peter later recounted to the Jerusalem church what had happened, he specifically recorded the divine promise to Cornelius about Peter, namely that ''he will declare to you a message by which you will be saved'' (Acts 11:14). And the Jerusalem church reacted to Peter's account by saying: ''then to the Gentiles also God has granted repentance unto life'' (11:18). It is clear then that, although in some sense ''acceptable'' to God, Cornelius before his conversion had neither ''salvation'' nor ''life.''

In his two sermons to heathen audiences, in Lystra and in Athens, the apostle Paul spoke of God's providential activity in the pagan world. Although in the past God had allowed all the nations ''to walk in their own ways,'' he said, yet even then ''he did not leave himself without witness,'' for he ''did good'' to all people, especially by giving them rain, fruitful seasons, food and happiness (Acts 14:16, 17).

To the Athenian philosophers Paul added that God the Creator was the sustainer of our life (''since he himself gives to all men life and breath and everything'') and the lord of history (''having determined allotted periods and the boundaries'' of all men's ''habitation'') intending that men ''should seek God in the hope that they might feel after him and find him.'' For ''he is not far from each one of us'' since, as heathen poets had said, ''in him we live and move and have our being'' and ''we are indeed his offspring.'' What these truths and the Athenians' knowledge of them did, however, was not to enable them to find God but rather to make their idolatry inexcusable. For, having overlooked it in the past, God ''now... commands all men everywhere to repent'' (Acts 17:22–31).

This sketch Paul filled out in the early chapters of Romans. He affirms there very clearly the universal knowledge of God and of goodness in the heathen world. On the one hand, God's ''invisible nature, namely his eternal power and deity'' are ''clearly perceived in the things that have been made,'' God having ''shown it to them'' (Romans 1:19, 20). On the other hand, men know something of God's moral law, for he had not only written it on stone tablets at Sinai; he had written it also on men's hearts, in the moral nature they have by creation (2:14, 15). So to some degree, Paul says, all men know God (1:21), know God's law and ''know God's decree'' that lawbreakers ''deserve to die'' (1:32). This revelation of God to all men, called ''general'' because made to all men and ''natural'' because given in nature and in human nature, is not, however, enough to save them. It is enough only to condemn them as being "without excuse" (1:21; 2:1; 3:19). For the whole thrust of the early chapters of Romans is that, although men know God, they do not honour him as God but by their wickedness suppress the truth they know (1:18, 21, 25, 28).

We turn now to John, and especially the prologue to the Fourth Gospel. Here he describes Jesus as "the Logos of God," and "the light of men" (John 1:1-3). He also affirms that the light is continually shining in the darkness and that the darkness has not overcome it (v. 5). Next he applies these great axioms to the historical process of revelation. He says of the Logos whom he later identifies as Jesus Christ: "The true light that enlightens every man was coming into the world." Indeed, "he was in the world" all the time (vv. 9, 10). Long before he actually "came" into the world (v. 11) he "was" already in it and was continuously "coming" into it. Moreover, his presence in the world was (and still is) an enlightening presence. He is the real light, of which all other lights are but types and shadows, and as the light he "enlightens every man." Thus "every man," Scripture gives us warrant to affirm, possesses some degree of light by his reason and conscience. And we should not hesitate to claim that everything good, beautiful and true, in all history and in all the earth, has come from Jesus Christ, even though men are ignorant of its origin. At the same time we must add that this universal light is not saving light. For one thing it is but a twilight in comparison with the fulness of light granted to those who follow Jesus as "the light of the world" and to whom is given "the light of life" (John 8:12). For another thing, men have always "loved darkness rather than light because their deeds were evil." Because of their wilful rejection of the light men are under condemnation (John 3:18-21).

The witness then of Peter, Paul and John is uniform. All three declare the constant activity of God in the non-Christian world. God has not left himself without witness. He reveals himself in nature. He is not far from any man. He gives light to every man. But man rejects the knowledge he has, prefers darkness to light and does not acknowledge the God he knows. His knowledge does not save him; it condemns him for his disobedience. Even his religiosity is a subtle escape from the God he is afraid and ashamed to meet.

The Place of Elenctics

We do not therefore deny that there are elements of truth in non-Christian systems, vestiges of the general revelation of God in nature. What we do vehemently deny is that these are sufficient for salvation and (more vehemently still) that Christian faith and non-Christian faiths are alternative and equally valid roads to God. Although there is an important place for "dialogue" with people of other faiths (as I shall shortly argue), there is also a need for "encounter" with them, and even for "confrontation," in which we seek both to disclose the inadequacies and falsities of non-Christian religion and to demonstrate the adequacy and truth, absoluteness and finality of the Lord Jesus Christ.

This work is technically called "elenctics," from the Greek verb *elengchein,* to "convince," "convict" or "rebuke," and so to call to repentence. J. H. Bavinck devotes the whole of Part II of his book *An Introduction to the Science of Missions* (Hodder and Stoughton 1954) to this subject, and describes the nature, place, task and main lines of elenctics. He defines it as "the science which unmasks to heathendom all false religions as sin against God, and . . . calls heathendom to a knowledge of the only true God" (p. 222). So important does he consider this science to be that it ought, he urges, "to have a respected position within the context of a theological faculty" (p. 232). For a full understanding of his thesis I must refer the reader to the fifty pages in which he carefully elaborates it. I wish only to draw attention now to a few of his main points.

First, the purpose of elenctics is not to "show the absurdity of heathendom," still less to ridicule other religions or their adherents. It refers chiefly "to the conviction and unmasking of sin, and to the call to responsibility" (p. 226). "In all elenctics the concern is always with the all-important question: 'What have you done with God'" (p. 223).

Next, the justification for this task is the Bible itself, for "the Bible from the first page to the last is a tremendous plea against heathenism, against the paganizing tendencies in Israel itself, in short, against the corruption of religion." The Bible also teaches us "concerning the human heart and its sly attempts to seek God and at the same time to escape him" (p. 244).

Thirdly, elenctics is not the harsh or negative activity it may sound. It "can actually be exercised only in living contact with the adherents of other religions." So "in practice I am never concerned with Buddhism, but with a living person and *his* Buddhism, I am never in contact with Islam but with a Moslem and *his* Mohammedanism" (p. 240). Further, this living contact must also be a loving contact.

> As long as I laugh at his foolish superstition, I look down upon him; I have not yet found the key to his soul. As soon as I understand that what he does in a noticeably naïve and childish manner, I also do and continue to do again and again, although in a different form; as soon as I actually stand next to him, I can in the name of Christ stand in opposition to him and convince him of sin, as Christ did with me and still does each day. (pp. 242–3)

A fourth and final point is that ultimately elenctics is the work of the Holy Spirit. It is he who "convicts" of sin, righteousness and judgment (John 16:8–10). "He alone can call to repentance and we are only means in his hand" (p. 229).

The very concept of "elenctics" is out of accord with the diffident, tolerant mood of today. But no Christian who accepts the biblical view of the evil of idolatry on the one hand and of the finality of Jesus Christ on the other can escape it. Further, only those who see the need for elenctics can also see the need for dialogue and can understand its proper place. Only when we are assured that a true Christian dialogue with a non-Christian is not a sign of syncretism but is fully consistent with our belief in the finality of Jesus Christ, are we ready to consider the arguments by which it may be commended. They are four.

The Argument for Dialogue

First, true dialogue is a mark of *authenticity*. Let me quote the Uppsala statement:

> A Christian's dialogue with another implies neither a denial of the uniqueness of Christ, nor any loss of his own commitment to Christ, but rather that a genuinely Christian approach to others must be human, personal, relevant and humble. In dialogue we share our common humanity, its dignity and fallenness, and express our common concern for that humanity. (Report II, para. 6)

If we do nothing but proclaim the gospel to people from a distance, our personal authenticity is bound to be suspect. Who are we? Those listening to us do not know. For we are playing a role (that of the preacher) and for all they know may be wearing a mask. Besides, we are so far away from them, they cannot even see us properly. But when we sit down alongside them like Philip in the Ethiopian's chariot, or encounter them face to face, a personal relationship is established. Our defenses come down. We begin to be seen and known for what we are. It is recognized that we too are human beings, equally sinful, equally needy, equally dependent on the grace of which we speak. And as the conversation develops, not only do we become known by the other, but we come to know him. He is a human being too, with sins and pains and frustrations and convictions. We come to respect his convictions, to feel with him in his pain. We still want to share the good news with him, for we care about it deeply, but we also care now about him with whom we want to share it. As the Mexico report put it, "true dialogue with a man of another faith, requires a concern both for the Gospel and for the other man. Without the first, dialogue becomes a pleasant conversation. Without the second, it becomes irrelevant, unconvincing or arrogant" (*Witness in Six Continents*, 1964, p. 146). Dialogue puts evangelism into an authentically human context.

Secondly, true dialogue is a mark of *humility*. I do not

mean by this that proclamation is always arrogant, for true proclamation is a setting forth of Jesus Christ as Saviour and Lord, and not in any sense or degree a parading of ourselves. What I mean rather is that as we listen to another person, our respect for him as a human being made in God's image grows. The distance between us diminishes as we recall that if he is fallen and sinful, so are we. Further, we realize that we cannot sweep away all his cherished convictions with a brash, unfeeling dismissal. We have to recognize humbly that some of his misconceptions may be our fault, or at least that his continuing rejection of Christ may be in reality a rejection of the caricature of Christ which he has seen in us or in our fellow Christians. As we listen to him, we may have many such uncomfortable lessons to learn. Our attitude to him changes. There may after all have been some lingering sense of superiority of which we were previously unconscious. But now no longer have we any desire to score points or win a victory. We love him too much to boost our ego at his expense. Humility in evangelism is a beautiful grace.

Thirdly, true dialogue is a mark of *integrity*. For in the conversation we listen to our friend's real beliefs and problems, and divest our minds of the false images we may have harboured. And we are determined also ourselves to be real. Bishop Stephen Neill distinguishes between dialogue and an "amiable discussion." In an article about Bangkok published in *The Churchman* in December 1973 he wrote:

> Anyone brought up in the Platonic tradition of dialogue knows well the intense seriousness involved; Socrates and his interlocutors are concerned about one thing only—that the truth should emerge. This is the concern of the Christian partner in dialogue. If Christ is the Truth, then the only thing that matters is that Christ should emerge, but Christ as the Truth makes categorical demands on the individual for total, unconditional and exclusive commitment to himself. It may well be that I may discover in dialogue how inadequate my own self-commitment is; but, out of respect for the freedom and dignity of the partner, I may not hope and ask for him anything less than I ask and hope for myself. As experi-

ence shows, it is extremely difficult to find in any of the non-Christian religions and anti-religions a partner who is prepared to engage in dialogue on this level of seriousness.

Yet such integrity is essential to true dialogue.

Fourthly, true dialogue is a mark of *sensitivity*. Christian evangelism falls into disrepute when it degenerates into stereotypes. It is impossible to evangelize by fixed formulae. To force a conversation along predetermined lines in order to reach a predetermined destination is to show oneself grievously lacking in sensitivity both to the actual needs of our friend and to the guidance of the Holy Spirit. Such insensitivity is therefore a failure in both faith and love. Dialogue, however, to quote from Max Warren "is in its very essence an attempt at mutual 'listening,' listening in order to understand. Understanding is its reward" (from an unpublished paper entitled *Presence and Proclamation*, read at a European Consultation on Mission Studies in April 1968). It is this point which was picked up in the Lausanne Covenant, which contains two references to dialogue. On the one hand it says firmly that we "reject as derogatory to Christ and the gospel every kind of syncretism and dialogue which implies that Christ speaks equally through all religions and ideologies" (para. 3). But on the other it says with equal firmness that "that kind of dialogue whose purpose is to listen sensitively in order to understand" is actually "indispensable to evangelism" (para. 4).* The principle was stated centuries ago in the Book of Proverbs: "If one gives answer before he hears, it is his folly and shame" (Proverbs 18:13).

*See "The Lausanne Covenant," in *Mission Trends No. 2*, pp. 239–48
—Eds.

Differences and Common Ground

Yves Raguin, S. J.

True dialogue reaches beyond words and ideas to a communication between persons, and that begins with the participants standing "at ease" on the same common ground of human, religious experience, not with immediately offering what is "specific of a religion." So insists Yves Raguin, a French Jesuit, now Professor at the Ricci Institute for Chinese Studies, Taipei, Taiwan. "If we start a dialogue by arguing that Christ is the only one in whom and by whom man can be saved, there is no real possibility of dialogue. Dialogue is dead from the start." The common ground, according to Raguin, is our common destiny. "We know that God, when He wants to dialogue with man, stands on that ground of human nature where man is made in the likeness of Himself." Even though Christians do not compromise faith in Christ as God's ultimate revelation, they are "still dialoguing with Him" and that will go on until the end of the world. "If we really want to bring people to recognize in Christ the ultimate Saviour and the Word of God, we ourselves have to first discover who He is. And in this discovery people of other faiths may help us tremendously." Father Raguin gave this address to the consultation on "Dialogue in Community," sponsored by the World Council of Churches at Chiang Mai, Thailand, in 1977. It is reprinted from the published proceedings of that meeting, *Faith in the Midst of Faiths*, edited by Stanley J. Samartha (Geneva: WCC, 1977).

The following reflections on dialogue have arisen from a long search for an understanding of the religious mentality and spirituality of the people of East-Asia, especially the Chinese. This paper will reflect not so much an effort to dialogue with a certain number of people as a real desire to understand the fundamental beliefs and inner attitude of believers outside of the Christian world of faith, particularly the Buddhists.

Dialogue in Depth

As there is no real dialogue with other people if we remain on the level of words, so it is for dialogue with other beliefs and religions. To have a real dialogue we have to confront each other's experiences on a deeper level than in words, a level beyond any possible expression. Dialogue is ultimately a communication, an exchange, an understanding beyond words.

Similar words may cover different ideas, beliefs, experiences. Different words may be ultimately the expression of a similar experience. This is why, for a real dialogue, we have to try to come to this level where we apprehend ourselves in an immediate and intuitive way. When we have arrived there, we will be able to come to a real awareness of others.

If we want to be honest we have to make dialogue on an equal level, which means that we don't compare what is deep in our belief with what is shallow or superficial in other people's faith or experience. But this is possible only if we try to really understand the faith and religious experience of others in all honesty and sincerity.

For all these reasons we should not fight with words, as we do too often, taking the "Word of God" as a weapon. If we do this, the word becomes a dead word, and we are far from what Christ says—that His words are life: "The words which I have spoken to you are both spirit and life" (Jn. 6:63). This level of spirit and life is where dialogue can take place. We see in the Gospel of John, chapters 5, 6, 7 and 8, that Jesus could not really dialogue with the Jews, because they were not standing on the same ground.

Dialogue on a Common Ground

There is no dialogue possible if there is no common ground to stand on, in order to start. This common ground has to be a "place" where both can stand at ease and be relaxed. This is what we call "common" ground. This ground may be very small, or may seem very small, at the beginning, but at least it is common. If there is no initial understanding there is no possibility of dialogue.

If we start a dialogue by arguing that Christ is the only one in whom and by whom man can be saved, there is no real possibility of dialogue. Dialogue is dead at the start. What is specific of a religion cannot be the starting point, because it is not "common" ground.

We may be very quick in using the arguments of revelation, because we have been raised in Christianity where we believe that God spoke to us in an "objective" manner, as expressed at the beginning of the Letter to the Hebrews. But this notion of revelation is totally foreign to the Buddhists. There is no God, the way there is one in Christianity. Here we should not argue that they give to God another name because for them there is no God to be named.

Here we come to the paradox that there is no dialogue possible unless we realize the magnitude of the differences, and try from this to find a common ground. This is of course a very painful experience, which may be discouraging at first. But under all the differences built up by the development of religious ideas, there remains the subject of all religious experience, man. So, it is there, at the level of human experience, that we will find this common ground on which to stand, or sit, in order to dialogue.

The Common Search of God

The common ground is that all people are bound to God by a destiny which is inscribed at the depth of their being. It is what we mean when we say that man is made in the image of God, that he is the image of God. This is the ultimate common ground, on which we can start a dialogue. It is precisely on this ground that God started dialoguing with man and this is still going on. When we think of salvation in Christ and by Christ, we should not forget this fundamental order on which the whole plan of salvation is built.

Christ is unique, but God has been inspiring all people to

search for Him, in many different ways. This is the mystery we have to accept if we want really to dialogue with people of other faiths. Men may have misused their fundamental capacity to search for God and to find Him, but this fundamental aptitude remains, in most cases, the only common ground on which we can stand to start dialoguing. God wants everyone to be saved. Since Christ came late in time, and in every definite place of earth, it seems impossible to me to hold that there is no salvation unless there is a positive knowledge and acceptance of Christ. If we hold this from the start there is no dialogue possible.

We know that God, when He wants to dialogue with man, stands on this ground of human nature where man is made in the likeness of Himself.

From this awareness of being the image of God, man has been searching endlessly, and sometimes with great suffering. We know, we Christians, what this search means. Although we have Christ, and His revelation, the search is still painful, because we are not sure that the Christ we figure out is the real Christ.

If we want to start a fruitful dialogue we all have to acknowledge that we are searching. If we have this humble attitude of one who is searching for the real meaning of what he believes, and for the real face of the one in whom he believes, dialogue will be easy with the faithful of other religions. We will not have the arrogant attitude of those who believe or pretend to ''have'' the truth. This attitude of possessiveness makes dialogue impossible from the start.

Appreciation of the Differences

In order to make dialogue easier we may tend to minimize the differences. But with such an attitude of mind, there is also no real dialogue. We may be afraid of leaving the common ground in order to keep the dialogue going in full harmony. But this is not real dialogue.

While standing on the common ground we should be able to appreciate the differences between our beliefs and religious experiences and the beliefs and experiences of others. Dialogue means first a right judgment on our own positions. This is the only way to proceed in full light. After all we must agree that there are many ways to search for God and to be saved, while believing that Christ is the ultimate revealer of God and Saviour of men. The fact that we see Him as the absolute Way does not mean that there are no other ways. These other ways are like the Law, they are not abolished but will find their fulfilment in Christ.

The first aim of dialogue is not converting other people to our own ideas, but understanding. This means that dialogue is first listening to the other, asking, trying to understand. There is no dialogue until we have begun to grasp other people's faith and experience. It is why we have to first make a bridge between us, and making a bridge means that we have the capacity of dwelling in the inner world of his thoughts and beliefs. This is the only way to be sure that I understand what he says and that he understands what I say.

In fact we have many common grounds on which we can meet. And by accepting, in a humble way, the ideas of others we may come to a deepening and widening of our understanding of the ways of man towards God and of God towards man. This will lead to a common acceptance of the different ways. We will discover that the Buddhist is as sure of his way as we are sure of our own. From this security, which is necessary, we may start looking in all objectivity to the beliefs and experiences of others. Then we will be able to have a fruitful dialogue.

Dialogue and the Finding of the Ultimate Way

We believe that in Christ we have the ultimate revelation of God to mankind, but at the same time we have to admit that we do not know Him yet. God in Christ became man. This is the great fact of our history.

When we come to dialogue with people of other faiths we have to be very careful in the way we present Christ. We cannot, for the sake of making the dialogue easier, renounce our belief in Christ as the ultimate Saviour. This is what we believe because Christ presented Himself this way. He told us that He is the Way, the Life and the Truth. This we believe, this we must hold.

But we cannot claim that the Christ we present is Christ in the fullness of His personality. We ourselves are still dialoguing with Christ, because we want to know who He is. And this dialogue of Christians with Christ will go on until the end of the world. As long as mankind has not completed its history, the knowledge we have of Christ will be incomplete. We cannot, we Christians, pretend to know Christ and tell others that they should believe in Him. The Christ we have to offer them may not attract them. It is difficult to convince them that Christ is the full revelation of God and the Saviour of man.

If we really want to bring people to recognize in Christ the ultimate Saviour and the Word of God, we ourselves have to first discover who He is. And in this discovery people of other faiths may help us tremendously. This is one of the most wonderful results of a real dialogue with people of other faiths. They help us to understand better what they believe, and, at the same time, they help us to deepen our understanding of Christ.

If we continue this dialogue with people, we are helping each other to understand what we believe, and since there is only one God, one eternal Word of God, a day may come when the dialogue of all believers will bring man to recognize the One who is the perfect image of God. But this means that every person must search for the truth by himself or herself and with the help of others.

III: Interfaith Relations in Practice

Guidelines and Suggestions for Catholic-Jewish Relations

Vatican Commission for Religious Relations with the Jews

In its 1965 *Declaration on the Relation of the Church to Non-Christian Religions (Nostra Aetate)*, the Second Vatican Council devoted a chapter to the Jewish people. Previous to this, in May 1964, Pope Paul VI established the Secretariat for Non-Christians; but he confided the religious aspects of Jewish concerns, with a special desk, to the Secretariat for Promoting Christian Unity. In October 1974, however, the Commission for Religious Relations with the Jews was papally created "to implement, correctly and effectively, the express intentions of the Council." On December 1, 1974, this new Commission issued *Guidelines and Suggestions for Implementing the Conciliar Declaration "Nostra Aetate" (N.4)*, over the signatures of the Commission's president and secretary, John Cardinal Willebrands and Pierre-Marie de Contenson, O.P. The pragmatic guidelines explain "real dialogue" about "the spiritual bonds and historical links binding the Church to Judaism," bonds which "condemn . . . all forms of anti-semitism and discrimination." Common elements of Christian and Jewish liturgy should be considered in Catholic liturgical reform, especially in dealing with commentaries on biblical texts and with liturgical explanations and translations. Catechisms, religious textbooks, history books, and mass media should reflect recent church teachings and the research of scholars in biblical exegesis, theology, history, and sociology. The Vatican document also urges Jews and

Christians, "in the spirit of the prophets," to work willingly together, "seeking social justice and peace at every level—local, national and international." The English translation of the original French text appeared in the *Information Service* of the Secretariat for Promoting Christian Unity (Via dell'Erba, 1, 00193, Rome), no. 26 (1975). In its introductory note, the Commission hopes that "our Jewish brothers too may find in [the document] useful indications for their participation in a commitment which is common."

The Declaration *Nostra Aetate,** issued by the Second Vatican Council on 28 October 1965, "on the relationship of the Church to non-Christian religions" (n. 4), marks an important milestone in the history of Jewish-Christian relations.

Moreover, the step taken by the Council finds its historical setting in circumstances deeply affected by the memory of the persecution and massacre of Jews which took place in Europe just before and during the Second World War.

Although Christianity sprang from Judaism, taking from it certain essential elements of its faith and divine cult, the gap dividing them was deepened more and more, to such an extent that Christian and Jew hardly knew each other.

After two thousand years, too often marked by mutual ignorance and frequent confrontation, the Declaration *Nostra Aetate* provides an opportunity to open or to continue a dialogue with a view to better mutual understanding. Over the past nine years, many steps in this direction have been taken in various countries. As a result, it is easier to distinguish the conditions under which a new relationship between Jews and Christians may be worked out and developed. This seems the right moment to propose, following the guidelines of the Council, some concrete suggestions born of experience, hoping that they will help to bring into actual existence in the life

---

*References are to the Second Vatican documents' first two Latin words, their official titles. Thus, *Nostra Aetate* (On the Relation of the Church to Non-Christian Religions); *Ad Gentes* (On the Missionary Activity of the Church); *Dignitatis Humanae* (On Religious Freedom); *Dei Verbum* (On Divine Revelation).—Eds.

of the Church the intentions expressed in the conciliar document.

While referring the reader back to this document, we may simply restate here that the spiritual bonds and historical links binding the Church to Judaism condemn (as opposed to the very spirit of Christianity) all forms of anti-semitism and discrimination, which in any case the dignity of the human person alone would suffice to condemn. Further still, these links and relationships render obligatory a better mutual understanding and renewed mutual esteem. On the practical level in particular, Christians must therefore strive to acquire a better knowledge of the basic components of the religious tradition of Judaism; they must strive to learn by what essential traits the Jews define themselves in the light of their own religious experience.

With due respect for such matters of principle, we simply propose some first practical applications in different essential areas of the Church's life, with a view to launching or developing sound relations between Catholics and their Jewish brothers.

1. Dialogue

To tell the truth, such relations as there have been between Jew and Christian have scarcely ever risen above the level of monologue. From now on, real dialogue must be established.

Dialogue presupposes that each side wishes to know the other, and wishes to increase and deepen its knowledge of the other. It constitutes a particularly suitable means of favouring a better mutual knowledge and, especially in the case of dialogue between Jews and Christians, of probing the riches of one's own tradition. Dialogue demands respect for the other as he is; above all, respect for his faith and his religious convictions.

In virtue of her divine mission, and her very nature, the Church must preach Jesus Christ to the world (*Ad Gentes*, 2). Lest the witness of Catholics to Jesus Christ should give offense to Jews, they must take care to live and spread their

Christian faith while maintaining the strictest respect for religious liberty in line with the teaching of the Second Vatican Council (Declaration *Dignitatis Humanae*). They will likewise strive to understand the difficulties which arise for the Jewish soul—rightly imbued with an extremely high, pure notion of the divine transcendence—when faced with the mystery of the incarnate Word.

While it is true that a widespread air of suspicion, inspired by an unfortunate past, is still dominant in this particular area, Christians, for their part, will be able to see to what extent the responsibility is theirs and deduce practical conclusions for the future.

In addition to friendly talks, competent people will be encouraged to meet and to study together the many problems deriving from the fundamental convictions of Judaism and of Christianity. In order not to hurt (even involuntarily) those taking part, it will be vital to guarantee, not only tact, but a great openness of spirit and diffidence with respect to one's own prejudices.

In whatever circumstances as shall prove possible and mutually acceptable, one might encourage a common meeting in the presence of God, in prayer and silent meditation, a highly efficacious way of finding that humility, that openness of heart and mind, necessary prerequisites for a deep knowledge of oneself and of others. In particular, that will be done in connection with great causes such as the struggle for peace and justice.

II. Liturgy

The existing links between the Christian liturgy and the Jewish liturgy will be borne in mind. The idea of a living community in the service of God, and in the service of men for the love of God, such as it is realized in the liturgy, is just as characteristic of the Jewish liturgy as it is of the Christian one. To improve Jewish-Christian relations, it is important to take cognizance of those common elements of the liturgical life (formulas, feasts, rites, etc.) in which the Bible holds an essential place.

An effort will be made to acquire a better understanding

of whatever in the Old Testament retains its own perpetual value (cf. *Dei Verbum*, 14–15), since that has not been cancelled by the later interpretation of the New Testament. Rather, the New Testament brings out the full meaning of the Old, while both Old and New illumine and explain each other (cf. *ibid.*, 16). This is all the more important since liturgical reform is now bringing the text of the Old Testament ever more frequently to the attention of Christians.

When commenting on biblical texts, emphasis will be laid on the continuity of our faith with that of the earlier Covenant, in the perspective of the promises, without minimizing those elements of Christianity which are original. We believe that those promises were fulfilled with the first coming of Christ. But it is none the less true that we still await their perfect fulfilment in his glorious return at the end of time.

With respect to liturgical readings, care will be taken to see that homilies based on them will not distort their meaning, especially when it is a question of passages which seem to show the Jewish people as such in an unfavourable light. Efforts will be made so to instruct the Christian people that they will understand the true interpretation of all the texts and their meaning for the contemporary believer.

Commissions entrusted with the task of liturgical translation will pay particular attention to the way in which they express those phrases and passages which Christians, if not well informed, might misunderstand because of prejudice. Obviously, one cannot alter the text of the Bible. The point is that, with a version destined for liturgical use, there should be an overriding preoccupation to bring out explicitly the meaning of a text,[1] while taking scriptural studies into account.

The preceding remarks also apply to introductions to biblical readings, to the Prayer of the Faithful, and to commentaries printed in missals used by the laity.

III. Teaching and Education

Although there is still a great deal of work to be done, a better understanding of Judaism itself and its relationship to Christianity has been achieved in recent years thanks to the teaching of the Church, the study and research of scholars, as also to the beginning of dialogue. In this respect, the following facts deserve to be recalled.

—It is the same God, "inspirer and author of the books of both Testaments" (*Dei Verbum,* 16), who speaks both in the old and new Covenants.

—Judaism in the time of Christ and the Apostles was a complex reality, embracing many different trends, many spiritual, religious, social and cultural values.

—The Old Testament and the Jewish tradition founded upon it must not be set against the New Testament in such a way that the former seems to constitute a religion of only justice, fear and legalism, with no appeal to the love of God and neighbour (cf. Deut. 6:5, Lev. 19:18, Matt. 22:34–40).

—Jesus was born of the Jewish people, as were his Apostles and a large number of his first disciples. When he revealed himself as the Messiah and Son of God (cf. Matt. 16:16), the bearer of the new Gospel message, he did so as the fulfilment and perfection of the earlier Revelation. And, although his teaching had a profoundly new character, Christ, nevertheless, in many instances, took his stand on the teaching of the Old Testament. The New Testament is profoundly marked by its relation to the Old. As the Second Vatican Council declared: "God, the inspirer and author of the books of both Testaments, wisely arranged that the New Testament be hidden in the Old and the Old be made manifest in the New" (*Dei Verbum,* 16). Jesus also used teaching methods similar to those employed by the rabbis of his time.

—With regard to the trial and death of Jesus, the Council recalled that "what happened in his passion cannot be blamed upon all the Jews then living, without distinction, nor upon the Jews of today" (*Nostra Aetate,* 4).

—The history of Judaism did not end with the destruction of Jerusalem, but rather went on to develop a religious tradition. And, although we believe that the importance and meaning of that tradition were deeply affected by the coming of Christ, it is still nonetheless rich in religious values.

—With the prophets and the apostle Paul, "the Church awaits the day, known to God alone, on which all peoples will address the Lord in a single voice and 'serve him with one accord' (Soph. 3:9)" (*Nostra Aetate*, 4).

Information concerning these questions is important at all levels of Christian instruction and education. Among sources of information, special attention should be paid to the following:

—catechisms and religious textbooks

—history books

—the mass-media (press, radio, cinema, television).

The effective use of these means presupposes the thorough formation of instructors and educators in training schools, seminaries and universities.

Research into the problems bearing on Judaism and Jewish-Christian relations will be encouraged among specialists, particularly in the fields of exegesis, theology, history and sociology. Higher institutions of Catholic research, in association if possible with other similar Christian institutions and experts, are invited to contribute to the solution of such problems. Wherever possible, chairs of Jewish studies will be created, and collaboration with Jewish scholars encouraged.

IV. Joint Social Action

Jewish and Christian tradition, founded on the Word of God, is aware of the value of the human person, the image of God. Love of the same God must show itself in effective action for the good of mankind. In the spirit of the prophets, Jews and Christians will work willingly together, seeking social justice and peace at every level—local, national and international.

At the same time, such collaboration can do much to foster mutual understanding and esteem.

Conclusion

The Second Vatican Council has pointed out the path to follow in promoting deep fellowship between Jews and Christians. But there is still a long road ahead.

The problem of Jewish-Christian relations concerns the Church as such, since it is when "pondering her own mystery" that she encounters the mystery of Israel. Therefore, even in areas where no Jewish communities exist, this remains an important problem. There is also an ecumenical aspect to the question: the very return of Christians to the sources and origins of their faith, grafted on to the earlier Covenant, helps the search for unity in Christ, the cornerstone.

In this field, the bishops will know what best to do on the pastoral level, within the general disciplinary framework of the Church and in line with the common teaching of her magisterium. For example, they will create some suitable commissions or secretariats on a national or regional level, or appoint some competent person to promote the implementation of the conciliar directives and the suggestions made above.

On 22 October 1974, the Holy Father instituted for the universal Church this Commission for Religious Relations with the Jews, joined to the Secretariat for Promoting Christian Unity. This special Commission, created to encourage and foster religious relations between Jews and Catholics—and to do so eventually in collaboration with other Christians—will be, within the limits of its competence, at the service of all interested organizations, providing information for them, and helping them to pursue their task in conformity with the instructions of the Holy See.

The Commission wishes to develop this collaboration in order to implement, correctly and effectively, the express intentions of the Council.

NOTES

1. Thus the formula "the Jews," in St. John, sometimes according to the context means "the leaders of the Jews," or "the adversaries of Jesus," terms which express better the thought of the evangelist and avoid appearing to arraign the Jewish people as such. Another example is the use of the words "pharisee" and "pharisaism" which have taken on a largely pejorative meaning.

Christian Witness, Proselytism, and the Jews

World Council of Churches

There are different understandings about the "authentic and proper forms of Christian witness in our relations with the Jews." Nevertheless, all agree that the rejection of proselytism, as distinct from authentic witness or mission, is more urgent today, since "Jews are rightly sensitive towards all religious pressures from outside and all attempts at proselytizing," both "in its gross and more refined forms." So declared the World Council of Churches' Consultation on the Church and the Jewish People that met in Jerusalem, June 1977. The original statement, from which is extracted here the section on "Authentic Christian Witness," was published in *Christian-Jewish Relations in Ecumenical Perspective*, edited by Franz von Hammerstein (Geneva: WCC, 1978).

1. Proselytism, as distinct from mission or witness, is rejected in the strongest terms by the World Council of Churches: "Proselytism embraces whatever violates the right of the human person, Christian or non-Christian, to be free from external coercion in religious matters, or whatever, in the proclamation of the Gospel, does not conform to the ways God draws free men to himself in response to his calls to serve in spirit and in truth" (*Ecumenical Review* 1/1971, p. 11).*

---

*From the Study Document, "Common Witness and Proselytism," recommended by the Joint Working Group between the Roman Catholic Church

We now realize more than ever before that the world in which we live is a world of religious pluralism. This demands from us that we treat those who differ from us with respect and that we strongly support the religious liberty of all.

2. This rejection of proselytism and our advocacy of respect for the integrity and the identity of all peoples and faith-communities is the more urgent where Jews are concerned. For, as stated above, our relationship to the Jews is of a unique and very close character. Moreover, the history of "Christian" anti-Semitism and forced baptisms of Jews in the past makes it understandable that Jews are rightly sensitive towards all religious pressures from outside and all attempts at proselytizing.

3. We reject proselytism both in its gross and more refined forms. This implies that all triumphalism and every kind of manipulation are to be abrogated. We are called upon to minimize the power dimension in our encounter with the Jews and to speak at every level from equal to equal. We have to be conscious of the pain and the perception of the others and have to respect their right to define themselves.

4. We are called upon to witness to God's love for and claim upon the whole of humankind. Our witness to Christ as Lord and Savior, however, is challenged in a special way where Jews are concerned. It has become discredited as a result of past behavior on the part of Christians. We therefore are seeking authentic and proper forms of Christian witness in our relations with the Jews. Some of us believe that we have to bear witness also to the Jews; some among us are convinced, however, that Jews are faithful and obedient to God even though they do not accept Jesus Christ as Lord and Savior. Many maintain that as a separate and specific people the Jews are an instrument of God with a specific God-given task and, as such, a sign of God's faithfulness to all humankind on the way towards ultimate redemption.

and the World Council of Churches, May 1970. The document is in *Mission Trends No. 2* (1975), pp. 176–187. —Eds.

Evangelistic Outreach to the Jewish People

School of World Mission, Fuller Theological Seminary

Under the deanship of Dr. Arthur F. Glasser, the faculty of the School of World Mission, Fuller Theological Seminary, in Pasadena, California, chose the 28th anniversary of the third commonwealth of Israel (May 1976) to "call upon the Christian community to renew its commitment to share lovingly the Gospel of Jesus with the Jewish people." The statement urges the church "to do more than merely include the Jewish people in their evangelistic outreach"; priority should be given "to the Jew first" (Rom. 1:16). Pointing out that those most engaged in "Jewish missions" have often unwittingly encouraged Jewish converts to divest themselves of their Jewish heritage and culture, this evangelical mission faculty calls on "Jewish believers in Christ" to maintain their cultural ties for the enrichment of the whole church. The statement is reprinted by permission of *Missiology: An International Review*, where it appeared in vol. IV, no. 4, October 1976. This is the quarterly journal of the American Society of Missiology, edited by Arthur F. Glasser.

We of the School of World Mission faculty of Fuller Theological Seminary feel constrained to address ourselves and the Church at large concerning the Jewish people. Particularly so at this time when the third commonwealth of Israel is celebrating its 28th anniversary and when we find ourselves much in prayer that the Jewish presence in the

Middle East shall become under God an instrument for reconciliation and peace.

We are profoundly grateful for the heritage given to us by the Jewish people which is so vital for our own Christian faith. We believe that God used the Jewish people as the sole repository of the history-centered disclosure of Himself to mankind. This revelation began with Abraham and continued to the Jewish writers of the New Testament. Not only were the oracles of God committed to them (Romans 3:2), but it was through this people that God chose to bring Jesus Christ into the world. We believe that He is the only hope of salvation for the Jewish people, and for all mankind. Indeed, we continue to pray that through the mercy and blessing of God, the Jewish people shall turn to the Messiah Jesus and become once again a light to the nations, that His salvation may reach to the end of the earth (Isaiah 49:6).

We wish to charge the Church, as a whole, to do more than merely include the Jewish people in their evangelistic outreach. We would encourage an active response to the mandate of Romans 1:16 calling for evangelism "to the Jew first." For this we have the precedent of a great Jewish missionary, the Apostle Paul. Though sent to the Gentile world, he never relinquished his burden for his own kinsmen after the flesh. Wherever he travelled, he first visited the synagogue before presenting Christ to the Gentiles. So it must be in every generation. We must provide a priority opportunity for our Jewish friends to respond to the Messiah. They are our benefactors and it was they who first evangelized us. Furthermore, the Gospel we share with them must be carried to all tribes and peoples and tongues.

We regret exceedingly that Christians have not always shared this Gospel with the Jewish people in a loving and ethical manner. Too often, while interested in Jewish evangelism in general, we have demeaned the dignity of the Jewish person by our unkind stereotyping and our disregard for Jewish sensitivities. How un-Christlike we have been!

Likewise, we have unwittingly encouraged Jewish converts to divest themselves of their Jewish heritage and culture. For this too, we would repent and express our regret that

the Western influence on our beliefs has precluded the original Jewish context. The Church is culturally and spiritually
poorer for it.

In our day we are encouraged that thousands of Jewish
people are coming to the Messiah. This being so, we cannot
but call upon the Christian community to renew its commitment to share lovingly the Gospel of Jesus with the Jewish
people. And we heartily encourage Jewish believers in Him,
including those who call themselves Messianic Jews,
Hebrew-Christians, and Jews for Jesus, to retain their Jewish
heritage, culture, religious practices and marriage customs
within the context of a sound biblical theology expressing
Old and New Testament truth. Their freedom in Christ to do
this cannot but enrich the Church in our day.

More, we feel it incumbent on Christians in all traditions
to reinstate the work of Jewish evangelism in their missionary
obedience. Jewish-oriented programs should be developed.
Appropriate agencies for Jewish evangelism should be
formed. And churches everywhere should support those
existing institutions which are faithfully and lovingly bearing
a Christian witness to the Jewish people.

Christian-Jewish-Muslim Relations

Monika Konrad Hellwig

Christians, Jews and Muslims have "competing truth claims." For the dialogue between these three world faiths, Professor Monika K. Hellwig suggests four common departure points or assumptions: worship of the one and same God who intervenes in history to judge and redeem; that history has a goal—the comprehensive salvation of all peoples who are summoned to find their own fulfillment in doing God's will (thus offering a base also for social justice); the election or calling "to a way of life that is a communion with God and a call to community or peoplehood with prescribed patterns of relationships and duties toward others"; and "the heritage of biblical lore and spiritual ancestors." This Roman Catholic professor of theology at Georgetown University, Washington, D.C., argues that there are three unique Christian convictions which also affect this dialogue: (1) the central place of Jesus of Nazareth in Christian faith; (2) the divided condition of the church, with the problematic political status of the Roman Catholic Church; and (3) the Trinity with its proclamation of the divinity of Jesus. Hellwig suggests the appropriate model for this interfaith dialogue is the biblical concept of the covenant or alliance of God with people, since covenant-language is common to all three faiths. The author was born in Breslau, with a Jewish, Lutheran, and Catholic background (see her "theological autobiography" in *Journeys*, edited by Gregory Baum [New York: Paulist Press, 1975]). She is associate editor of *The Journal of Ecumenical Studies*, in which this long extract appeared (vol. XIV, no. 3, Summer 1977) under the title "Bases and Boundaries for Interfaith Dialogue: A Christian Viewpoint."

It is the very nature of the Christian's commitment to proclaim the experience of Jesus of Nazareth as Savior and Word of God that propels the Christian community to dialogue with respect for the freedom and the truth of the others. More particularly, it propels Christians to a dialogue with other communities claiming a message of universal salvation. Among these the dialogue becomes more immediately urgent with those whose proclamation of universal salvation stems from the same biblical roots but branches out into quite different interpretations of history.

If Christians could regard Jesus as savior of a statically defined Christian sector of the human race, there would be little urgency or theological need for dialogue. Christians could then live side by side with those of other persuasions, quietly minding their own business, inquiring perhaps into the folkways and beliefs of other communities for diplomatic or purely academic reasons. Such dialogue would remain forever peripheral to Christian theology and Christian identity. It is precisely because they proclaim a universal salvation, and proclaim the centrality of Jesus of Nazareth as a saving power in the history of the whole human race, that Christians are driven to dialogue by a systematic and practical exigence that arises out of the very center of the Christian understanding and commitment. The Christian understanding and commitment cannot be authentically maintained within the Christian community if it is not in fact engaged in the continuous dynamic of serious dialogue with outsiders.

The subject matter of such dialogue obviously is not a debate over the conflicting truth claims of different traditions. Sober reflection on the nature of religious language and religious experience and on the cultural and epistemological bases of religious claims has long since convinced thinking persons of all traditions that there is no "unbiased" procedure by which to judge among the conflicting truth claims of different traditions. The subject matter of such dialogue from the Christian viewpoint must be concerned with the nature of salvation. Because Christians are committed to proclaiming salvation in Jesus the Christ, they are required by their own commitment to seek an understanding of what that salvation is, why it is linked to the person of Jesus, and how it can be universally meaningful. Christians are bound to tell their story and to listen in order to learn what others hear in it. Likewise they are bound to listen to the stories of the other traditions, to try to find out what their understanding of salvation is; why it is linked to particular persons, events, and teachings; and how it can be meaningful in terms of their own experience. They are bound to this simply by the demands for inner coherence of their own stance.

Thus far the need for dialogue would direct Christians equally toward Hindus, Buddhists, and even Marxists. But the demands become very much more urgent in relation to Jews and Muslims, though the pattern is not quite symmetrical in these two relationships. The Christian community looks toward the Jews with the claim that the Christian community, though still looking forward to a final fulfillment, has already experienced through the person of Jesus the definitive realization of the promises and hopes of Israel. For its own self-understanding, therefore, the Christian community is required to search not only for the sense in which those hopes and promises were understood by Israel before the time of Jesus, but also for the way they are understood now by those who expect salvation in the Jewish tradition and not through the person of Jesus of Nazareth. In other words, without intent to proselytize but rather for their own understanding of their own position, Christians are driven to ask Jews what it is that they expect and do not see in the person and the followers of Jesus of Nazareth.[1]

When Christians turn in the direction of the Muslims, their question and their quest are somewhat different. In effect they must ask themselves, and therefore they must ask the Muslims, why the message of salvation in Jesus the Christ with its universal claim has in the course of history been complemented by a vast people, gathered from many nations, coming likewise to worship the God of Israel, but in a distinctively different tradition that denies the universality of the Christian claim. For their own self-understanding, Christians must ask themselves what the experience of being called to salvation is for those who are brought into submission to the one God as followers of the Prophet. They must ask wherein lies the difference between Christians and Muslims in the interpretation of the ancient hopes and promises passed on to them from Israel.

Of course, these questions to Jews and Muslims could be asked simply in the context of ethnology and of social and political and cultural history, and within these contexts they could be answered. But if these answers were to be taken as complete, they could lead only to a sense of the cultural relativity of all convictions and a certain cynical indifference to the truth claims of one's own tradition. The questions must be asked seriously in a theological context, expecting further insight into the various ways that the need for salvation is experienced and understood, and into the various ways that persons, events, and teachings promising salvation have been experienced and understood.

The dialogue concerning the meaning of salvation can not and does not take place in a vacuum, however. It assumes the meaning of some common terms and understandings and the need to explain some unique terms. . . .

Chief among the common points of departure is certainly our understanding of the One God, transcendent, benign, provident, all-powerful, intervening in history to judge and redeem, self-revealing to those who seek, forever mysterious but offering the possibility of personal relationship in prayer and the direction of one's life. To know that others claim self-revelations from the same God that we ourselves worship is an invitation to discover the content of the revelation as perceived by the others. To know that others worship the same God that we worship is to know also that somewhere in our experience there lie possibilities for common prayer, though it may only be a prayer of wordless quiet. To hold that this God intervenes in history to judge and to redeem implies a willing ear for testimonies expressing perceptions from other traditions of the judgments and the redemption.

of dialogue. The self-interest and mutual distrust of power groups may pose almost insurmountable obstacles, but the religious bases for dialogue on these issues exist in the teachings concerning a goal for all history, the ultimate unity of the whole human race before God, and the divine demand for social justice that does not exclude the poor and powerless.

Again, it must be noted that such a common base does not appear so clearly from positions more or less approximating the fundamentalist one. When it is understood that the law of God and the plan of God have been set forth once and for all, explicitly and in every detail, there can be little room for moral questions about new situations that arise in the course of time, and obedience to the divine will is readily reduced to private lives of individual persons and to certain archaic patterns of association in groups within the tradition. For dialogue among traditions there can be even less room. Yet it must also be noted that such a common base seems to be equally absent in certain liberal positions which see almost all elements of the tradition as culturally relative and expendable, simply because such positions adapt very readily to fit the national or partisan interests of their own group, and they read the situation from that vantage point.

A third common base or point of departure is closely linked to the second, but does appear to be a different point. This is the election or vocation of each person and the election or vocation of the community. It is a calling to a way of life that is a communion with God and a call to community or peoplehood with prescribed patterns of relationship and duties toward others. The three traditions make reference to the same basic vocation stories concerning Noah, Abraham, and Moses, which are models of individual election but also of the election of the people. Each tradition interprets histor rather differently in the light of these stories, in applying election or calling to itself. Yet this appears as a comm point of departure and as a conviction that rather pere torily impels the traditions to dialogue with one anoth has indeed happened, peacefully or otherwise, since r times).[2]

A community which claims to have been chosen

The basis for assuming that the three traditions are i sense on common ground here is that for all three God ultimately inscrutable mystery, and the self-revelation that received is never exhaustive of the reality. Nor is that sel revelation ever apprehended in strictly appropriate concep or in univocal images; religious language can only be th language of poetry, of analogy, of subtle hints of the inex pressible. From a fundamentalist position in which this is not admitted, there can be but little meaning to dialogue with a tradition other than one's own. If the assumption is made that not only the revelation, but all the language in which it is apprehended and expressed, is divinely guaranteed as time-less, changeless, beyond critical examination, having intrin-sic and exclusive validity quite independent of historical and cultural conditioning, then there cannot be a common ground from which dialogue between traditions can take place.

A second common point of departure is the (often unspo-ken) assumption that history has a goal, that time is not only cyclic (which it assuredly is) but also linear, that salvation is not only a salvation of the human spirit from the world but is quite comprehensively salvation of the world. The god of the biblical religions is not seen as other than Master of the uni-verse, Lord of history, Lord of all being, and Ruler of the day of reckoning. All history is under God's judgment, and all peoples are God's people summoned to find their own fulfillment in doing God's will. That will is recognized con-stantly as justice—justice on a grand social scale, not only a certain relative justice in one-to-one relationships.

This common base seems to offer very clear grounds for dialogue among the three traditions on matters of social jus-tice and the relief of large-scale human suffering and depriva-tion. At least in theory, it offers a basis for meaningful dia-logue in matters as thorny and urgent as colonial oppression, racial oppression, remnants of slave trading, the State of Israel, the plight of the Palestinians, various liberation strug-les, societal role restrictions on women, deprivation of civil ghts of certain groups, and so forth. These obviously are not ints at which dialogue might be expected to begin, but ither may they be categorically ruled out as possible areas special way as God's instrument of redemption of the world is compelled to ask itself how it stands in relation to other communities that claim a similar election from the same God, if only because of the need to define its own claim for its own members. Yet each community can really only come to an authentic answer to its own question in the process of open dialogue that solicits testimony from the other communities as to how they interpret their traditions and their election in the changing contexts of the present. There is no other way to distinguish oneself or one's position from others than that which begins with an attentive inquiry into the nature and the characteristics of the others.

It may seem paradoxical, yet it seems that it is the very universality and apparent mutual exclusivity of our claims that provides the necessary basis for a fruitful and substantive dialogue. Any position that attempts to reduce or obscure the claim to a unique election related to the universal plan of God would seem to reduce rather than enhance the foundations for dialogue. So, of course, will any position that sees the doctrine of election as simple, fully explicit, and univocal, and as having attained a timeless formula capable of direct and universal application. Any position between these two moves naturally into dialogue in its quest for a more comprehensive and coherent understanding in the contemporary context.

A fourth common base has been quietly assumed in the presentation of the preceding three. This is the common heritage of biblical lore and spiritual ancestors. There is an available common language of symbols (found in persons and events), and an available common pool of models and points of reference. The biblical stories that form the common lore seem also to be precisely those that offer the most basic and universal insights and understandings, the most archetypal images and visions. Moreover, these biblical stories with their symbolism have remained both foundational and explicit in all three traditions. They carry assumptions and attitudes that may not be underestimated, as to creation, the providence of God in history, the nature of the faith response, or submission and obedience. It is, for instance, quite clear to Christians that when Jews and Muslims speak to each other about Isaac and Ishmael, each may not like what the other is saying, but they both understand very well what it is that they are discussing. Likewise, when Christians invoke the Pauline understanding of Isaac as the child of the promise, and claim thereby to be the true children of Abraham, Jews may object to the exegesis, but they object because they understand it. All of this offers a not insubstantial base for effective dialogue on important issues for the three traditions concerned.[3]

Having given brief consideration to these four points of common basis, one is left with the task of considering those unique convictions or positions of Christianity which are bound to affect the possibilities of dialogue with the other two traditions. First and most obvious among these is the Christian perception of revelation and redemption as focused in the person of Jesus of Nazareth. At first sight this seems to be primarily a hindrance to dialogue, something for which the Christian community should apologize, explaining that it can do no other than to hold and proclaim this, but that it nevertheless wishes to enter into dialogue with its biblical neighbors.

Such an admission and apology would seem to be premature. If the aim in dialogue is a fuller understanding of the position of the other, in order the better to grasp the inner logic of one's own position and in order to achieve some clarity and authenticity in relations with the other tradition, then the central and constitutive claim on which one's own tradition rests must be placed centrally in the dialogue also. As such, it offers a rather solid platform for an exchange of perceptions and perspectives. In confrontation with Jews and Muslims, Christians must either be silent or must give an account of what the revelation and redemption are that they have experienced in the person of Jesus of Nazareth, and they must attempt this account in language other than the technical "churchy" language which already assumes the experience. They must attempt to account for their experience and conviction in language that is experientially meaningful to those who are outsiders to the Christian tradition.[4] Such attempts cannot but be sources of thoroughgoing renewal within the Christian community itself, although they will be regarded as dangers to "the Faith" by those holding more fundamentalist positions in which the technical "churchy" language stands in its own right as divinely guaranteed. Likewise, such dialogue cannot but be a source of more coherent relationships with the outsiders to the tradition, although certain more liberal elements within the Christian tradition will see a danger to the ecumenical or dialogic endeavor whenever the unique claims and teachings are put forth as subject matter for interfaith conversation.

At this point, some crucial limits or restricting boundaries to the dialogue may be noted. They are not doctrinal but practical. Christians cannot speak very clearly about revelation and redemption experienced in Jesus of Nazareth, in the presence of Jews, because centuries of anti-Semitism and oppression obscure the testimony. Likewise, Christians have considerable difficulty inquiring of Jews concerning the Jewish understanding of revelation and redemption, because Jews tend to suspect a proselytizing drive and are conscious of being a minority for whom the possibility of discrimination, contempt, and outright persecution is never remote. Even in Israel today, the situation cannot be said to be substantially more favorable; Jews readily interpret such inquiry as judgmental on the conduct of the State of Israel and its relations with the Palestinians, while Christians are embarrassed by being unable in conscience to give the unconditional approval to everything Israel does, which is often demanded as a prelude to serious dialogue.[5]

When Christians address themselves to Muslims in dialogue concerning revelation and redemption experienced in Jesus the Christ, and revelation and redemption as experienced according to the teachings of the Prophet Mohammed, there are again obstacles which are not doctrinal or theological, but rather practical and historical. Christian voices are heard by Muslims in the context of the Crusades and of colonialism under Christian auspices, so that any message of peace, humility, reconciliation, and forgiveness sounds quite hollow. Moreover, the Christian gospel advocacy of simplicity of life and the blessedness of the poor is seen as ludicrous in the context of the colossal economic imperialism of the

"Christian" West against which all Third World nations must contend. At the same time, the situation is not much better in the other direction, because Christians are likely to hear anything the Muslims say in the context of a fear of Holy Wars, internal violence in Muslim countries, terrorism, despotic governments, oppression of women, and harsh persecution of non-Muslims. Much as this may be a caricature, it does in practice tend to cloud and obscure testimonies concerning the true nature of Islam.

These practical considerations may not be underestimated. The possibility for any genuine dialogue at all certainly depends on the willingness of some scholars and religious representatives to achieve a psychological distance from these historical and practical stumblingblocks, by willingness to consider not the achievements of the other parties but the aims and desires intrinsic in the religious position of each. More habitually each group evaluates its own position by its ideals and the position of the others by their performance. From this nothing but further prejudice and failure of understanding can arise.

Yet even when these problems have been somewhat overcome by persons and groups particularly dedicated to dialogue, there remains at all times the question as to the extent to which they represent their respective communities. It is a frequent experience that groups with a mandate from their communities to engage in dialogue draw up a coherent and far-reaching statement that represents real progress in mutual understanding among the partners to the dialogue, only to find at the end of their labors that the respective mandating authorities in their own communities will not approve the statement. Such statements are then frequently reduced to rather unsatisfactory evasions and compromises that were already in vogue before the dialogue was set up.[6] What seems to be at stake is the question whether dialogue with the other traditions can be delegated to specialized groups or whether it must be conducted at the heart of the religious and theological enterprise of each community.

Having noted the negative aspects that restrict dialogue concerning the central issue for Christians, one must note two further unique convictions from the Christian viewpoint which play an important role in dialogue. One of these is the role of the church or, more accurately, of the many Christian churches which exist today in a state of considerable ambivalence toward one another. Though the churches do act jointly on some issues, and although there have been great ecumenical advances in the contemporary experience, it must frankly be admitted that the Christian churches, claiming to live by the same gospel of Jesus the Christ, are in a condition of rather extensive dissociation from one another. There is a double disadvantage for interfaith dialogue in this condition of dissociation. Not only does the dialogue tend to represent and speak for some churches and not others, but the very concept of church and the understanding of the role of the church in the society at large and in the redemption do in fact vary widely from church to church. The primary referent in this essay is the self-understanding of the Roman Catholic Church.

The role of the church is bound to present problems to Jewish and Muslim partners in dialogue inasmuch as it is not coextensive with a people racially, ethnically, culturally, or politically. In fact, theologically, the church can only be understood as that community of witnesses that mediates between Jesus the Christ and the final realization of the Reign of God among all human persons and peoples which Jesus proclaimed and promised. The church may be understood as an assembling or a movement of such witnesses in history, although it most obviously appears as an institution and usually as a rather powerful hierarchic structure.[7] As many reflective Christians view it today and have viewed it in the course of history, the church is necessarily a counterculture force, a critique of any established regime and social structure, a radicalizing force that judges every situation in relation to the vision of the promised Reign of God.[8] Clearly this is by no means the way the church (or the larger churches taken as a group) has in fact conducted itself in most matters throughout the history of Christianity. Therefore, although it may puzzle and antagonize the outsider to the Christian tradition, Christian partners in the dialogue may say without any sense of hypocrisy or inconsistency that "the church does not condone" actions and situations which the outsider sees being done by Christians and perhaps even by those who appear as church representatives.

The church claims to be the gathering of those who have been "reborn" in the experience that Jesus who was crucified and died has burst forth again in irrepressible and unquenchable vitality that permeates the whole human race and all history with new and undreamed-of possibilities of fulfillment, reconciliation, and community. In Christian theology such persons become a witness community in a double sense: they have witnessed in the rebirth in their own lives the coming of the Reign of God, and they bear witness to others by their community life, their hope, their service, and their transforming impact. They do this, ideally, "from within," that is, in community with similarly "reborn" persons—all willingly and creatively changing their relationships with one another to express what they have experienced.[9]

In this ideal picture, the "elect among the nations" who are called to this witness function are not thereby cut off from their diverse cultural and political affiliations, though these all become relativized in the light of an over-riding interest in the community of all the human race—an interest which is most particularly concerned with the poor, the outcast, and the suffering, as perennially represented by the Crucified.[10] The issue is of course immensely complicated by the fact that through the centuries, sometimes by conquest, sometimes by princely "conversion" of whole peoples, there came about the identification of Christianity with the whole of Western culture and with the political structure of Europe, which we named Christendom, which was in due time extended also to the whole of the North and South American continents. It is quite common to speak of these as "Christian nations," and indeed governments often invoke Christian beliefs in their support, as in the power struggles of the West with the Communist countries, but from the point of view of most Christian ecclesiologies (which strongly favor separation of church and state) the term is almost meaningless.[11] Most Christian spokespersons, whether church officials or theologians, will not accept the actions of their governments as attributable to the Christian community as such.

The clarification of this position is obviously rather important to interfaith dialogue, because both Jews and Muslims envisage as the ideal an integrated peoplehood in which the religious convictions are expressed in political, legal, economic, and cultural as well as religious ritual forms. This sets some limits or boundaries to the dialogue, which again involves practical, historical, as well as theoretical, problems. It may be very puzzling and irritating to Jews that Christian nations and even Christian churches have stood so aloof in the Lebanese civil strife, instead of leaping to the defense of their "Christian brothers and sisters" against the Muslims of that country. Israeli Jews may find it hard to understand that the so-called Christian nations do not experience any particular bond with the Christians of Lebanon, while all Jews may be horrified that the churches have generally been more concerned to disentangle the questions of social justice involved in the conflict than to support "their own."

A parallel problem arises in dialogue with Muslims, who frequently ask why Christian nations and Christian churches express support for the State of Israel when they should be supporting and defending their Arab Christian brothers and sisters from aggression, land expropriation, exile, deprivation of political rights, and harsh oppression.[12] Thus Jews and Muslims use the same argument as an obstacle to dialogue, though for diametrically opposed practical purposes. The strong and fairly monolithic alignments of interest in the case of both Jews and Muslims on a worldwide basis render it urgent, but also difficult, for Christians to represent their own total allegiance to the gospel as taking priority over their qualified allegiance to any particular group. It may well be that it is only in the context of a three-way interfaith dialogue that this particular element of dialogue can be put in its proper perspective.

The last and most crucial point to be made concerning the unique claims and teachings in the Christian tradition is of course that of the Trinitarian conception of God and the claim of divinity made on behalf of Jesus of Nazareth. It may seem at first sight that the very admission of these two doctrines simply vitiates all that has gone before. It seems so because the history of previous encounters over the centuries may suggest that interfaith dialogue comes to an impasse at that point. But previous encounters were conducted with a frame of reference much closer to simplistic fundamentalist positions, and much less aware of the cultural relativity and analogous nature of all religious language. It would seem to be supremely worthwhile to re-engage in dialogue precisely on these points, remembering again that the point of the dialogue is not proselytizing but the clarification of one's perception of the position of the others, in order thereby to clarify one's perception of one's own position and engage in more realistic and authentic relationships.

It should be no secret to Jews and Muslims that the doctrines of the Trinitarian Godhead and of the divinity of Jesus have been and are the subjects of searching inquiry, reflection, and renewed attempts at appropriate formulation by Christian scholars within their own circles, quite apart from the demands of interfaith dialogue.[13] At the risk of over-simplification within this limited space, it may be said very briefly what the minimal formulations of these ancient doctrines are.[14] As to the Trinitarian "image" or conception of God, one may say with Josef Ratzinger that Christian faith is at pains to preserve at all costs a paradox it is not able logically to resolve—a paradox that reflects as faithfully as it can certain irreducible elements of the Christian experience. Christians worship the transcendent God of Israel, yet they know that in Jesus they had a self-validating experience of what it is to be in the presence of God uttered or expressed within history and within the human community, and at the same time they know that their experience of the presence and the power of God was not only in the person of Jesus long ago in history, but is in the Spirit that is alive and active now within the community of believers. Moreover, Christian faith is committed to the confident conviction that these divine self-revelations may be trusted, that God is in inner reality truthfully as God is revealed to us in history, though the reality clearly transcends what human knowing and imagining can grasp.[15] Jesus is experienced as the fullest possible, and therefore the definitive, self-expression of God in history and within the human community. Yet it must be said quickly that Jesus is not seen dissociated from the rest of the human race, but rather as "heading" or incorporating the human race within his own person and experience—a process that is seen as being yet unfinished.[16]

The scandal of the particularity of the claims made for Jesus certainly stands at the heart of Christian faith, and raises the question as to the possibility of dialogue. Inasmuch as the religious language of the divinity claim—Son, Word, Image, light from light, one in being with the Creator, and so forth—is capable of the most varied and nuanced interpretations, much careful exploration of the meaning would seem to be appropriate in interfaith dialogue. However, the appropriate pathway into this exploration is by way of that which can be judged by outsiders by reference to their own experience. With reference to Christology that approach is through the experiential analysis of what is meant by salvation and why Christians claim a foretaste of salvation in their association with Jesus as the Christ.

Is there a language or a model that might serve in such interfaith dialogue as has been envisaged here? A language and model that would seem to be appropriate from the point of view of all three traditions is the biblical notion of the covenant or alliance of God with the people. As presented in the Hebrew scriptures, there appears to be only one covenant, expressed in various modes of participation—the covenant of creation realized in the Noachic covenant, very precisely focused and explicitly expressed in the intimate participation of the Abrahamic and Mosaic convenant. Jews have been willing to grant that Christians and Muslims participate in the Noachic covenant, but both Christians and Muslims claim rather a complementary participation in the Abrahamic covenant, and each claims in its own way to bring that covenant to its consummation. Inasmuch as all three traditions own and understand this language of covenant, it seems to provide an appropriate arena for an exchange of the alternative interpretations of the history of salvation (and the salvation of history).[17]

There is a further image that seems to offer a very viable context for dialogue, and that is the image of the seed and the tree with the two great branches, proposed by Yehuda Halevi.[18] Israel sees itself as a witness people for God and as situated at the heart of the redemptive process, yet does not generally reach out in proselytizing efforts. Christianity and Islam see themselves as rooted in the revelation and promised redemption inherited from Israel, but as sent out to embrace all the nations. This much has not changed since the time of Yehuda Halevi, and the image appears to be as generative now as it was then.

NOTES

1. This thesis is consonant with the potentially significant but actually little noticed dialogic ecclesiology set out by Pope Paul VI in his inaugural encyclical letter, *Ecclesiam Suam*, August 6, 1964, *A.A.S.* 56 (1964):609–59, available in English translation, *His Church* (Huntingdon, Ind.: Our Sunday Visitor Inc., 1964).

2. This theme is set out rather clearly by James Kritzeck, *Sons of Abraham* (Baltimore: Helicon, 1965).

3. *Ibid.*

4. Contemporary Christian theology is already well stocked with efforts to do this in relation to the existentialist perceptions (e.g., the works of Moltmann, J. B. Metz, G. Gutierrez, and J. L. Segundo), and in relation to many other currents of thought and experience.

5. This observation is based on the author's own experience in Jerusalem among academics well disposed toward and well prepared for interfaith dialogue, during the academic year 1975–76.

6. This can certainly be said for the Jewish-Christian statement that was drawn up before Vatican II, in relation to what appeared in the approved texts, and again for the repeated efforts of the Vatican's post-conciliar commission.

7. These conflicting models are expressed very clearly in Vatican II's *Lumen Gentium* [*On the Church*].

8. Cf. Hans Küng, *Structures of the Church* (Notre Dame, Ind.: Univ. of Notre Dame Press, 1964), and *The Church* (New York: Sheed & Ward, 1967). Also, J. B. Metz, ed., *The Church and the World of Politics* (New York: Paulist Press, 1967).

9. For an analysis of the various models and perceptions of the church, see Avery Dulles, *Models of the Church* (Garden City, N.Y.: Doubleday, 1974). And cf. Pier Cesare Bori, *Koinonia* (Brescia: Paideia Editrice, 1972).

10. Cf. J. B. Metz, "The Future in the Memory of Suffering," in J. B. Metz, ed., *New Questions on God* (New York: Herder, 1972), pp. 9–25.

11. This has not always been so and is not universally so now. For example, Spanish and Portuguese colonialism were officially sanctioned by the Catholic Church, while the Church of England is nationally established in a bond of mutual support with the government.

12. Expressed vigorously to the author by Muslim Arabs both in the U.S. and during a stay on the West Bank.

13. E.g., in Paul Tillich, *Systematic Theology* (Chicago: Univ. of Chicago Press, 1951); in Karl Rahner, *Theological Investigations,* especially vol. 13 (New York: Seabury, 1975); in Jürgen Moltmann, *The Crucified God* (New York: Harper, 1974); in the various Christologies of the "process theologians"; etc.

14. There is no possibility for present unanimity among Christians on this point; therefore, particular and generally accepted authors are followed here.

15. Josef Ratzinger, *Introduction to Christianity* (New York: Herder, 1970), part I, chap. 5.

16. Cf. *ibid.,* especially part II, and Piet Schoonenberg, *The Christ* (New York: Herder, 1971).

17. Cf. Kritzeck, *Sons of Abraham.*

18. *Ibid.,* p. 227.

The Muslim Convert and His Culture

Harvie M. Conn

Traditional missionary responses to evangelization among Muslims largely depended on the evangelist's viewpoint of the relationship between Christian conversion and culture. Harvie M. Conn, Associate Professor of Missions and Apologetics at Westminster Theological Seminary in Philadelphia, outlines these responses, and then reflects on the interactions between theological and sociological barriers to Muslim conversion. Among evangelicals, understanding conversion as "one-step decisionism," which downplays or loses altogether the daily process for the entire renewal of the person, has helped to create "nominal Christianity" among Muslim converts. The over-emphasis on an "individual decision" has ignored "the multi-personal, infra-group judgments" or communal nature of the decision process within "the ethnic microcosms that constitute Islam." " 'Personal' cannot be equated with 'individual.' " Furthermore, if conversion be understood as "purely spiritual," and not as "a sign of the Kingdom of God come in Christ and the Lordship of Christ over the whole of life," then the "gospel for Islam" does not in fact "make the total claims for all of life that Islam itself makes." Conn concludes that a more comprehensive understanding of the Gospel of the Kingdom, of Christian conversion, and of the diverse, authentic motives in coming to Christ, offers the evangelical missionary wide-ranging ways of presenting Christ as Lord and Savior, without restriction to a single formula. Until 1972, the author had spent twelve years as a missionary of the Orthodox Presbyterian Church in Korea. He edited and co-authored *Theological Perspectives on Church Growth* (Nutley, N.J.: Presbyterian and Reformed Publishing Co., 1977). This revision of his presentation to the North American Conference on Muslim Evangelization (Colorado Springs, October 1978) was published in the proceedings of that conference, *The Gospel and Islam*, edited by Don M. McCurry (Monrovia, Calif.: MARC/World Vision International, 1979), and is reprinted with permission.

How does the evangelical missionary's perspective on the relation between Christian conversion and culture affect the ways by which one approaches evangelization among Muslims? Do different viewpoints, for example, play a part in the planting of Millat 'Issawi (churches as Jesus fellowships) and the development of a Muslimun 'Issawiyun (submission to Jesus) movement? Are the barriers to fruitful evangelism "primarily theological" or "primarily sociocultural"? What steps should the cross-cultural evangelist take on his side of the barriers to erode those obstacles in the strength of the Holy Spirit?

I. A Traditional Evangelical Response

Until recently, one could expect often negative emotional responses to such terminology. To some, the terms connote the evangelist's unwillingness to disassociate the convert from the religion of Islam. To others, the terminology supports resistance to public confession and baptism in secret. To still others, such terms veil the syncretistic baptism of Islamic ritual and belief—a euphemism for Christian casuistry in the interests of convert-numbers.

On the lips of some theorists, these charges could no doubt be real. And no doubt, in the practical outworking of such theories, the dangers of syncretism and casuistry can become more than merely dangers. At the same time, behind these fears may also lie the remnants of a 19th-century apologetic approach which pits Christianity as a monolithic system over against Islam as a purely theological construction, both relatively untouched by the ethnic world-views with which religion is integrally bound.

Without this sensitivity to the relation between religion and cultural world-view, the Christian approach to Islam was often conceived of as the confrontation of one linear, rational, universal system with another linear, rational, universal system. Kept by the Christian naiveté of compassion and respect for the whole person from plummeting into something worse, allegiance to the truth as purely rational has kept evangelical apologetics from ascending into something better. With such presuppositions, evangelism becomes polemics, rather than elenctics, the call to repentance and faith that repeatedly asks, "What have you done with God?" (Bavinck 1960: 221–272).

Contemporary publications dealing with evangelism among Muslims continue to show this same struggle, though not as blatantly as older materials. Reinforced by a long pattern of resistance on the part of the Muslim to the gospel, evangelism retreats further into a pattern of ideology comparisons aimed at breaking down "misunderstandings" and "misconceptions" (Elder n.d.:1). C. R. Marsh is deeply sensitive to the need for conveying the gospel "in such a way that he will be able to understand and grasp it" (Marsh 1975:7). But, in keeping with the conflict inherent in the older tradition, that concern for the gospel being "heard" is understood in rational categories, conveying "the message to his mind." Marsh tells us that "the whole man must be reached," but that is defined in terms of dealing with "theological problems," and prefaced by the sentence, "We must show him that our faith is logical" (Marsh 1975:10).

May we not recognize in this language the remnants of an older model of approach which presumed a monolithic concept of culture as a more or less static macrocosm united in an impregnable way to its "primitive," "heathen" center? Too often the terms "primitive" and "heathen" have been used in the colonialist, western sense of "non-civilized." And this "hidden curriculum" was combined with the pietistic roots of evangelicalism into a "Christ-against-non-western-culture" mould that made no effort to transform or possess Islamic culture for Christ. There was little "eye for what God has spared in his mercy" from the complete deterioration of sin. There was little awareness of the historical, sociological shifts in culture's histories. Through those shifts, what a theologian might call the "common grace" of God, culture's components, though basically an indivisible whole integrated by man's relationship to God, became more detached from that coherence, losing their original character.

Reflections of this mentality are multiplied in the collection of testimonies edited by Muriel Butcher from North Africa. Malika resisted the compromise of her young faith by calmly saying, "Christians don't keep the fast" (Butcher n.d.:14). Jamel's "spontaneous joy" was sapped by disobedience and compromise in keeping the fast and smoking (though refraining from both in the presence of the missionaries) (Butcher n.d.:41–42). Aziza's lack of a clear stand during Ramadhan is related to the near death of her daughter and her daughter's recovery to her eventual acknowledgment that "God was punishing me for keeping the fast." "She could never again follow Christ *and* Islam" (Butcher n.d.:68–69). . . .

Increasing evidence is mounting to question the simplism of these older efforts. Frederick and Margaret Stock, analyzing a 97 percent Muslim Pakistan, comment, "Too often we assume that theological differences are the primary barriers to winning Muslims. This has been repeatedly disproved. Many are theologically convinced of Christianity, but cannot hurdle the social and cultural obstacles to faith" (Stock 1975:202). Following Donald McGavran's emphasis on sociological barriers as the primary obstacle to faith, the Stocks may be guilty of falling into another kind of simplism here and overplaying sociology at the expense of "theology." At the same time, we recognize they are speaking of Pakistan and not other cultural settings; their statement is a corrective to the tendency of past methodology to isolate religious commitments from their sociological and cultural dimensions. This corrective is reinforced by Avery Willis, Jr., in his extensive study of Javanese church growth in the last decade, a movement comprising "the largest group of people ever to become

Christians out of a Moslem background'' (Willis 1977:4). Willis fears that growth will be impeded as the Church tends to view ''theology'' as the antithesis of culture and the call for conversion in terms of a radical rejection of any Javanese enculturation (Willis 1977:203–204). Peter McNee, writing of Bangladesh, dreads ''to think of ... how many Muslims have been turned away because of their inability to adjust to the Hindu thought forms through which Christianity is expressed in Bangladesh, or consider how many Muslims have reverted because they were never trusted in a Hindu convert church'' (McNee 1976: 122).

Written testimonies of converts thus echo a Muslim identification of Christianity not simply with theological kufur (blasphemy) but with colonialism and western culture. Butcher's collection of biographies from North Africa provides several examples. Malika's refusal to fast is met with the angry rejoinder of her brother, ''You've been eating at the missionaries' home; they're turning you into a European.'' She is accused of becoming a ''blasphemer and a European dog'' (Butcher n.d.:14). Norria's family meets her new faith with warnings against ''the false religion of the Europeans.'' ''Didn't she know that Mohammed was her prophet and Jesus the prophet of the Europeans?'' (Butcher n.d.:21). Erik Nielsen, the former General Secretary of the Danish Missionary Society, remarks, ''How often has it not happened that I would talk with a person, for example, in Indonesia and ask him whether he was a Moslem. He would say 'Yes.' And I would say, 'I am a Christian,' to which he would reply with a smile, 'Yes, that I can see.' He could see that by the color of my skin. To be a white man was to be a Christian'' (Nielsen 1964:222).

In these examples we are neither seeking to reduce or belittle the theological barriers between Islam and Christianity, nor arguing that the primary obstacles are simply sociological. We fear the simplism of the past that has reduced the conflict to primarily one of a purely ''religious'' sort, and the simplism of the present that can reduce the conflict to primarily one of a purely sociological or cultural sort. Religion is never that pure, neither is sociology. Both interact constantly in a cultural continuum. And in many situations, the sociological dimension of the continuum may be the more important as the "real" barrier to the gospel. The traditional evangelical approach, by its view of culture, inhibits us from seeing that continuum. How may this insight help us in correcting our understanding of the barriers?

II. Barriers to Muslim Conversion

A. Our Understanding of Conversion as One-Step Decisionism

Under the cultural impact of pietism, missionaries like India's Ziegenbalg have understood conversion as leading "a single soul belonging to a heathen people to God" (Christensen 1977:118). Though modified by a concern for man's social needs (Verkuyl 1978:176–181), this narrow individualism was reinforced by puritan moralism and Protestant scholasticism. In the process, conversion was reduced to merely an act of repentance, and faith was distinct from other isolatable categories like sanctification, adoption, etc.

The end result has been to downplay or lose altogether a sense of conversion as a comprehensive designation for the entire renewal of man (Calvin's view), conversion as a sign of the Kingdom come in Christ and into which we are *daily* engrafted. Conversion as the *process* of change of vesture (Eph. 4:24; Col. 3:9–10), conversion as metamorphosis over a period of time (Rom. 12:1–2), has become narrowed to its necessary initiating deed of transferal, the turning from idols and turning to God in Christ (I Thess. 1:9). In so doing, the Pauline perspective on conversion as an eschatological ongoing event begun with Christ's power encounter with the sinner but not consummated until the coming of his Son from heaven (I Thess. 1:10), has become isolated from glorification and narrowed to conversion as initiation. In this same perspective, repentance has become known by its fruits, though John clearly reminded his hearers that their deeds were not per se their repentance. "Bring forth, therefore, fruits worthy of repentance" (Luke 3:8) (Warfield n.d.: 94–95).

This strong focus on individualism and one-step decisionism as a feature of conversion was a cultural bias theologized by the pietist against a European background where there were large numbers of nominal Christians. The same can easily be repeated in the face of the nominalism which is also present in Christian communities in the Muslim world. McNee sees it as a grave hindrance to the cultivation of "people movements" among the Muslims of Bangladesh (McNee 1976:119–120). "Sound conversions" become largely limited to one-step transitions of allegiance. This step of initiation into the process is essential, but if it is isolated from the process of growing in understanding of what commitment to Christ means, we face again the onslaught of "nominal Christianity." Faith thus becomes devaluated to the act of one moment, rather than the attitude of a lifetime that has a beginning at a moment in time, but which for some people may not be capable of "western" definition. That apparently has happened in the Punjab where "Muslims are urged to make a personal decision for Christ that inevitably leads to ostracism and social dislocation, with all the psychological upheaval this involves" (Stock 1975:201).

Understanding conversion as a life-long allegiance process of conformity to Christ, initiated by a confession of submission to the resurrected Lord (Rom. 10:9), should help us in seeing that the initial allegiance is not an absolute degree of attainment that proves a Muslim is a child of Abraham and not Ishmael. It is rather "discernable progress *in the right direction*" (Taber 1976:3). Conversion must be genuine, but its genuineness will be tested by a lifetime of fruitbearing. It is not a quick step to some altar rail more ideological than biblical. In that sense, we must distinguish between what *makes* a Muslim a Christian and what *shows outwardly* that the person is a Christian.

This one-step mentality can also reinforce the custom, in many circles, of delaying baptism until full instruction or lengthy fruit-testing has been completed. The effect reduces baptism from the sign and seal of our entrance into the Kingdom of God and the beginning of life-long training as Kingdom disciples (Shepherd 1976:71) and makes baptism the last stage of incorporation in our rite of passage from Islam to Christianity.

In too many "Jesus Muslim" communities, baptism is not so much the biblical mark of our initial passage from death to life in Christ, as it is the sociological mark of our culturally conceived notions of what constitutes "adequate understanding for sound conversion." Discipline, the God-given tool for discipling and for correcting nominalism, is virtually administered before the convert is initiated into the Kingdom community. The end result can be the encouragement of "secret believers." For "as soon as a Muslim becomes a Christian, we have to put him through a test; we have to teach him, teach him, teach him in order to baptize him. And this very often discourages him and he goes away, or he falls away" (Marzeki 1974:84). Conversion is conceived of simply as passing a point rather than as a process. This is then misunderstood by the Muslim community (Stock 1975:225). Baptism "is seen, not as a sign of the convert's new life and of a new and positive attitude to the Lord and to the community, but rather as the last vile step on the road to apostasy" (Anderson 1976:299).

In one of the testimonies contained in Mark Hanna's volume, *The True Path,* a convert approached a Christian; he requested baptism and met the reply, "How can I baptize you when I don't know you?" When the convert met the Christian elders, he was asked what errors he had seen in Islam. "I stated that it was not so much what is wrong in Islam as what is right in the Christian faith that brought me to my commitment to Christ" (Hanna 1975:4). After some clarification of the basis of his conviction, the convert was baptized. Wisely he was not turned away. But operative in the mind of the elders may have been more than the biblical demands of faith and repentance. In addition to these, may have been a concern that baptism required an intellectually formed articulation of what was wrong in one system rather than an affirmation of allegiance to Christ in the other.

B. Our Understanding of Conversion as an Individual Decision

Western cultural emphasis on the individual-centered nature of conversion is willing to concede the gathering of the fruits of conversion into the group solidarity of the Church. But, often like Jens Christensen, one warns against any similar expression of solidarity or group coherence in the turning of a whole *ethne* to Christ (Christensen 1977:128ff). "On the contrary, the covenant theme of the Old Testament and the household baptisms of the New Testament should lead us to desire, work for and expect both family and group conversions.... Theologically, we recognize the biblical emphasis on the solidarity of each *ethnos*, i.e., nation or people. Sociologically, we recognize that each society is composed of a variety of subgroups, subcultures or homogeneous units. It is evident that people receive the gospel most readily when it is presented to them in a manner which is appropriate and not alien to their culture and when they can respond to it with and among their own people" (Willowbank Report 1978:22).

Muslim evangelization must continue to stress the necessity for a personal relationship to Christ as an essential part of conversion. But in the world's cultures such personal relationships are entered into not always by isolated "individual" decisions in abstraction from the group but more frequently, in multi-personal, infra-group judgments. "Personal" cannot be equated with "individual."

Christians have long recognized that this sense of community within the Islamic decision process is a barrier to conversion, but this recognition, combined with an insensitivity to the diversities of cultural ethnicity in their impact on Islam, has augmented the myth of Muslim impregnability by the gospel (Conn 1977:6). Such a myth has deadened awareness that Islam's cultural continuum may extend far enough for an adherent to be an atheist but still call himself a Muslim. Deep doubts may be veiled "under a cloak of external conformity to traditional Islamic practices and customs," the fast of Ramadhan observed "primarily because of social pressure and the fear it induced" (Hanna 1975:43).

Islamic objections to the gospel in some cultures may be as much cultural barriers as theological. So Don Corbin writes of evangelistic effort among the Muslims of Senegal, "We have to go through Islam and into black culture as well, into the tribal setting that [sic] Islam exists in Senegal.... Islam, for the Sengalese, is black'' (Corbin 1974:40). Martin Goldsmith bemoans his failure to revisit a remote village of about 200 people in the Muslim area of south Thailand. ''It was a Muslim village, but it had no *imam* or religious establishment of any sort. . . . It was, in fact, an ideal situation for a possible group turning to Christ'' (Goldsmith 1976:319). Avery Willis notes that ''The majority of converts to Christianity,'' in Indonesia's recent history, ''have come from . . . syncretistic, Javanistic Islam rather than the orthodox *santri* variant. Of the 163 interviewees who were Moslem converts to Christianity after 1965, 63 percent specified that they were from the 'statistical Islam' or animistic Javanese background . . .'' (Willis 1977:48).

Increasingly, the analysis of Muslim conversion patterns is recognizing the communal nature of the decision process, and recognizing also that such conversions have taken place within the ethnic microcosms that constitute Islam. Too many hints and too much research still undone prevent us from simply saying that ''there have never been mass movements of any significance among Muslims in India or Pakistan'' (Inniger 1963:124). In the 1830s, 560 persons were baptized in the Nadia district of Bangladesh, drawn from a sect ''half Hindu and half Moslem'' (McNee 1976:106). Even the bleak picture of Muslim resistance drawn by Stock is not totally unsupportive of possibilities yet to be explored. Of the 43 adult baptisms registered by the United Presbyterian Mission from 1855 to 1872 in the Punjab, 9 were Muslims (Stock 1975:23). In the Sialkot area 53 converts were baptized from 1954 to 1964. Why not more? ''Significant church growth from the Muslim community is unlikely until some means can be devised of winning responsive segments of them in whole family units'' (Stock 1975:261). False assumptions of Islamic society as a monolith, and evangelization directed at individuals apart from their family environment reinforce a methodology not geared ''to win the natural leaders of potentially responsive segments of Muslim society'' and, through them, whole clans and sects, ''conversion . . . without severe dislocation'' (Stock 1975:201–202).

Even in cultures which have been Islamicized for half a

millennium, a new emphasis on the communal character of the gospel's good news, a careful and patient cultivation of Christian communities in Muslim societies, can be a living demonstration of redemption. And, in addition, it may supply what some now call "the redemptive analogy" to the communal nature of Islam.

C. Our Understanding of Conversion as Purely 'Spiritual'

The western bifurcation or separation of the sacred from the secular, combined with a pietistic hostility to the cultural side of the missionary task, has not helped us in seeing the totalitarian, radical demands of conversion as a sign of the Kingdom of God come in Christ and the Lordship of Christ over the whole of life. As a result, our gospel for Islam frequently does not make the total claims for all of life that Islam itself makes.

The fruits of this are displayed in a Christian community where Kingdom lifestyle is narrowed to the confines of an ecclesiasticized subculture wherein is little interest in the larger questions of culture and society. Turning to Christ is not always seen as also a turning to culture, where the believer rediscovers his human origins and identity, and a turning to the world in acceptance of the mission on which Christ sends the believer in eschatological pilgrimage (Costas 1978:17-20). In this process, conversion does not remake; it unmakes. The results of this are tragic for Muslim listeners.

The radical nature of conversion involves a recreation, through union with the resurrected Christ, a resurrection from spiritual death, the "putting off" of the old and the "putting on" of the new. But too often for the Muslim, that rupture with the spiritual "past" is interpreted as discontinuity with his culture, treachery to his or her own cultural origins. So, with the Kabyles, a Berber tribe of 1,000,000 in eastern Algeria. Though they represent what is the "only tribe in the once-Christian Maghreb to have in any way responded to the Christian faith in the present century," the acceptance of Christianity became identified not so much with allegiance to Christ, as "often coupled with the acceptance of French culture and civilization'' (Beaver 1973:248). The universal dimensions of the gospel are thus lost and Muslims continue successfully to represent the Christian faith as a white man's religion (Parshall 1975:75). A random sampling taken by Avery Willis in Java of non-Christians generally sympathetic to Christianity reveals that ''93.4 percent said lack of acculturation by the churches was a hindrance to their becoming Christians'' (Willis 1977:195). What is needed is a view of conversion and the believer's relation to the past ''as a combination of rupture and continuity'' (Willowbank Report 1978:21).

For the Christian, separating the conversion change from life creates cultural assumptions of what motivations are ''proper'' for conversion. ''Spiritual need'' is isolated from politics, social relationships, social unrest, and other ''secular'' questions. The Christian Church becomes wary of any conversions for motives other than ''spiritual'' ones. In so doing, the whole area of human ''felt needs'' troubling the Muslim, and often providing a more fruitful ''point of contact'' than technically ''religious'' ones, is unused. We concentrate on theological problem areas of the Trinity, the Sonship of Christ; we neglect what to many may be larger doors for opening—bitterness towards parents, guilt over immorality, frustrations on the job, loneliness.

The same reluctance that prompted the research of Waskom Pickett into the caste movements of India to Christ in the 1920's continues to inhibit the contemporary Church from utilizing other than ''spiritual factors.'' How can we use the discovery of Willis in Java that, from 500 interviewees, one-half were motivated by ''spiritual factors,'' but one-fourth came because of political factors and one-fourth from social factors (Willis 1977:212, 221-226)? The Pauline perspective that saw all of life as God's did not make conversion a signal to efface the forms of his culture, whether Jewish or Gentile (I Cor. 7:18-19), or even to abandon the social distinctions of slavery (I Cor. 7:21-23). The Pauline advice does not mean, ''Remain a worshipper of Zeus.'' Neither does it mean, ''Abandon all your culture since none of it can be used in the service of God.'' Paul still says to the evangelist within Muslim cultures, "Use those elements of your culture which adorn your calling in Christ and which do not endanger it" (I Cor. 7:24, 31). In all things that do not deny Christ, let each person abide with God.

All of this is simply to underscore the need for a fresh look at the understandings, motivations and expectations Muslims in their diverse cultures bring to the encounter with the Christian and with Christ. What are they looking for, and why? These understandings and motivations differ widely from Muslim to Muslim and from area to area. Yet they have also many common elements that only informed research can identify.

An increased awareness of the diversity of motivations in coming to Christ and of the comprehensive character of the gospel of the Kingdom means also that the communicator need not ever restrict himself to one formula in the presentation of Christ as Savior and Lord. The call to conversion in culture is a call to "present the message in such a way that people can feel its relevance . . . and can then respond to it in action" (Nida and Taber 1969:24).

The wide-ranging nature of the gospel (I Cor. 10:31) permits us easy access to any context in which the culturally conditioned hearer re-encodes the message within his own frame of reference. To the recently delegitimized Ahmadi sect of Islam, long an antagonist of Christianity but now rejected as a genuinely Muslim system, a new door of opportunity for evangelism might be opening. What effect will it be in their disenfranchisement to hear of Isa as the Builder of a new community? To the small coterie of Muslims in northern Nigeria, still loyal after persecution to their leader, Ibrahim, and to his prophecies that God would one day reveal the true faith to them concerning Isa, the Word of God, the Breath from God, the message in 1913 from a missionary concerning Jesus as Fulfiller turned them to Christ (Jarrett-Kerr 1972:319–320). From West Africa comes news of the Banu Isa, the Jesus People, "Large groups of Muslims who have been gathering at Bima Hill in the Gombe area of Bauchi State in Nigeria to await the coming of 'Isa the Mahdi' and who have requested the Evangelical Churches of West Africa to instruct them about Isa'' (von Sicard 1978:335–336). The appeal of a Christology built around Jesus as the Mahdi who breaks crosses by being broken on one, who kills swine by putting to death the impurities they symbolize. Under this Mahdi there will be eternal security and prosperity. Lions and camels, bears and sheep will live in peace and a child will play with serpents unhurt.

We are under no illusion in all of this that a new sensitivity to our own failings and to the cultural conditioning of Muslim responses to Christ will obliterate the ''stumbling block'' that the gospel will always be. Even when Christ came to ''his own,'' they received him not. His entrance into any culture always brings crisis. We are simply insisting that it must be Christ who is the ''stumbling block.'' Part of our task as effective evangelists is to seek the removal of any other ''stumbling blocks,'' whether cultural or social or ideological, so that the Muslim may fall on Christ alone. If for the Muslim the word ''conversion'' has become a verbal symbol of cultural denial, we must look for a verbal equivalent similar to the Jews-for-Jesus movement who speak instead of being ''completed in Christ.''

Hopefully, someone will undertake the study of the motivations behind conversions to Islam from animism or other systems. Why are people switching to Islam? Our goal in all this study and self-reflection must be a willingness to be ''all things to all men, that I may by all means save some'' (I Cor. 9:22). The changeless, comprehensive gospel must be made intelligible and relevant to Muslim contexts, to their felt needs (Conn 1978:75–76).

BIBLIOGRAPHY

Anderson, John D. C.
　　1976　''The Missionary Approach to Islam: Christian or 'Cultic.' ''
　　Missiology 4:285–300.
Bavinck, J. H.
　　1960　*An Introduction to the Science of Missions*. Philadelphia: Presbyterian and Reformed Publishing Company.

Beaver, R. Pierce, editor
1973 *The Gospel and Frontier Peoples*. South Pasadena: William Carey Library.

Butcher, Muriel
n.d. *By Faith—Character Cameos from North Africa*. Highgate: North Africa Mission.

Christensen, Jens
1977 *The Practical Approach to Muslims*. Upper Darby: North Africa Mission.

Conn, Harvie M.
1977 "Missionary Myths About Islam." *Muslim World Pulse* 6(2): 1–13.
1978 "The Cultural Implications for Conversion: Some Theological Dimensions from a Korean Perspective." Unpublished paper read at the Lausanne Consultation on the Gospel and Culture, January 6–13, 1978. Willowbank, Bermuda.

Corbin, Don
1974 "Demonstration of Resistance Problems." *Media in Islamic Culture*. C. Richard Shumaker, ed. Marseille: International Christian Broadcasters and Evangelical Literature Overseas, pp. 37–40.

Costas, Orlando
1978 "Conversion as a Complex Experience." *Gospel in Context* 1(3): 14–24.

Elder, J.
n.d. *Biblical Approach to the Muslim*. Houston: Leadership Instruction and Training International.

Goldsmith, Martin
1976 "Community and Controversy: Key Causes of Muslim Resistance." *Missiology* 4:317–323.

Hanna, Mark
1975 *The True Path. Seven Muslims Make Their Greatest Discovery*. Colorado Springs: International Doorways Publishers.

Inniger, Merle W.
1963 "Mass Movements and Individual Conversion in Pakistan." *Practical Anthropology* 19:122–126.

Jarrett-Kerr, Martin
1972 *Patterns of Christian Acceptance*. London: Oxford University Press.

Marsh, C. R.
1975 *Share Your Faith with a Muslim*. Chicago: Moody Press.

Marzeki, Jonathan
1974 "Amplifying the Problem." *Media in Islamic Culture*. C. Richard Shumaker, ed. Marseille: International Christian Broadcasters and Evangelical Literature Overseas, pp. 82–87.

McNee, Peter
1976 *Crucial Issues in Bangladesh*. South Pasadena: William Carey Library.

Nida, Eugene and Charles Taber
    1969 *The Theory and Practice of Translation*. Leiden: E. J. Brill.
Nielsen, Erik W.
    1964 "Asian Nationalism." *Practical Anthropology* 11:211–226.
Parshall, Phil
    1975 *The Fortress and the Fire*. Bombay: Gospel Literature Service.
Shepherd, Norman
    1976 "The Covenant Context for Evangelism." *The New Testament Student and Theology*. John H. Skilton, ed. Nutley, N. J.: Presbyterian and Reformed Publishing Company.
von Sicard, S.
    1978 "Maranatha: Advent in the Muslim World." *Missiology* 6:335–341.
Stock, Frederick and Margaret Stock
    1975 *People Movements in the Punjab*. South Pasadena: William Carey Library.
Taber, Charles
    1976 "When is a Christian?" *Milligan Missiogram* 3(3):1–4.
Vander Werff, Lyle L.
    1977 *Christian Mission to Muslims: The Record*. South Pasadena: William Carey Library.
Verkuyl, J.
    1978 *Contemporary Missiology*. Grand Rapids: William B. Eerdmans Publishing Company.
Warfield, B. B.
    n.d. "New Testament Terms Descriptive of the Great Change." Reprint from *The Presbyterian Quarterly*, pp. 91–100.
Willis, Avery, Jr.
    1977 *Indonesian Revival. Why Two Million Came to Christ*. South Pasadena: William Carey Library.
Willowbank Report—Gospel and Culture. Lausanne Occasional Papers. No. 2.
    1978 Wheaton: Lausanne Committee for World Evangelization.

Summary of Participant's Responses

"I wish I could understand this. It sounds *very* important."

Several respondents leveled good-natured barbs like this at Dr. Conn for his propensity to use difficult words and constructions in his excellent paper. Many agreed completely with him, and felt that if the conference did no more than deal with the three barriers he raised, it would have been worth the effort and cost. Many more agreed in general, but raised important specific questions about his approach or assumptions. A number of these comments clustered around the headings suggested below.

Jesus Muslims?

The most frequent reactions had to do with the author's references to "Isa the Mahdi," (Jesus the Guided One"), "Masjid Issawi" (Jesus Mosques), and "Muslimun Issawiyun" (Jesus Muslims). Some were highly favorable to the idea. One, going further perhaps than was being suggested by the author said, "Conn has shown masterfully that the barriers are not in Islam but in western Christianity and we can now move from apologetics to anthropology."

Others, however, objected. "It's improper," they said, "to compare Jews for Jesus with 'Jesus Muslims.'" There can no more be a "Jesus Muslim" than a Jesus Buddhist, a Jesus Hindu, or a Jesus atheist." Another argued that while Christians can accept all of the Jewish Scripture and the Jewish concept of God, we cannot accept all of the Quran or the Muslim concept of God. Two others were also critical, but approached from opposite directions:

—"We believe that much of Jewish culture was God-given . . . we do not believe that Muslim customs and cultures are in the same way God-given."

—"We don't need to dislocate them out of their cultures, but we do need to dislocate them out of their religion."

Perhaps most importantly, a Muslim convert asked if anyone had ever done research on this question of a "Jesus Muslim" movement. "Wouldn't it be wise," he asked, "to see if (the thousands of converted Muslims) *want* to be called "Issawiyun"?

On Theological Issues Not Being the Primary Barriers

Dr. Conn's statement that it has been repeatedly disproven that theological differences are the primary barriers to winning Muslims, also met with disagreement. One respon-

dent asked, "Where and how has it been disproved that
theological differences were not primary?" Others did not
like Conn's "belittling" the theological barriers between
Islam and Christianity. "Theology is God within a culture,"
they said, "and therefore the most significant of the cultural
barriers."

Others added:

—"Who is offended by the cross, they or we? Everything is offensive to the Muslim so we change it all. But
what shall we do with the cross? We cannot translate it,
we cannot change it. It will always remain an offense.
There is a danger of our becoming men of anthropology, sociology and culture but failing to be men of the
Spirit."

—"The motifs of Islam and Christianity are opposite—
the hijra and the cross. Thus the differences are more
than terminological—they are profoundly theological
and practical."

—"It's simplistic to say the theological barriers are not
primary—they are monumental."

Conversion as One-Step Decisionism

The first of Dr. Conn's "Barriers to Muslim Conversion" had to do with some people's understanding of conversion as a single decision. By far the majority of the respondents agreed that conversion is more than a once-in-a-lifetime
decision. They added that conversion is even more than a
process, saying that "It's an event, a process, and a relationship," and also stressed that there must be a specific moment
where there is a "power encounter."

The reaction against Dr. Conn on the conversion decision question was partly also a reaction to the statement by
Dr. Taber, quoted by Dr. Conn, that conversion is "discernible progress in the right direction." "Who," one asked, "is
to say what is the right direction?" "What is discernible
progress?" "Does it ever reach a stage of breaking with the

past?'' And, ''At what point can a man be considered a Christian, either by himself or those in the community?'' ''I'm afraid,'' one concluded, ''that in following this logic, it will be very difficult to ever say that any person is or is not a Christian believer in an Islamic culture.''

A Muslim Question to Christians: Why Do You Come to Live Among Us?

A Roman Catholic Study-Group in Tunisia

A Roman Catholic study-group living in predominantly Muslim Tunisia, discussed questions which their Muslim friends were constantly asking. The group formulated "a loyal answer, without evasions and ulterior motives," shared its draft with Muslims, then improved and published a final text. The questions and answers center on key doctrines (the Trinity; the Incarnation of the Divine; original sin, the cross and redemption; the written Word of God; the prophethood of Muhammed), and on Christian life (prayer, the liturgy, the vocation to religious life in community, with its freely chosen celibacy). Another frequent question is, Why do Catholic missionaries leave their homeland to go out "to love 'strangers' such as those who put these questions to them"? Behind the question is the deeply rooted suspicion of proselytism, the astonishment of leaving home for disinterested motives, and the conviction that "all other truth is even a threat and an attack on one's own truth." The group suggests possible responses; for example: My life among Muslims is meant to bear witness to the universal love of God, revealed in Jesus Christ, for the people of another race and another religion. The complete text of the Tunisian group statement appeared in *Encounter,* a documentation service for Muslim-Christian understanding, published by the Pontifical Institute for Arab Studies (Piazza S. Apollinare, 49, Rome, Italy 00186); nos. 39 (November 1977) and 45 (May 1978), from which this extract is taken.

The Muslim Question: Why have you come to live among us? Why did you leave your country, your family and relatives? What do you gain by doing this? Who pays you?

I. *The Mentality Behind the Question*

1. The suspicion of *tabshîr* (evangelization in the pejorative sense of proselytism). The Christian's true aim, formerly declared and now hidden, is to get Muslims to leave Islam in order to lead them to Christianity. All our activity, even the apparently most selfless of our institutions, have no other aim than that.

This suspicion is very deeply rooted among the best of our friends, at least as an ever-present question. It is objectively justified not only by ancient history (Crusades, Western imperialism) still very vivid in people's minds; and not only by recent history (colonization, the 1930 international Eucharistic Congress in Carthage); but also by the Church's teaching and practice until quite recently: our sole aim is to found the Church by the conversion and baptism of non-Christians, while rejecting any salvific value in their religions as such.

2. On both the Muslim and Catholic sides, each has a unilateral conception of truth which leads adherents to think they possess the whole of this truth; they have nothing to receive from others; all other truth is even a threat and an attack on their own truth. This threat and attack aims at both the cohesion of the Muslim social body and its religious unity: to abjure one's religion is to betray one's country.

3. Muslim astonishment, even scandal, which is caused by the missionary's leaving his or her own country, forsaking one's father and mother, in order to live in another country. Some Muslims are astonished at our leaving wealthy countries where it is so nice to live (a somewhat mythical view) and our coming to areas which lack so many things.

4. Muslims' seeking for some interested motive on our part, either religious (proselytism) or personal (Who pays us? A foreign embassy? The Vatican?).

5. But an evolution is taking place. Exchanges between peoples and different cultures are multiplying on the spot (bi-culturalism)) and by travel and staying abroad for study or employment. Religions, like cultures, are beginning to open up to one another and to acknowledge that to a certain point they are complementary. Above all, they find they confront the same problems (atheism, secularization, social problems, etc.). They feel the need to collaborate. Many believers, both Christian and Muslim, no longer consider their religion the sole, valid, salvific one. In certain milieux, especially of young people, the principle of freedom of conscience is proclaimed like that of all other freedoms.

II. *Muslim Teaching*

Islam is the only religion approved by God (Qur'ân 3,19). Whoever follows another religion will go to hell: 3,85; 3,83; 2,130. It is an immutable religion: 9,36; perfect: 5,3; 9,32; 61,8; which abrogates and recapitulates all other religions: 24,55; and must take the place of them all: 9,33; 48,28; 61,9. Even the "People of the Book" (Jews and Christians) who had received a true revelation and a true religion, "falsified" (*tahrîf*) their Scriptures: 4,46; 5,13,41; 2,75; and consequently they must believe in the Qur'ân: 4,47; 5,15,48; 98,1; and be converted to Islam: 3,20; 3,73; 3,95. The Muslim community (*umma*) is the best one of all: 3,110.

Consequently, the Qur'ân harshly condemns the Muslim apostate, doomed to hell: 3,85–90; 4,115.137; 16,106; 47,25–28; and already condemned below here to have one hand and one foot cut off and to be put on the gibbet (*salb*) (cf. Hallâj): 5,33; 7,124; 20,71; 26,49. It also harshly condemns those who "turn believers away from God's path"; they must be opposed and killed (the polytheists of Mecca who had forced the Muslims to make the *hîjra* [migration]: 2,217; 2,191.193; 9,12; since they attack religion, they will go to hell with no hope of pardon: 47,34).

On the other hand, the Qur'ân proclaims the principle of freedom of conscience, "no constraint in matters of religion" (*lâ ikrâh fî-l-dîn*): 2,256. Faith, the gift of God, is a free and personal act. The "People of the Book" have a right to a special status of "protection" (*dhimma*): 9,29. Their salvation is secure: 2,62; 5,69; 22,17. Christians are even the closest friends to Muslims: 5,82.

Several Muslim theologians (Ghazâli, taken up again by Md. 'Abduh and R. Ridâ) declare that whoever follows what one believes to be the truth in matters of religion and is unintentionally ignorant of the coming of Muhammed will be saved (cf. these texts in *Encounter* No. 31, January 1976). Many cultured Muslims think what is essential is for each one to follow one's conscience.

III. *Christian Teaching*

As defined by Vatican II (especially its *On the Church* and *On the Church in the Modern World*) and by subsequent theologians (Bourgeois, Duquoc, L'Arbresle), *current* reflection of the Church on itself and its relationship to the world can be expressed as follows:

By his person and his message, Christ came to bring to all humankind salvation and deliverance from all servitudes, from sin in all its forms, by calling each one to "conversion" (metanoia: cf. *tawba*): to get out of one's egoism and one's pride in order to open up to God, the Father of all humankind, and to fellow human beings, especially to the most disadvantaged (the "poor"). This is what the Gospel calls conversion to the Kingdom of God (here on earth). The Church, the communion of those who believe in Jesus Christ, has as mission, not directly to spread itself out until it embraces all men and women, but to bear this message of personal conversion to the world, to be the *ferment*, the sign of conversion to the Kingdom. This conversion can come about in many ways *within* the various "religions." Knowledge of Jesus Christ and explicit faith in his message have meaning only as a supreme requirement for personal conversion and testimony to our brothers and sisters. This message the church is to bear within "all nations," while respecting the religious progress of each individual and each people.

IV. *Our Possible Answers to the Question*

1. Relations between developed and developing countries, at least from the economic point of view, are among today's major problems, an essential decisive task of our day. I have chosen to come and live here and take part in this huge effort of development as my response to the Christian demand to prefer the poor and to struggle for their liberation and for more justice between countries.

2. Understanding between peoples and different cultures is also one of the major problems of our time. Living in a culture different from my own, I try to learn the language and to know the human values of this people. I should like to be its ambassador to European/North American peoples, who are ignorant of, and so often contemptuous of those who do not resemble them. Being a "bridge," even a modest one, between peoples, is an exciting task. For a Christian this is working for peace and reconciliation—essential values in the Kingdom of God on earth.

3. Relations between religions have entered a new phase. The time for wars of religion—a real sacrilege against God—is past. Islam and Christianity are more and more confronting the same problems: the faith of young people, religious education, the response of faith to the great problems of our day, and so forth. I have come to live in a Muslim country in order to take part in this dialogue and this collaboration between Christians and Muslims. Far from wanting to attempt anything against Islam, my dearest wish is for the Muslim faith to emerge victorious and more pure from the conflict with the modern world.

4. The essential revelation brought by Jesus Christ is the universal love of God, the Father of all humankind, who loves them all without distinction, Muslims as well as Christians, with a predilection for the most weak and disadvantaged. My life as a Christian among Muslims is meant to bear witness to this universal love of God for the people of another race and another religion.

5. The Gospel's invitation to conversion to the Kingdom of God must be borne to, and lived out in every nation. I have received the vocation to come and live that calling in a Muslim country. It is, first of all, a requirement of my own faith: to live out this conversion to the Kingdom. By living among Muslims, it can happen that my relations of friendship, my attitude in the face of some problems, in some circumstance or other, will provoke them to this conversion to the Kingdom, particularly by urging them to rediscover for themselves the calls to this conversion which are contained in their own religious tradition. My role as a Christian is strictly limited to this: working together with my Muslim brothers and sisters for our own conversions to the values of the Kingdom of God by scrupulously respecting each one's religious vocation, as God makes it known to each.

This in no way excludes my wish to make Jesus Christ and his Gospel message known. If I were to deny this, either I would not be sincere or would not be loyal, or else I would pervert the love which I claim to bear. When you love someone in truth, you cannot but desire to communicate to him or her all that by which you live, especially that which is the very basis of your life and your joy. Because I believe that the knowledge of Jesus Christ and of his Gospel is the most powerful factor for conversion to the Kingdom of God, and hence for the total fulfilment of mankind (while recognizing that there are other paths than this one), I can but desire this knowledge for my friends. But the paths and the means do not depend on me. This is the mystery of the relations between the Spirit and each conscience. My role is limited to bearing witness by my life to what this conversion through knowledge of Jesus Christ is. But it is a tremendous and demanding role. Mr. Talbi expresses differently but in an excellent manner this "logic of love" when he requires Christians to repudiate proselytism but to carry out their "duty of apostolate" by bearing witness to the truth they bear. ("Islam and Dialogue," *Encounter*, no. 11–12, Jan.–Feb. 1975).

6. As to what *interest* we might have in living in a country and among people other than our own, it is a real

interest, though not financial. It is the discovery of a different way of being human, of a style of human relations full of riches. It is at times the sharing of life with the poor which helps me to fulfil the evangelical ideal. It is the discovery of a great monotheistic religion whose essential values—the transcendency of God, adoration, submission to His will—have to be lived by the Christians, in order to give their full meaning to their strictly Christian values: Incarnation, intimate life of grace with God, two-fold love of God and neighbor. Only by living this Christian life in a non-Christian milieu does one really fathom Christianity.

7. Finally, for some Christians there are particular reasons for living here: Those who are born in this country have no reason to go and live the Gospel elsewhere; those who are dedicated, at least in part, to the service of Christians living here; those who are dedicated to research in Arabic and Islamics and would like to carry out their research in a living milieu.

Christianity Meets Traditional African Cultures

Peter K. Sarpong

In the judgment of the Roman Catholic Bishop of Kumasi, Ghana, "the Church has not become 'African' enough," and he hopes that the religious "symbols, imagery, signs, etc. that are clearly remnants of other cultures will be replaced by those comprehensible to the African." The African traditional cultures are deeply religious, even though they contain some objectionable elements which the Ashanti bishop lists. But areas of convergence are many and profound: godliness, fatherhood and religious authority; veneration of ancestors; extolled virtues of respect, hospitality, purity, truth, and hard work; and liturgical sensitivity about the "life cycle" or rites of passage. Sensitive in dialogue with these traditions, the evangelist discovers that one need not preach "a new God" but "an old God who has been revealed to us positively by his Son." Indeed, "there is a vast Christian theological potential in Africa, not simply in spite of contemporary change, but because of it." Peter K. Sarpong is a pastor, prolific writer and scholar, who holds degrees in theology from Rome's Angelicum and in literature and anthropology from Oxford University. The article from which these extracts are taken, appeared in *Worldmission* (vol. 30, no. 2, Summer 1979), a publication of the U.S. office of the Society for the Propagation of the Faith (366 5th Ave., New York, NY 10001).

The ordinary African is not "logical" in the Western sense. By and large he has no interest in cause and effect but in actual happenings. Neither does he reason along strict syllogistic lines. This does not mean that he is not a thinker or that he is unintelligent. In fact, he is a philosopher in his own right. But he philosophizes in the concrete, not in the abstract.

The African can pursue a particular cause or act in a definite pattern for, say, 20 years and when the Westerner has concluded that he will continue to do so for the rest of his life, he suddenly goes off at a tangent. To the non-African this is illogical, but not to the African who on the whole does not accept absolutes. To his way of thinking, behavior must be related to his needs, to what he considers good. So it is not wrong to tell a "lie" for a good purpose. Baptism is a good thing; then it should be permissible to have a person unfit for Baptism receive the Sacrament by concealing the truth about him. . . .

I am not by any means suggesting that the African has no appreciation of what is true and what is a lie. I am only trying to explain that his understanding of these concepts is more pragmatic. . . . The Catholic Church is the true Church founded by Christ, but if my petition is unanswered when I go to Mass then there is nothing wrong in praying in a Spiritual Church or falling back on the traditional magico-religious ritual for help. After all, religion is worthwhile only inasmuch as it helps man to get rid of the many inevitable hazards of life—childlessness, illness, poverty, death, disgrace, hunger, etc. In some African languages there are no abstract terms and one has to seek a concrete image to convey the thought.

The African believes in God and spirits, but he is not interested in defining these realities, and most of the theological terms used in such an exercise mean nothing to him. His interest stops with how God and the spirits influence his life and what good or evil they mete out.

Much has to be accomplished in studying the culture and institutions of different African societies and endeavoring to harmonize the authentic teaching of Christ with the everyday lives of people.

To my mind, the Church has not become "African"

enough. By "African" I am not referring to the skin or origin of people; I am not preaching racism. I am only expressing a concern that the Church truly become incarnated in the African soil, hoping that the symbols, imagery, signs, etc. that are clearly remnants of other cultures will be replaced by those comprehensible to the African.

The problem then is comprehending the unacknowledged and unanalyzed standpoints from which the African's views are taken.

The Vatican Propagation of the Faith in 1659 issued to missionaries in China and Indo-China the directives:

> Put no obstacles in their way; and for no reason whatever should you persuade these people to change their rites, customs, and ways of life unless these are obviously opposed to religion and good morals. For what is more absurd than to bring France or Spain or Italy or any other part of Europe into China. It is not these that you should bring but the faith which does not spurn or reject any people's rites and customs, unless they are depraved, but, on the contrary, tries to keep them... admire and praise what deserves to be respected.

My contention is that like all other cultures, African traditional cultures contain several objectionable elements. This is not to say that they do not or did not fulfill a social function now or in the past. A careful examination of many an African custom, no matter how repulsive it may be to modern man, will reveal that it once played or even now plays a role in the social life of the people.

In the light of the Christian message one can hardly justify the reign of terror of some chiefs in Africa. The tests of endurance that young boys and girls have to undergo during their initiation ceremonies, and widows during the funeral celebration of their husbands, amount to objective cruelty. Those being initiated are sometimes subjected to circumcision and clitoridectomy, deep cuts on the forehead and other parts of the body, and forcible extraction of teeth—all with very crude instruments. Some bleed to death or die through infection of their wounds. Widows are sometimes placed in solitary confinement for days on end, made to sleep for weeks with stones as their pillow, or have pepper thrown into their eyes.

In the past, the atrocities committed through traditional secret societies were so horrifying that, as far back as the beginning of this century, the Colonial Powers had to proscribe societies, such as the Ogbonu in Nigeria, from the purely humanitarian point of view.

Traditional cultures' estimation of women, even in strictly matrilineal societies, has always been very low. Often the woman is considered only a second-class citizen, the mother of the man's children. The Christian teaching of the equality of all human beings would have taken many African cultures a very long time to appreciate.

Christianity insists on our loving everyone, even our enemies. Traditional cultures regard the downfall of the enemy a desirable thing to be sought vigorously. Love is the cornerstone of Christian religion. Traditional cultures emphasize fear as sufficient motivation for doing good and for avoiding evil. Traditionally, religion is useful because, and insofar as, it helps man to solve the many problems that beset him in life. A religion that prepares man mainly for a reward after death is, at best, of dubious utility.

In the context of traditional cultures, the African could never rise to the lofty heights of revelation attained by Christianity. The Trinity, the Incarnation, the Eucharist and the Resurrection are theologically beyond the reach of "primitive revelations." Christianity gives meaning to suffering. Suffering has no place in traditional cultures except as the sign of the spirits' anger, the reward of man's inequity. Neither can traditional cultures understand the meaning of the virtue of humility. Traditionally, the African is by nature a proud person. He always feels more important than anyone else.

One could go on enumerating points of divergence between Christianity and traditional African cultures. Nevertheless, the areas of convergence appear to be many and profound. In fact, it looks as if the good Lord from all eternity has prepared the African soil for the reception of the Christian seed.

Godliness has always been part of the African tradition.

Indeed the attributes of the African God are so "Christian" that many 19th-century ethnographers doubted their originality. It is true that besides the Supreme Being, Africans venerate or even worship other spirits, human and non-human, and have belief in totems, witches, magic and taboos. But these are considered as manifestations of God, his functionaries who do his will. The preacher in Africa is therefore not preaching a new God; he is preaching an old God who has been revealed to us positively by his Son. If he studies and makes use of the belief of the Africans, then he is giving a new dimension to, rather than correcting, their religious conception. This belief is in fact basic to what is going to follow. As a matter of fact, in African traditional cultures there appears to be no distinction made between a person's religious practices and his other spheres of activity. Religion is a way of life, not a fashion. It permeates every aspect of a man's life, from cradle to grave. For the African, religion is not a subject to learn. Nor is it a subject for debate. Being part of ordinary life, it is accepted and absorbed in the normal cause of events. As an integral part of culture, it shares culture's compulsory, impersonal, objective and universal nature. Religion is part of African society. . . .

The structure of African societies may and sometimes does have effects which may be inconsistent with Christian aspirations. For example, Christianity would insist that marriage is primarily an institution of love between a man and a woman for their mutual happiness and the well-being of their children. In many African cultures, however, marriage may be regarded as a social affair between two lineages which agree to hand over their people in marriage primarily for the benefit of the group. If an uncle or father can say: "I have arranged a marriage for my nephew or son," then there should be no wonder that they sometimes control the marriage, interfere with it, help it to last or cause its disruption. . . .

The education of children may provide a serious point of conflict in African lineal cultures. Matrilineal fatherhood approaches the idea of the fatherhood of God more than the patrilineal fatherhood. For the matrilineal father has no juridical rights over his children and exercises authority over them only by virtue of a mystical bond that is supposed to exist between him and them. The patrilineal mother is in the same situation. Both love the children for the sake of the children. Here is love which does not ask for or expect something in return. It is love which is reminiscent of the words of the hymn: "My Lord, I love thee not because I hope for heaven thereby." But friction arises when Christianity advises that the education of the child is the responsibility of both parents. In African lineal cultures the responsibility falls on the lineage.

The patrilineal father and the matrilineal mother are the parents with authority over their children. They are not likely to neglect the training of their children. They guard and protect the children from harm. The children, in turn, develop the virtue of reverential fear towards them. However, parental or filial love of the kind expected between a Christian and God is strained. The son, especially the eldest son, is a sort of rival to his father for his property. In some African societies, the threat posed by an eldest son against his father is so feared that it is counter-balanced by a strict regulation making it illegal for a king's or chief's eldest son to succeed him. The absence of specialization of work which in Euro-American societies helps the child to become easily independent, coupled with the group sense which makes the child regard his father's possessions as his by right, makes him the potential "usurper" of his father. He is, therefore, looked upon askance by the father.

However, even here the concept of fatherhood is pregnant with "Christian" ideas. God indeed is our master, he possesses power and authority over us. He is provident, looking after us, guarding and protecting us from bodily as well as spiritual harm. He is jealous for our service and undivided loyalty. But his intolerance of man's infidelity is always altruistic, rather than egoistic. There can be no question of a strained relationship between us and God. His love for us increases precisely when we try to "inherit" his Kingdom.

Consequently, the very comparison and contrast between the two types of "African" fatherhood could be extremely useful in instructing catechumens. They project God's personality better on the catechetical screen.

Among other by-products of African social systems is

the tendency to unfair play. Social structure alone cannot adequately explain the high incidence of bribery and corruption, nepotism and favoritism everywhere in Africa. However, in any society it should be difficult for a person conducting an interview not to give first consideration to ten candidates for whose education he feels responsible in some way. I would not like to be a judge in Ghana. The number of clansmen appearing before me expecting to be treated leniently, the number of the friends of these relatives in the same situation, not to count those on my wife's side, would leave very few people upon whom I could test my integrity!

But to be a little charitable to African social structures, let me explain that they do not always obstruct the practice of the Christian religion. On the contrary, they are capable of being used to promote the Christian cause. For one thing, the idea of authority in the lineage to whom lineage members look for direction and whom they willingly obey is a good example of the hierarchy in the Church. The communal spirit that ideally should reign supreme in a lineage and the mutual assistance given by and to members of the same lineage remind us of the early Christian communities described for us in the Acts of the Apostles, the spirit of which unfortunately appears to be found nowadays only among the Religious in their communities. Theoretically, no single person should die of hunger, nakedness or lack of shelter. What belongs to one clansman belongs to another.

In African societies, terms like "father," "mother," "brother" and "sister," which, elsewhere, are employed to refer to strictly biological relations, have much wider practical and sociological connotation and application. At a time when so much is being said and recommended about "basic communities," a fresh look at African traditional cultures could point the way to the true salvation of mankind. . . .

The veneration of lineage tutelary gods and ancestors may be compared with our Christian cult of angels and saints. Here again we are strongly reminded of the doctrine of the Communion of Saints. African social structures well-utilized could afford us traditional ways of securing good relationships among members of our Christian communities. Their effects on marriage could be commendable, for loyalty to the lineage exercises a restraining influence on its married members.

African traditional cultures extol the values of respect, honor, hospitality, magnanimity, purity, truth and hard work. Traditional cultures demand that all citizens have *character*, and live in conformity with their conscience. Without these, a person is not a human being. He is clothed only in the skin of a human being. If people in practice do not live up to the expectations of culture, this is because, as St. Paul tells us, they cannot understand their own behavior. They find themselves doing the very things they know they should not do. Moreover, African traditional religions lack the concept of grace, enabling weak and frail man to act in accordance with his nature and convictions, to do what is right.

The need to utilize the African's culture for the benefit of Christianity cannot be over-emphasized, especially in the area of the Liturgy. Africans want to enjoy a liturgical situation. They want to play an active and meaningful role in what is happening. Singing and dancing have always formed a constitutive part of their religious celebrations. What takes place must be relevant to their life. They seek room for spontaneous expressions of filial sentiments towards God. They desire the minister to be personally interested in them. To treat the individual as only one in a crowd, and as an impersonal, unnoticed, unacknowledged and unaided spectator is to refuse to fulfill the innermost craving of his heart.

In reflecting on African cultures in relation to Christianity, one must mention the "life cycle" or rites of passage. These rites, which are very much religious in character, are found everywhere in Africa. Because of their varying complexity, my comments are based mainly on my Ashanti experience.

Until these rites of passage have been carefully analyzed and all their implications truly ascertained, we would do well to refrain from equating them with the Sacraments. The thought is tantalizing because the rites contain elements which on the surface are similar to features in the Sacraments. For instance, the rites are performed at crucial turning-points in a man's life—in particular at birth, puberty and death. The same seems to be true for at least some of the Sacraments. Rites of passage are meant to produce what they symbolize. So also are the Sacraments. Each of the rites may be performed only once for any one person. Baptism, Confirmation and the Priesthood too are received but once by any one individual. In the performance of the rites, material objects accompanied by words are employed, and the Sacraments, in scholastic terminology, are constituted of matter and form, and so on.

The two sets of ceremonies contain somewhat similar ideas indeed, but they are not therefore identical—the rites should not be regarded as some sort of primitive Sacraments, since the discrepancies between them are notable. Baptism, for Christians, is a new birth, which renders one a child of God, and an heir of his Kingdom. It produces its effects on the recipient alone. It is not necessarily received in babyhood—a 100-year old man may be baptized just as validly as a one-day old baby. Baptism, therefore appears to be different from child-naming or outdooring ceremonies. The latter are not regarded as a new birth, but a "ratification" of the old. They are not thought to benefit the child alone, but its mother, father and the whole community; and they cannot be postponed until adulthood.

The same view may be expressed on puberty or initiation rites. Their effects are not intended only for the novices. True, a girl neophyte is prayed for in order that she may be pleasing to the ancestors, have a happy and especially fruitful life, and grow old. But it would appear that the main motive behind her initiation is to change an alarming condition from a calm but unproductive girlhood to potentially dangerous but fertile adulthood. The adults in the community do not want to associate with an "unclean" girl at their level and thereby suffer from famine, plagues, child-death, etc. They cleanse her from her "impurity" before admitting her into their company. The rites are as important to them as to her. I therefore do not see which of the Sacraments can be favorably compared with initiation rites.

Funeral rites are probably the best example of ceremonies performed for the sake of community, and not those for whom ostensibly they are meant—the dead. In the first place they are rites of passage performed after the person has given up his soul. They are cautiously gone through lest the deceased become annoyed and visit the living with various calamities. Even when references are made to the dead, they are not necessarily meant to benefit them. The living are sorry that they no longer enjoy the good services of the dead; they petition them for things, ask them to protect them and so on. Therefore, one cannot by the wildest stretch of imagination, claim that funeral obsequies are comparable to the Sacrament of the Sick, which is advantageous to the dying, not the dead. A close study of widowhood and other funeral rites will confirm this opinion.

So the Sacraments differ from rites of passage, but here again my intention is not to give the impression that they are so opposed that they cannot be reconciled. I want only to guard against the hasty and probably false hope that we have in Africa specimens of the Sacraments.

I am all for purifying the rites and then preserving them if only because of the good pragmatic effects they produce. They engender the spirit of solidarity in a community; funerals are attended by all and sundry and while in progress, disagreements and hatreds are buried. Puberty or nubility were once the mainstay of juvenile or premarital purity, not to say virginity. Even now it is the painful truth that the morally good girl or boy is more difficult to find among literate Christian children than among pagan children who still hold fast to their traditional beliefs. The same rites focussed attention on the girl, and gave her the publicity through which she hoped to attract a husband. They further served as an instrument of instruction in the qualities of a wife, in motherhood and in maternal attributes. Educators of children used them to maintain the accepted standards of morality and good behavior. They also acted as sanctions against bad husbands.

Another "African" theme of importance to Christianity is that of fecundity. Because of their fundamental humanity, Africans place a great value on physical generation, on life and the sharing of life. In the Western world, the "good life" is equated with proficiency in science and technology. It is a dehumanizing equation. Africa might assist in the process of revaluation.

Closely linked with the theme of fecundity is that of "man-in-community." Pope Paul VI, in his letter to Africa of 1967, pointed out that this has three characteristics: the spiritual view of life, the sense of the family and the sense of community.

Finally, Africa has the potential to place a much-needed priority on a theology of relationships between human and spiritual beings, particularly between the living and the dead. As Aylward Shorter points out, this is a strong preoccupation of traditional religious systems in Africa and it could well provide an enrichment for the Christian idea of the Communion of Saints.

It is evident that there is a vast Christian theological potential in Africa, not simply in spite of contemporary change, but because of it. That is why it behooves Christianity in Africa to heed the exhortation:

> Prudently and lovingly through dialogue and collaboration with the followers of other religions, and in witness of Christian faith and life, acknowledge, preserve, and promote the spiritual and moral good found among these men, as well as the values in their society and culture (Vatican Council II, *Nostra Aetate,* 2).

Christian Awareness of Primal World-Views

Anastasios Yannoulatos

This Greek Orthodox Bishop from Athens writes from his experience of direct contact with African religions. He reflects on their specific world-views and primal religious experiences, and recognizes the traps the outsider must avoid: an uncritical underestimation which leads to indifference or contempt; an equally uncritical admiration which comes from "an almost adolescent passion for all things primal"; and an uncritical judgment which overemphasizes the differences and overlooks the basic unity of human nature. Nevertheless, the Christian encounters people of primal world-views in the belief that "'primal' is not 'final.' There is something essential they are entitled to receive from the Christian community." Bishop Anastasios, Professor of Missions at the University of Athens, draws on his own Eastern tradition to answer: Have Christians made available to those of African traditional religions "all of the twenty-century-old tradition of the Church, not least that of the first centuries when Christians lived in a comparable climate of primal world-views? Or have missionaries only tried to transplant the Christianity and the problems of the western Europe of the 16th century onwards?" The Greek Orthodox missiologist also questions some practical interpretations of the "indigenization" slogan which could lead to isolationism and weaken the sense of the "common essence of mankind." He concludes, "the basic Christian doctrine of the Holy Trinity provides the theological infrastructure for the co-existence of a plurality of persons and of a common essence." This article was published in *Primal World-Views: Christian Involvement in Dialogue with Traditional Thought Forms,* edited by John B. Taylor (Ibadan, Nigeria: Daystar Press [P.O. Box 1261], 1976), the proceedings of a conference on the theme at the Institute of Church and Society in Ibadan, September 1973.

Any approach to primal cultures can be a source of interest and curiosity. But the actual mental and physical experience of entry into such a community is fraught with a singular sense of mystery not unlike the fascination of the virgin tropical forest.

The Survival and New Vitality of Traditional Forms

It has been pointed out before that the so-called "primal world-views" are far more complex and sophisticated than outsiders had suspected until recently. The cultures and primal religious experiences of primal societies present, to my mind, an analogy with that other basic function of emerging humanity: speech. Both the religion and the language of primal societies have already evolved, albeit along the lines of different patterns. Their present state, far from representing the first steps of a straightforward ascending ladder, reflects a much higher position on a cultural staircase of different architecture. To try to understand them by analogy to other patterns can be a mistake.

What we are faced with is not merely an involved past, but mainly an intricate present. The traditional world-views are in a state of dynamic change characterized by a very high degree of flexibility leading to the creation of ever new forms. Contrary to the oversimple conviction of many, the old religious certainties do not yield so easily to modern technological civilization. The cold northern breath of western technology can freeze the old nightmares in their existing patterns or into new patterns which are of deep interest to the careful investigator. In the market place of even the largest Nigerian cities, I was shown that you can buy, along with transistors, batteries and other goods of our technological age, "patent medicines" such as monkey and bird skulls, animal bones, roots, leaves, feathers, shells, crocodile and snake hides. Some of these will be used for traditional ceremonies and spell-breaking rites.

While traveling with three Nigerians from Ibadan to Lagos, I had an opportunity to attend a formal evening sacrifice to *Ògún*, the god of iron. This involved oil libations, the sacrifice of a chicken, and the offering of various roots and shells. It culminated in the sacrifice of a dog and the partaking of its blood by the participants. For the purposes of this note, I will pick out one characteristic detail: among other iron objects prominent on the altar of *Ògún* was the carcass of an old motor car engine, a bumper and other automobile parts. These products of European industry have been incorporated in the old religious rite. Three days later, I went back to the same small town to collect more information on this ritual, and I was granted an audience by the king of the area. I wondered if a car manufactured in a European or American factory was a suitable material for an altar of *Ògún*, a god of the Yoruba. "Any iron thing," he answered, "no matter where it is or where it comes from, belongs to *Ògún*."

A few days later, while I was walking in the main street of Lagos, I was cordially approached by a well-dressed gentleman carrying an attache-case inscribed with his name: "Chief A...". He was one of the officiators at the *Ògún* sacrifice and indeed the one who had actually sacrificed the animal. I received from him firsthand information that the so-called herbalists or diviners have their own professional associations which provide them with identity cards and diplomas. The holder of such a diploma will display it in his home, much in the way of a university diploma, to enhance his status. Large numbers of people breathing the air of modern technological civilization still seek divinations and offer sacrifices to various gods, *Ògún*, for example, as the god having jurisdiction over iron, is regarded as the patron of motorists.

Modern Attitudes Towards Primal Forms

In trying to understand and evaluate the elements of primal world-views, one becomes aware of a number of traps to be avoided:

(*a*) *Uncritical underestimation, leading to indifference or contempt.* Fortunately, an increasing awareness of the maturity and wisdom of primal cultures has already initiated a tendency away from this supercilious reaction.

(*b*) *Equally uncritical admiration.* Some people, not least outsiders, develop an almost adolescent passion for all things primal. "Naturally living man" they say, "will react in this or that way. Let us re-discover the lost treasure, the lost sensitivity and spiritual experience." However, there is nothing to guarantee that the lost "treasure" is not just another human illusion, the passing of which we should have no reason to regret. This idealizing tendency can lull our discriminatory and selective powers to sleep.

A sober and correct attitude should keep equally clear of unquestioning acceptance, indifference or rejection, and be one of respect for those other dimensions of human life and history, which are revealed by primal world-views.

(*c*) *Uncritical differentiation.* It is often directly stated or indirectly implied that people living in the spheres of primal world-views are "different." By overemphasizing this being "different," we run the risk of overlooking the basic unity of human nature, which in turn may lead to other forms of racial discrimination. Whenever we admit that certain things, certain principles, certain beliefs, are unsuitable for us, but are, after all, quite good for *them,* we do in effect adopt very questionable anthropological criteria.

Many of these primal world-views were our own before they were superceded by subsequent reformulations. Why should others be expected to adhere to them for ever? Is that not a kind of derogatory discrimination too? In physical terms, the main functions of the human body are always the same despite existing differences in body build, color and facial features. To be sure, every person, and by extension, every family and every nation, have their particular inherited characteristics. But these differences are of secondary importance and by no means justify classifications into sealed anthropological compartments. Far more important is the unity of the human race.

Christian Rejection or Re-discovery of Primal Elements

These considerations are directly connected with the issues involved in the encounter between Christians and the people of primal world-views. With all due respect for the past, and for the wisdom and sensitivity of our brethren as expressed in their best creations which reflect the secret light of the image of God they carry in their beings, it is clear that "primal" is not "final." There is something essential they are entitled to receive from the Christian community.

(*a*) The cities and villages of Nigeria today throng with products of the West—cars, photographic equipment, radios, electric fans, etc. No one asks whether these constitute western influences and no one seems to be concerned whether or not such western products ought to be banned. When it comes to religion, on the other hand, the need to preserve the indigenous character may be strongly defended. Can a distinction be made between technical and spiritual culture? But again the universities have adopted western educational systems with amazing faithfulness. What is the particular element which is felt to conflict and jar with the local culture? This greater resistance in the area of religious beliefs and experiences is undoubtedly due to the deeper roots of these things in the human soul because of their intimate relationship with primal human functions. It should, then, be useful to investigate and define the latent selection criteria in order to arrive at those that should rightly apply. On which principles is one thing accepted and another rejected?

(*b*) This problem of selection criteria faces the Christians themselves with a critical question: Have we offered the people of primal world-views the best we have? Have we made available to them all of the twenty-century-old tradition of the Church, not least that of the first centuries when Christians lived in a comparable climate of primal world-views?

Or have missionaries only tried to transplant the Christianity and the problems of the western Europe of the 16th century onwards? Can it be true that, owing to these inadequacies, Christians from primal societies, as in Africa, were not given all the possibilities and all the material that would have enabled them to make an appropriate selection, and were therefore forced to seek to re-discover in their traditional religious rites some vital elements of the religious experience—such as the sense of total devotion, of being cut to the heart, *katanyxis,* of deep symbolism, or of participation of the whole person in worship? Were they offered all the wealth of the tradition of the first millennium of the Church ''extending from end to end of the *oikumene,* '' or were they presented only with a dry, moralizing type of Christianity?

Tragically, some of the new churches in Africa and Asia are unaware of the depth of Christian experience and quality of worship developed by the early indigenous churches of these continents. In some local African churches which have evolved from Protestant groups, a member of the Eastern Orthodox Church is conscious of a certain anxiety in such vital matters as Christian symbolism, participation of the total human being in worship, the desire to transcend the here and now by a spiritual elation and not merely with ideas. One gets a feeling that despite the excellent intentions of many missionaries, what was often achieved was a shrunken sort of religion reminiscent rather of a school, complete with school books and school events. And that readily explains the reaction of some Independent African churches with their spontaneous addition of a multitude of liturgical elements, such as incense, water sanctification, fasting, special vestments and clothing, exorcising oil, and their respect for profound spiritual experiences, schematically expressed by visions and other images—all of which elements have never been missing in the eastern liturgical experience, and which are close to the life of the churches developed in the early period in the triangle of Asia-Europe-Africa.

(*c*) I would not wish my reference to the liturgical experience of the Eastern Orthodox Church construed as an affirmation that everything in contemporary Orthodoxy is perfect, and that the only problem is how to offer it to the people of primal world-views! During my participation in the worship of some local Nigerian churches, I envied them some things: the wholehearted group participation, the ardent fervor and deep spiritual involvement of the community in prayer, the overwhelming sense of God's presence and guidance, the certainty of His protection, the healing power of prayer.

Many bespectacled European Christian leaders with their thick wise books and university degrees could learn a great deal from the religious passion for God and man of some African religious leaders who, with the sensitivity of oriental monks in matters of prayer, fasting and chastity, are amazingly effective in freeing their people from the webs of devilish powers. If we approach these communities with nothing but the ideas of a standardized European Christianity with its often mutilated spiritual experiences, we are bound to be critical of many things—even shocked.

The Ibadan Consultation and direct contact with traditional religious life have helped me to understand what I saw, for example, at the Cherubim and Seraphim indigenous church, Bar Beach, Lagos (where I was invited following the visit of their leader in Greece). Especially moving were their insistent invocation of the angels, their need for guidance through the mazes of their lives by the prophecies of some charismatic members of the community, and the fervor of the congregation in prayer for the salvation of the whole man and his delivery from his nightmares.

Many of these experiences imply indeed an enviable sensibility, the possession of an antenna which existed in the early Christian era, but which we have lost and must seek to regain. After all, what evidence is there that the rational western interpretations are more authentic than these people's existentialist interpretations and certainties? I believe in the possibility of a mutual offer of experience and mutual enrichment, for I am finally convinced that despite our many different cultures there is at the back of it all the essential unity of human nature. I doubt if there exists a civilization so great and self-sufficient that it has nothing to learn from other, even lesser, civilizations.

The Universal Relevance of Primal World-Views

At this point I would like to come back to what I said earlier concerning uncritical differentiation, with particular reference to the now much-discussed question of "indigenization." This concept of indigenization appeared first as a slogan of independence, to allow African or Asian Christians to express their religious experiences unrestricted by the limited western forms introduced by some missionaries. But is the so-called "indigenization" the solution? And how can such an indigenization be conceived at a time when the world tends towards a uniformity of life? The search of self-affirmation of a people's personality should not lead to isolationism.

In stressing the particular "essence" of separate peoples, it would be a mistake to weaken the sense of the "common essence" of mankind. Of course, the final forms will not be defined by just one, say the European, set of concepts. All cultures have something to contribute. The basic Christian doctrine of the Holy Trinity provides the theological infrastructure for the co-existence of a plurality of persons and of a common essence. The indigenization drive may reflect and highlight some common human aspects which have perhaps remained underdeveloped in European Christianity. The recruitment and mobilization of all the particular qualities and assets of a nation, its self-awareness and expression in worship, cannot be the end of the journey. It can only be another step toward the "new," "universal" man, who will embody the universal experience of the Church extending "from end to end of the *oikumene*" (St. Basil's Liturgy), from end to end of time.

A person, a local Christian community, should become the best they can be. But after that they should not remain closed unto themselves, unto what they are. They should open up creatively, spread, and participate in the sum total of human possibilities, in the sum total of the gifts of the Church under the guidance of the Holy Spirit. It is precisely this profounder and more essential search for the spiritual experiences of the whole mankind that will contribute to a more personal and more universal discovery of the "wholeness of human life."

Hindu Impressions of Christ and Christianity

Roger Hooker

An Anglican missionary-pastor of a congregation in Varanasi, India, lists here the impressions and evaluations of Christ and Christian churches which he has gathered from Hindu friends and magazines. Behind much of Hindu thinking, with no real distinction between history and legend, is the assumption that Mother India is the source of all the world's wisdom; so, for example, some claim that Jesus must have been taught in India. Hindus question Christian assertions about creation, the origin of evil, human freedom, and God's saving acts within history. Educated Hindus "commonly see Christianity as a philosophical system, yet as such it seems limited, intolerant and vastly inferior to what Hinduism has to offer." One problem in solving this situation is that there are relatively few good books written in Hindi to explain Christian faith and church history to Hindus. Roger Hooker, with the Church Missionary Society, worked in India from 1965 to 1978, and is now on the staff of Crowther Hall—the CMS training college—at Selly Oak Colleges, Birmingham, England. His article is reprinted from *New Fire* (no. 30, Spring 1977), which is published by the Society of Saint John the Evangelist, in Oxford, England.

What do Hindus know of Christ and Christianity? How do they respond to what they know? There are many possible answers to those questions. For example, in *The Acknowledged Christ of the Indian Renaissance* (SCM 1970), M. M. Thomas has described something of the impact made over the last century and a half on a number of important Indian thinkers who have written in English. Here, however, I attempt a much more local and contemporary answer. I limit myself to the city of Varanasi, which is where I live, and to Hindus whom I know personally, who know little if any English, and who think and speak in Hindi. I also refer to articles in contemporary Hindi magazines and newspapers.

As a student of Sanskrit I spend much of my time in the company of traditional pundits. These men normally have a profound grasp of their own subject but very little general knowledge. "Where was the Lord Christ born?" one of them once asked me. I told him. "So he was not a European?" he said with surprise. A Jain pundit was no less surprised to discover that Jesus' mother tongue was not English.

Hindus can sometimes make the same assumptions about Christians. A member of my congregation told me of Hindu reactions to his family when they first arrived in the city: "Our Hindu neighbours were amazed that my wife wore a *saree* and not a frock and that we both spoke Hindi."

It is universally believed that Christian missionaries make converts by offering gifts. "If I become a Christian will I have a motor scooter like you?" an office clerk once asked me. "If I become a Christian what advantages will I get?"— this was from an officer of the local CID. A Hindu friend once said to me: "Muslims make converts at the point of a sword, you people by gifts and inducements." In part this attitude springs from the fact that a Hindu is born and not made, and he thus finds it difficult if not impossible to understand how anyone could wish, as he sees it, to leave his ancestral religion and join another, for genuine reasons. When such a change is made it can therefore only be in the hope of material gain. Most Christians in India come from poor and outcaste groups. Material help offered by foreign missionaries who have been moved by Christian compassion at the plight of the poor is seen as something very different by a suspicious Hindu.

There is a widespread and growing popular belief that Jesus visited India in the so-called 'hidden years' before his ministry began, and that he sat at the feet of some Hindu saint

from whom he derived his teaching. I recently came across a
different version of this in a Hindi magazine article. Buddhism spread to Europe (sic) where it influenced the Essene
sect. Jesus was probably an Essene during the hidden years.
On the cross he did not die but only swooned, and then set off
for the east. He reached India and, said the article, according
to a manuscript discovered in a Tibetan monastery, sat at the
feet of Buddhists, Jains and Brahmins and studied their scriptures. Thus, "It is clear that Jesus Christ not only spent a long
time in India acquiring education, but also became a follower
of the Hindu *dharma*."

A refinement of this view was published in a local Hindu
daily paper on Christmas Day 1976. When a book establishing the above case was first published in the Marathi language, it was suppressed by the then British government of
India, for "How could they tolerate the idea that anyone
living under their rule should prove that the one whom they
worshipped was fundamentally Hindu or Indian?"

Two factors lie behind this kind of thinking: the first is
the Hindu assumption that Mother India is the source of all
the world's wisdom. Further, for the Hindu mind there is no
real distinction between history and legend. Hindus are very
ready to admit that Jesus was a great teacher—indeed the first
magazine to which I referred printed a large section of the
Sermon on the Mount as the first article in the same number—so Jesus must have got his teaching from India.

The second factor is the ambivalent relation between
church and empire which not unnaturally led Hindus, who
themselves make no distinction between religion and society,
to identify the two. An elderly Hindu friend once described to
me a conversation he had had many years previously with a
British missionary. The missionary asked why more people
did not come to hear him preach, to which my friend replied:
"Because you criticise Hinduism under the protection of
British bayonets." It is also fair to add that much criticism by
foreigners and even by missionaries was and still is no less
prejudiced and ill-informed than the articles which I have just
described.

I have several times been invited to address groups of

Hindu scholars in Hindi on aspects of Christianity. Sometimes these audiences have contained a number of Tibetan Buddhist monks for whom this has literally been their first encounter with Christianity. Some of the Hindus have also said: "We know nothing about this religion and want to learn." Though there is now plenty of material available in English about eastern religions, there are hardly any good books about Christianity written in Hindi for Hindus. Other members of these audiences are not wholly ignorant and may have read parts of the Bible in English or in Hindi.

These addresses are always followed by questions which afford valuable insights into the Hindu mind, into the impressions which my hearers have already gained of Christianity, and into their reaction to my own presentation.

The questions are of broadly three kinds. Some are of a mainly speculative nature. An address on the Christian doctrine of creation produced the following: "If God is the efficient cause of the world what is the material cause?" "If God is the creator then how did evil get into the world?" "Will God's plan (of which I had spoken) reach fulfilment within this world or beyond it?" "Do Christians believe in other forms of life beyond those which are visible to us such as men and animals?" "Is there life in other universes?"

These questions were all plain matter-of-fact requests for information. I suspect that behind them was the assumption that Christians claim that their scriptures and their doctrines provide knowledge which cannot be obtained by empirical methods. Until comparatively recent times most western Christians shared that assumption. It is still almost universally held in the intensely conservative Indian church. My theology, by contrast, is inductive. I fear my answers must have seemed hesitant or even evasive, for to me these were all profound questions where language must tremble on the edge of mystery. Also I had been at pains to point out that the biblical understanding of creation was a "projection" from the historical experience of the Hebrews and of the early church, but I failed to get this across; indeed, even well-informed Hindus very rarely appreciate the significance which history has for Christians.

The second type of question asks why Christianity makes man a sinner and the slave of God, both of which are taken to imply a limitation on human freedom. I would tentatively trace this to two sources. The first is the narrow and somewhat distorted interpretation of man and his sin which the church still presents. The second lies within Hinduism itself which finds the origin of man's predicament not in his sinfulness but in his ignorance. Further, in Hindi and Sanskrit the normal word for "free" means literally "under one's own control," while the word for "unfree" means "under the control of another." Thus a man can be described as one or the other but not as both. Paradox is an unfamiliar concept to the Hindu; such a phrase as "whose service is perfect freedom" is strictly meaningless. So the Christian God is seen as a potentate who restricts the liberty of man.

The third type of question has remained unspoken. My replies have frequently provoked the comment: "It is very enclosed." At the level of philosophy there are far more options open to a Hindu than to a Christian. To a Hindu our theology seems to bear a family resemblance to the theistic stream of his own tradition, but this represents only one of a large number of possible interpretations of the mystery of the universe. Thus, when we Christians claim that our view alone is the correct one, we appear to be narrow and intolerant.

This account of the impact of Christianity on contemporary Hindus in Varanasi is, of course, incomplete and impressionistic. I draw from it three provisional conclusions. The first is that although there has been a continuous Christian presence in this city since at least 1815, astonishingly little accurate information about Christianity has percolated through to the educated Hindu of today. Those who can speak and read English are better informed than those who do not, and the old generally know more than the young; yet in Varanasi today there has been no significant meeting between the Hindu and Christian mind. Partly this is because for many years national and expatriate Christians have devoted most of their time and energies to the maintenance of the church and its institutions rather than to meeting Hindus. Here, as in other countries, we have submitted too easily to the tyranny of what is immediately urgent at the expense of what is of long-term importance.

The second conclusion is a practical one. The church and the individual Christian must be, and must be seen to be, politically weak and vulnerable. All foreign missionaries now require a residential permit which is renewable every year by the Indian government. This is a positive symbol of such weakness. The church also needs to be much more Indian in its attitudes and *mores,* but it is not easy to see how this can be achieved. A respected church leader of outcaste origins once said to me: "The church is completely caught up in its institutions and is therefore unwilling and unable to experiment, but you must also remember that for us the customs of Western Christianity which we have adopted spell freedom. To adopt Hindu customs would be to return to the slavery from which the Gospel has delivered us." One should therefore not wonder that calls for indigenization—which usually come from missionaries—meet with little response. Yet this very situation gives a unique opportunity and responsibility to the foreign missionary, who, precisely because of his foreignness has access to Hindus whom his national colleagues cannot reach. As a Hindu pundit of mildly liberal views bluntly put it to me on a recent visit: "I can come and eat and talk with you, but not with Indian Christians who are all of low caste and became Christians to improve their position in society."

Third, educated Hindus commonly see Christianity as a philosophical system, yet as such it seems limited, intolerant and vastly inferior to what Hinduism has to offer. Can we present it instead as a pattern of interpretation which might open up for the Hindu new dimensions into the meaning of being human today? . . . A Christian who can humbly offer his or her faith as affording insights into our common perplexities is much more likely to gain a sympathetic hearing than one who can only repeat traditional assertions.

Proclaiming the Inner Christ of Hinduism

An Interview with Paul Sudhakar

Paul Sudhakar, a high-caste Menon from Kerala, South India, had been a Hindu until his Christian conversion in 1947. Three years later he left a government post to give his life completely to personal evangelism among educated Hindus. A layman with no formal theological education, he is a member of the Church of South India. He is not an employee of the church, but since 1950 has been a "faith missionary" to his fellow Hindus. Al Krass, a convert from Judaism and former missionary in Ghana, interviewed Sudhakar in March 1975. Sudhakar still maintains a Hindu philosophy, and believes that Christ is "the answer and hope of the Hindu religion." In conversations and public meetings with Hindus, he preaches that the Hindu reality of God finds its fulfillment in the historical Christ, the only Lord and Savior; but he presents this to the Hindu "in such a way that it will be a discovery for him, rather than [doing] all the thinking for him." The ideal Hindu conversion occurs when one is not so much converted *from*, as *to*—the Christ. Al Krass is Associate Editor of *The Other Side* magazine in Philadelphia, PA. His interview was published in *Beautiful Feet* (vol. 4, no. 4, June 1975), from the Office of Evangelism, United Church Board for World Ministries (475 Riverside Drive, New York, NY 10027).

Krass: Paul, who was responsible for your conversion?
Sudhakar: Another Hindu philosopher, Dr. Radhakrishnan, the former President of India. I was studying under

him as his private disciple and I was attracted to his philosophy. He gave me great interest and respect and admiration for Jesus Christ. When I became a Christian I didn't feel any break with Hinduism as such.

Krass: Is Hinduism not a religion?

Sudhakar: Hinduism can be a religion, but then it can turn into idolatry—or temples, polytheism, pantheism, etc. But there is a distinct Hindu philosophy that is in the Upanishads and the Vedas.

Krass: You maintain a Hindu philosophy?

Sudhakar: Yes, just as what you find today in Western theology is the marriage of the Christian-Jewish faith in Jesus Christ and Greek philosophy. I still maintain that I can hold on to the Hindu philosophy and interpret Jesus Christ.

Krass: Did Hindus and Christians accept this decision of yours and understand it?

Sudhakar: Hindus are accepting to a large extent, but my problem is with the Christian people, the Westernized Christian people. They are still sold out to all that Christianity has been told in the West and they think that Christology has ended.

Krass: And you believe there can be a Hindu doctrine of Christ?

Sudhakar: I believe there will be.

Krass: How do you go about your work? Where do you speak? in churches?

Sudhakar: Three or four churches join together in a city and arrange a big meeting where I speak to Hindus from the background of Hindu scriptures, showing that Christ is the answer and the hope of the Hindu religion. I put topics like "The Bhagavad Gita and the Gospel" or "The Upanishads and the Gospel." So just for the curiosity of what I'm going to do, whether I'm comparing or contrasting, Hindus come.

Krass: Do you have large attendances?

Sudhakar: Some places I get only small groups, like 100–200, but in many places I get 3,000–4,000. They come regularly for four, five days; in one place they came for one full week.

Krass: What response do you get?

Sudhakar: They listen, they agree, and the balance has to be done by the church.

Krass: Why is it that Hindus can so easily agree with what you teach?

Sudhakar: Hinduism is tolerant, but Hindus are intolerant of the exclusiveness of the Christian preacher.

Krass: What are some of the things that Christian preachers say which offend the sense of universality of the Hindu?

Sudhakar: Hindu tolerance is based upon a philosophical principle that truth is never the monopoly of one religion, that there are different ways of knowing truth, that God can be known in many ways. Then when a Christian preacher comes and says that Jesus is the only Savior, Jesus is the only Lord, Hindus think that he is bigoted, narrow-minded, arrogant, and he's just selling his goods.

Krass: But don't you believe that Jesus is the only Lord?

Sudhakar: Jesus is the only Lord and Savior; but it all depends upon how you tell it. If you want to present Jesus as the only Savior you must work up to your position as a conclusion. Don't introduce this point as a propositional statement to fling upon him. Let him arrive at his own conclusions. But preach in such a way that he will realize it, that it will be a discovery for him, rather than that you'll do all the thinking for him.

Krass: Many young people in our country have adopted a very tolerant view of religion. Some of them are following in the various Hare Krishna groups. I heard one young woman say to me that she could accept Jesus Christ as Lord but she would accept Krishna as lord also. Is this the position you would feel Hindus could come to?

Sudhakar: No, not at all. I think when you talk of your country, they do it because they have not understood Hinduism, nor even Christianity; they have only a superficial knowledge. They must be tired of what they find in the denominational churches, of their form and ceremony, something outward—they have not found the power of God. When they turn to the Hare Krishna movement, they don't know what they mean by it. They accept some superficial experiences and mistake them for mysticism. But when the Hindu says Krishna (I mean the educated Hindu, not the average Hindu) he knows what it means, because there is a scripture for him; especially there is a *Gita,* and if he understands what he means by Krishna, then he follows the *Gita.*

Krass: Now, as you read the *Gita,* do you understand Krishna as presented in the *Gita* as the Lord in the same way in which Jesus is presented in the Scriptures of the Christian faith?

Sudhakar: If you ask me, frankly, the *Gita's* Krishna is the Lord and the only Savior.

Krass: Then how do you deal with that when you talk to an audience of Hindus?

Sudhakar: You have to convince the Hindu and open his eyes to point out who Krishna was. There are so many ways in which Hindus are looking at Krishna, just as it is with your people. They say Krishna without knowing where he lived, who he was, whether the story about Krishna is really historical, whether the things that are told about him are really reliable. In other words, if the type of New Testament criticism (higher criticism and form and textual criticism), if this criticism that has gone into the New Testament, if one-hundredth of that goes into the Hindu scriptures, 99% of the gods and goddesses of Hinduism will disappear.

Krass: That was President Radhakrishnan's approach, wasn't it?

Sudhakar: Yes.

Krass: And so you apply textual criticism to the *Gita* and show that Krishna is not really a historical being?

Sudhakar: Something similar to that. It's making an average Hindu into a real Hindu.

Krass: Now what would a real Hindu be by your understanding?

Sudhakar: A real Hindu is someone who is not following mythological stories—which in Hinduism are just like the Greek legends. We must work to bring the Hindu beyond those mythological stories to the Upanishads and the Vedas, where God is only explained in terms of Ishvira and Brahma. No names are even given to him. And then to the *Gita.* In the

Gita you'll find a Krishna, but that Krishna is only symbolical, allegorical, mystical—but not historical. Maybe a historical Krishna may have existed, but that has nothing to do with the Krishna of the *Gita*. So you have to say that what is written in the *Gita* is true, that Krishna is only the symbolical expression of the Hindu reality of God, and *that* Hindu reality of God finds its fulfillment in the historical Christ.

Krass: What are the basic truths in the legends about Krishna?

Sudhakar: He is a personal god. He is a loving god. He is a god who forgives people. He is a god of grace, a god who is willing to reveal himself to anybody who comes to him, a god who is dear and near to everyone, so close! And I think that's the reason why Krishna of all the Hindu pantheon has become the most popular deity in Hinduism.

Krass: And now what you say to Hindus is, this one who is symbolically presented as Krishna has really come in the form of Jesus Christ?

Sudhakar: Jesus Christ, the Word that became flesh. In other words Hinduism has the word and Christianity is the Word become flesh. I won't enter into the argument that Hinduism is speculation and Christianity is revelation. I believe that God has revealed himself to Hindus also. Maybe a different kind of revelation. In the Jewish revelation, in the Old Testament, it may be what we call revelation through events in history. In the New Testament it is revelation through a person that is God who became man, Jesus. But in Hinduism we have revelation through philosophy—I even see philosophy as a type of revelation. I don't like to distinguish between philosophy, reason, and revelation. It is very difficult to find the dividing line between reason and revelation. Even in revelation people use reason and they reason out revelation.

Krass: Do you hope the Hindu will be converted in the traditional sense?

Sudhakar: I don't think he'll become converted in the traditional sense (in which the prodigal came back and said, 'Father, I have sinned'). He may not accept all of the doctrine of atonement, but he will come to Christ and, having come to

Christ, when he looks back upon himself he may realize he's a sinner.

Krass: What are some of the ways in which you see that Hindus have been converted in the past?

Sudhakar: There are three types of conversion that I find. One is the type of convert who, though formerly a Hindu, now finds nothing in Hinduism. He rejects it 100%. He thinks that idolatry is wrong, the caste system is wrong, all the Hindu gods and goddesses are wrong. He makes a complete break and becomes a Christian. But he doesn't become a Christian in the biblical sense of the word. He becomes a denominational Christian. He becomes more denominational-minded than even the denomination into which he has come! In other words, he is more of a liability to the church.

The second type is an individualist. He has come to Christ because of the vacuum in his heart. He feels the need of Jesus Christ. He doesn't find anything in Hinduism and so he comes. But when he comes to Christianity, already he has come broken away from Hinduism, and he yearns for fellowship. But then his culture—his former culture—and the Christian community and culture into which he has come are so different. So he cannot adjust. So he walks a lonely road. Then he becomes an individualist. He doesn't belong to any church. Sometimes in extreme cases he forms his own denomination and, though he's coming to Jesus Christ the Lord of the world, he ends up with his own lord.

Krass: And you say that there is a third type of conversion?

Sudhakar: Yes, there is a third type of conversion where he is not converted so much *from* but he's converted *to*. He has no break with Hinduism. He has not felt as if he has broken away from Hinduism. And so when he looks back there is no break. There is no crisis, there is no tension in him when he comes to Christ. So when he comes to Christianity also, to the Christian church, he doesn't come with tension, he comes as a full person. Then he begins to contribute to the accumulated knowledge of the Christian church.

That third type is the ideal conversion. And if this type of conversion is coming along in India, I am sure the biggest prejudice of Hindus towards Christianity will go away.

Krass: And that Hinduism will become a very different thing? It will become filled in Christ?

Sudhakar: I believe in that case, instead of the Hindu getting converted to Christ, Hinduism itself will be converted.

Krass: And that's your hope?

Sudhakar: That's my hope—more than my hope, my conviction!

Conversion:
An Asian Woman's Experience

Marianne Katoppo

The author—a theology graduate, free-lance journalist, and novelist—comes from the Minahassa region of Indonesia. Descendant of a tribal priestess, she describes the ancient religion there, the 19th-century evangelization by German Pietists, and today's social situation in her native area which is one of Indonesia's wealthiest, and 99 percent Christian. She ponders that "we [have] somehow substituted technology and GNP [Gross National Product] for the tribal gods," and today offer a different variety of human sacrifices "to the anti-god of an ever-increasing GNP." The freedom that is of Christian conversion today "is not freedom from the tribal gods—trees, stones, mountains, cosmic forces of the past, but freedom from the modern gods—money, hedonism, systems, and structures that enslave people today." Ms. Katoppo is now working with the Gossner Mission in Mainz, West Germany. Her article, which she subtitles "From Tribal Priestess to Social Critic," was published in the *International Review of Mission*, a quarterly journal of the World Council of Churches in Geneva, Switzerland (vol. 67, no. 270, April 1979).

The Tribal Priestess

One of my great-great-grandmothers was a tribal priestess. Actually, that is somewhat of an understatement. In my native region of the Minahassa (North Sulawesi, Indonesia) the four major tribes were very closely related to each other ethnically, linguistically and culturally. They were all descendants of *Luminuüt*, the great mother who divided the land at Watu Pinawetengan (The Stone of Division), giving each tribe a fair share.

Each tribe has a great many priests, ranging from hunters to those who communicated directly with the *opo*, i.e. the ancestors (who were the tribal gods). Only one tribe—the Tontemboan—believed in the ordination of women and reserved the office of priesthood exclusively for women.

Among those priestesses, there was one who was the *Walian Wangko*, the *Priestess Supreme*. She was a figure of great authority and power. Priests of other tribes submitted to her, and chieftains dared not take any steps without consulting her. Such a one, then, was my maternal grandmother's grandmother.

We do not even know her real name, the name given to her by her own people. We only know the name given to her by Schwarz, that indefatigable East German Pietist, when he finally succeeded in baptizing her. He called her Lydia. She had resisted conversion until late in life for she belonged to the fiercely proud mountain people, who tolerate no intrusion.

Her world was that of ancestor worship to ensure cosmic balance. Head-hunting and human sacrifice were part of this, *not* primarily because of a lust for blood, but because this was what the ancestors demanded. Human sacrifice—usually captives from other tribes—was a salvific ritual in which the whole community participated. The beautiful *kulintang* (bamboo xylophone) music was originally intended to accompany the stabs of the priest's knife.

Marriage, with persons moving from one clan to another, could seriously upset the cosmic balance. Therefore, one had to try to make amends and restore the balance through gifts of a high mystical content, such as human heads.

Cannibalism was also practiced in order to absorb the qualities and virtues of the victim, usually an enemy.

There was not a single act in Lydia's world which was not directly rooted in or related to her religious beliefs. There was no compartmentalization of "religious" from "secular" life; nor was one subordinated to the other.

The Evangelization of the Minahassa

In the coastal regions of the Minahassa, such as the cities of Manado and Amurang, Christianity was introduced by the Portuguese in the 16th century, surviving after a fashion until Riedel and Schwarz, "the Apostles of the Minahassa," arrived in 1831.

They were working class Pietists from Eastern Germany, sent by the Dutch Missionary Society. There was a great deal of work for them to do: Riedel in Tondano in the north, Schwarz operating from Langowan on the southwestern side of the lake. Schwarz used to ride his horse far into the deep south, to places where no white person had ever ventured before.

This took great personal courage. Although the Minahassa chieftains had signed a treaty with the Dutch some fifty years before, giving their solemn word that they would "henceforward desist from the abominable practices of cannibalism and headhunting," this treaty—as indeed so many others—was by no means a guarantee for one's personal safety. It was as late as the 1850's that Linemann remarked in the Dutch mission journal, *Mededeelingen vanwege het Nederlandsche Zendeling Genootschap (MNZG)*, that the Minahassa had become a safe place to travel.

I think it was Schwarz's courage that impressed Lydia as well as his sincerity. He inculturated himself with the people by marrying a "native" woman, a fact referred to with some horror by Ida Pfeiffer in her travelogue. Actually, Mrs. Schwarz was Eurasian.

Many Minahassan women, besides Lydia, resisted Christianization. Often they were the tribal priestesses, who stood to lose everything by adopting the "Western" faith. It was not an appealing prospect to give up one's position of authority and power in order to be relegated to the position of *hausfrau*. The *MNZG* records cases of women throwing their husbands out of the house for having converted to Christianity.

On the other hand, once they had become Christian, women were the most ardent supporters of the Church. The *MNZG* also records that women personally lugged timber to the church-site in Tomohon, putting to shame the men who were afraid to act against the local authority's orders.

Lydia saw the inconceivable happen: her world was changing, yet it did not fall apart. Her values were being proved false; she had to relinquish the power, which at any rate was already slipping from her.

Did she, in her turn, experience the liberation of so many others of her people: the joy, in being set free from the inexorable claims of the ancestors, in being persons in the sight of God instead of units in the cosmic make-up of the universe?

I think she did; otherwise she would never have let herself be baptized. She saw the words of Schwarz come true. She knew him to be a person of great courage and sincerity: a *do-er*, not just a *preach-er*. They had great respect for one another, which is evident in the name he gave her: Lydia (Acts 16).

Since Lydia's day, the Minahassa has become one of the acceptedly Christian regions of Indonesia. The population is 99% Christian, the remaining 1% are migrants or settlers from other regions. Education has been one of its most important assets. Illiteracy is virtually unknown. The first school for girls, *de Christelijke Meisjesschool,* was opened in 1881, when Kartini who is often mistakenly called "the pioneer of women's education in *Indonesia*" was barely two years old in far-away *Java!*

A Social Critique of the Minahassa Today

In the past it was copra. Today it is cloves. The Minahassa has always been one of the most wealthy regions in Indonesia. Last year its GNP [Gross National Product] was estimated to be US $600 [per capita], almost three times that of the rest of Indonesia (US $250).

Last year I went to see Schwarz's grave in Langowan. Barring church historians, very few people in the Minahassa today are aware of the contributions of either Riedel or Schwarz to their present affluence.

The road from Sam Ratulangie Airport in the north into the capital city of Manado displays a fair share of statues erected to commemorate cultural or political heroes and heroines. As one then follows the road up into the mountains, one realizes that the Minahassans like this kind of monument. There are even statues to legendary *opo* (the tribal gods).

In Langowan, I found Schwarz's grave in a corner of a plot now used as a football-field, right in the center of the city. The cross was partly broken, the stone slab invisible because the whole was overgrown by weeds. People had also taken advantage of the comparative seclusion afforded by the tall weeds to defecate there.

I turned away, unable to control the tears of anger that sprang into my eyes. The religion of my people attached great importance to the veneration of ancestors. In a way, Schwarz was a spiritual ancestor, yet how shamefully he was treated!

I know that it would not have been important to him, for he worked for the kingdom of God, not for his own personal glory. But would he have recognized the kingdom of God in the high literacy rate and the material prosperity of the Minahassa today?

My mother recalls that the house of her grandfather (Lydia's son) was adorned with human heads, which were only taken down after he died. The mere sight of them made her shudder, as they would many of us.

Yet the Foreign Correspondents' Club in Hong Kong, for example, a fashionable restaurant, which erudite and civilized people frequent, boasts of a wall of photographs at its entrance which are only slightly less unsettling than human heads. They are award-winning photographs, almost life-size. Nearly every single one of them portrays a violent death: a murder, a suicide. The best-known is probably that of the Buddist monk burning himself to death. The photos are not known to affect the appetite of the correspondents or their guests.

Lydia believed human sacrifices were necessary in order to maintain cosmic balance. The *opo*, as guardians of the tribe's welfare, had to be placated.

Returning from Langowan to the Minahassan Church Synod's Office in Tomohon, we drove past mountain-slopes verdant with cloves. Tomohon's main road was jammed with cars, buses, horse-carriages and other means of transportation, linking Tomohon with the other cities of the Minahassa. Within Tomohon itself, of course, one could walk. Yet many preferred to take the car.

I could not help thinking that we had somehow substituted technology and GNP for the tribal gods. Coconut plantations have to make way for industrial plants. Fishing-villages disappear in the face of luxury hotels. The sensual fertility feasts of old have given way to the prostitution racket. Pollution and consumerism are the order of the day.

The small farmers or fishing villagers, the prostitute and the cheap laborer, are they not human sacrifices we offer to the anti-god of an ever-increasing GNP?

Conversion in my case is not marching down the streets shouting "Halleluia!" at the top of my voice. Rather, it is consistently saying "No!" to the anti-god who demands these human sacrifices, who ruthlessly reduces living human beings to so many factors making up a higher GNP.

Conversion means, for example, drinking home-grown tea, instead of trans-nationally produced soft drinks. Wearing native *batiks*, instead of imported fabrics. Using locally-made sandals, instead of Kickers or Bally shoes purchased in Hong Kong or Rome.

Conversion means being constantly aware that we are because of what we *are*, not what we *have;* that, in relinquishing power, we demonstrate our authority, i.e. competence to communicate freedom.[1]

This freedom we communicate is not freedom from the tribal gods—trees, stones, mountains, cosmic forces of the past, but freedom from the modern gods—money, hedonism, systems and structures that enslave people today.

It is a sin to sacrifice even a few in order to serve the mode of existence of the majority. To turn from this, and to turn to the Living God, in whose sight every person is precious, that is conversion.

NOTE

1. Aloysius Pieris S. J., "Towards an Asian Theology of Liberation: Some Religio-Cultural Guidelines." Paper presented at Asian Theological Conference, Holy Family Convent, Wennapuwa, Sri Lanka, 7–20 January 1979.

The Real Threat of the Moonies

Harvey Cox

The Holy Spirit Association for the Unification of World Christianity—commonly known as the Unification Church, and its members popularly called Moonies by non-members—offers a genuine theological challenge, according to Harvey Cox, who teaches at Harvard Divinity School. The Unification's challenge comes at three levels: (1) going beyond "the particularism of historical Christianity" to a higher stage of spiritual development which combines the great religious traditions into one. What is the Christian response to global religious pluralism? (2) Bridging the modern dichotomy between religion and science. Recent Christian theology has turned toward religious experience and social issues but "has left the vital issue of the relation between religion and science relatively unattended." (3) The vision of a new world order guided in its economic and cultural life by religious teachings. Is the Unification's appeal "a reflection of the death of social action in churches and synagogues and the failure of theology to provide a credible basis for the struggle for the Kingdom'"? Cox offers his reflections and questions after attending a long weekend workshop sponsored by the Unification Church. He concludes: "Here is a movement which manages to combine religious universalism, pentecostal immediacy, a warmly supportive 'family' and a program for allegedly building the Kingdom of God on earth. Such a potent admixture cannot be dismissed lightly." One of Harvey Cox's more recent books is *Turning East: The Promise and Peril of the New Orientalism* (New York: Simon and Schuster, 1977). This article first appeared in *Christianity and Crisis* (537 W. 121st St.,

New York, NY 10027), November 14, 1977, and is reprinted with permission.

The Boston Headquarters of the Unification Church is an elaborately constructed old mansion on Beacon Hill, occupied during the Gilded Age by the family of the founder of the Jordan Marsh department store. From its steep windows and grilled balconies the members of the Reverend Sun Myung Moon's organization can gaze at a plaque erected on the Common in 1930 during the administration of the late Mayor James Michael Curley to commemorate the 300th anniversary of the founding of the City of Boston. The plaque carries part of the famous sermon of Governor John Winthrop, preached on board the *Arabella* just before landing, in which he declared the settlers had been called by God to "build a city set upon a hill," a new commonwealth which, under God's providence, would establish his righteous reign in the virgin wilderness.

There is something singularly appropriate about this juxtaposition, for in the Unification Church an old idea that both Winthrop and Curley believed in their own different ways has returned like the Ghost of Christmas Past. The idea is simply that God has a special purpose in mind for America, and that if America misses its destiny, it will be an affront to the very nature of God. For Winthrop this providential vision was derived from a stoutly Calvinistic belief that God's hand had guided the settlers to the new world. For Curley it was a hope, sprung no doubt from his Catholic parish and parochial school training, as well as from his own experience as an Irish-American, that America should be the place where what he called "the newer races" would find a place in the sun. That badly battered idea, called by some the "American civil religion" and recently seen to be faltering, is back again in a surprising new form in the teaching of Moon, a former Calvinist and a member of what Curley would surely have thought of as one of his "newer races."

Earlier this fall I attended one of those notorious Moonie weekend workshops, held in this headquarters building. Friends and family bade me farewell, some joking about how long they should wait before dispatching a deprogrammer, others voicing mild or serious misgivings about whether I should get involved with such people. My reason for wanting to go was mainly curiosity. I teach one course at Harvard on new religious movements and another on heresy, and the Moonie movement seemed to be a fine example of both. Also, I had heard and read a lot about the Reverend Moon, his Unification Church and the weekend workshops where innocent young post-adolescents were allegedly brainwashed into docile robots. I had done a lot to oppose the deprogrammers. Now I wanted to see for myself; so I called the local Unification Church headquarters and registered for a weekend.

The workshop began with a supper of hamburger and noodles. While we ate, some of the brothers and sisters in the "family" sang several songs. I noticed a high proportion of young people of Oriental background (almost all Japanese, it turned out) among the singers and hosts. Later, when the 23 people who had gathered introduced themselves, we discovered that we represented seven different countries including Germany, Kenya, Japan, England and Jamaica. Most of the people were already members. Only about eight were new recruits. One workshop attender was a sympathetic mother whose son had joined the church a few years before and who had joined it herself recently. The master of ceremonies was a lively, sharply dressed, young Japanese who first introduced a sextet and then a sister who sang "Green Fields." Then he himself sang the theme song from *Exodus*. After a few more songs sung by the whole group, some sisters emerged from the kitchen carrying trays of banana splits.

Uniting Religion and Science

While we ate, the director of the center, an Irish-American, gave a lecture on the Divine Principle. His approach was cheerful, confident and articulate. He explained that this lecture was "only a taste," a sample designed to persuade those still undecided to attend the workshop which was then beginning. (Only later did I learn what a small taste his lecture was and how gigantic a full helping can be.) His main argument seemed to be that we can no longer perpetuate the division between science and religion, but that religion must be brought up to date in order to meet the intellectual and social challenges of the modern world. He added that although in some movements one goes off to meditate alone in order to meet the divine, here, since people are created in the image of God, we meet the divine by meeting each other. He did not ask for questions and none were asked. After a few more songs we were asked to get to bed—it was already 11:45—and to be up for group exercise at 7 a.m. The men and women were ushered off to different floors.

At 7 a.m. the chords of a Bach fugue swelled through the building and the participants tumbled out onto the linoleum floor of a large room on the second floor to exercise. After 20 minutes of stretching, we breakfasted on orange juice, fried eggs, sliced tomatoes and toasted rolls. The morning session began at about 9:30 with more songs led by the energetic MC. Then the director began another lecture on the Divine Principle.

The lecture was unbelievably complex, elaborate and long. After an hour and 20 minutes my head began to ache; my buttocks had already gone numb. We had heard about the negative and positive valences of atoms and molecules; the feminine and masculine aspects of plants and animals; the need for a new development in Christianity; the pattern of Creation-Fall-Restoration-Last Days-Resurrection; the duality of God's being; the similarities and differences between Oriental philosophy and the Divine Principle. Were people actually listening? Although they seemed to be, I could not help wondering where minds were wandering. When I began to look a little tired after nearly two hours of the lecture, the Japanese woman seated next to me smiled and began to pound lightly on the back of my neck and massage my shoulders, apparently in a sisterly effort to keep alert.

At about noon, after I had almost given up hope that the lecture would ever end, the director announced a coffee break (*not* lunch) after which the "second part of the lecture" would begin.

We were back in the lecture room by 12:30 and at 2:30 the lecturer was still going strong. My stomach was screaming for lunch. I wondered how people were bearing it. Long before this, my own students would have reminded me that we had gone on far too long. The "Four Position Foundation," the "Three Blessings," the relation of the spiritual to the physical world, the reasons for the failure of Christianity to bring in the Kingdom of God, the need to establish a newly perfected family—it all poured out in cascades of words, analogies, biblical quotations and scientific allusions. I wondered what had ever happened to the "brainwashing," the group pressures, the subtle indoctrination. To me it seemed like a clear example of philosophical overkill. At first I was totally unable to recognize what the appeal could possibly be.

But appeal there is—and it is in large measure a theological-intellectual one at that. In his book, *Sun Myung Moon and the Unification Church*, Frederick Sontag has tried to discern what the appeal is. In order to do so he spent an entire year traveling and studying the Unification Church in Europe, the US and the Orient. His book is almost obsessively "objective," setting forth the roots of the Moon movement in Korea, its amazing growth in Japan, Europe and America, the teachings of the Divine Principle, the brainwashing and deprogramming controversy and the future prospects of the movement. Sontag relies very heavily— perhaps too much so—on interviews with a large number of church members, including early disciples in Korea. His book also includes a lengthy interview with the Reverend Moon. It does not probe very deeply beneath the replies.

What Sontag glaringly leaves out is any reference to the cloud of political accusations that have hung over Moon almost since his arrival in the US. Some readers will find this to be a fatal flaw in the book. I did not, however. There is very little hard evidence to be found, and at the time Sontag wrote the book the Fraser Committee's investigations of South Korean influence peddling (which, in any case, have not yet turned up much on Moon) had not even begun.

A Three-Tiered Challenge

Whether or not these investigations turn up evidence about Moon himself, I do not believe the whole movement is merely a political front. In fact, I believe some of the liberal critics of the Moon movement do us all a great disservice by seeing the Moonies *entirely* in terms of a political threat (which they may in fact be), thus failing to come to terms with the genuine *theological* challenge the movement poses. I think this theological challenge comes at three levels, no one of which can be dealt with by attempting to reduce the appeal of Unification to behavioral control or political subterfuge. These three levels are: (1) Unification's bid to transcend the particularism of historical Christianity and combine the great religious traditions into one; (2) Its programmatic effort to go beyond the dichotomy between religion and science; and (3) Its vision of a *novus ordo seculorum* guided in its economic and cultural life by religious teachings.

(1) *Beyond traditional Christianity.* One of the things about the Unification Church which most confuses and angers traditional Christians is that it claims to be a Christian church—thus meriting membership in the National Council of Churches—and at the same time a movement which goes beyond Christianity to a higher stage of spiritual development, a stage it claims the human race is now ready for. This is not a new challenge. Mormons, Christian Scientists and others have made it in the past. But the threat it poses to almost all present forms of theology is a formidable one. The question, simply put, is: Can there be new revelations, or are all such revelations *ipso facto* heretical? Pastor John Robinson in his farewell sermon to the Pilgrims declared that "God has yet new light to break forth his Holy Word." The underlying question of what "new light" is and how it relates to the "Holy Word" has never been solved. Catholics have generally been a bit more open to progressive revelations than have strictly *schriftmassig* Protestants. Witness the evolution of Marian devotion and the revelations at Lourdes and Fatima. But Christians who emphasize the Holy Spirit more than either Catholics or Protestants do have tended to be even

more open to religious ideas not derived solely from the original revelation. Lamentably, the failure of orthodox theology to deal with the claims of the Unification Church betokens a larger puzzlement about the independent churches of Africa and the burgeoning Pentecostal movements. Maybe that is why the National Council of Churches' recent critique of the Divine Principle sounds so implausible at many points. At least the Moonies, performing the historic function of heresies, have forced the NCC to make its theology a bit more explicit. The problem is: Now that it's explicit, how adequate is it?

I have no doubt that at the core of Unification's appeal to many young people is its claim to permit them to remain Christian, but to subsume the particularity of Christianity in a larger and more comprehensive world faith. Moon's teaching combines such characteristic Oriental elements as Yin and Yang, a kind of modified version of karma called "indemnity," the role of the guru and—especially—the centrality of the family in transmitting a spiritual tradition. The volumes of Dr. Yung Oon Kim, the principal theologian of the movement, deal in a fundamentally sympathetic way with the major spiritual traditions of the world. In the research I did for *Turning East* I ran across hundreds of young people who wanted to be religious, even Christian, but who felt both attracted by Oriental ideas and practices and at the same time confused by the bewildering plethora of religious claims around them.

I do not believe Christian theology can continue to dodge this challenge of global religious pluralism much longer. Unification theology is surely not the answer, but until Christian theology comes up with a religious vision that transcends the particularism (if not parochialism) by which it is currently harnessed, nothing is to be gained by condemning Unification thought, because it tries to cope with one of the major facts of life in the late 20th century: global religious pluralism.

(2) *Beyond the conflict between religion and science.* Why did two dozen reasonably intelligent people, including a nuclear engineer from MIT and a graduate fellow in physics from Harvard, sit through those interminable lectures at the

weekend workshop I attended? I think the reason is that the Divine Principle was presented not just as an authoritative religious teaching but as a system of ideas substantiated by modern science. Time after time I was reminded of the books of Teilhard de Chardin. Many of the ideas are similar: a frank acceptance of evolution, a fascination with the "inside" and the "outside" of all phenomena (called "sung sang" and "hyung sang" in Moon's theology), the notion that we stand today at a crucial turning point in the unfolding of human consciousness.

Dubious Analogies

As the lectures proceeded, the appeals to science came less frequently, and there was even an occasional tendency to resort to proof-texting. I am not saying the appeal to science was persuasive. It was not, at least not to me, although I do not have much scientific training. Also, the science-oriented people present seemed quite unsophisticated in the problems related to the analogical applications of biological or chemical theories to other fields. Consequently they seemed more persuaded by the lectures th' . I thought they should be. Still it made me wonder about l ow much theology has ducked the issue of scientific reasoning recently by accepting this division of realms, while many young people want to find a single holistic approach to all questions. In any case, the lecturer continually stressed the need to bring religion and science back together, and his listeners obviously liked the idea and believed it would be possible if worked at assiduously enough.

This aspect of Moon's teaching explains to some extent why he is willing to expend such huge amounts of time and money on the annual International Conference on the Unity of Science which is scheduled to take place this year in San Francisco and will concentrate on the "search for absolute values." The roster of this year's conference includes the usual number of Nobel laureates, as well as one prominent Marxist philosopher, Adam Schaff. I have been invited to attend this controversial and lushly arranged gathering nearly every year since its inception and have always turned it down, in part because like many others I have been suspicious of its actual intent. As I have looked into the Moon movement more carefully, however—and this observation is sustained by Sontag's more thorough study—I have come to believe that the Science Conference, though it obviously produces a large public relations pay-off, is not just a front or a subterfuge. Moon and his followers devoutly believe that science, ethics and religion must be brought back together. Although I have alerted uninformed colleagues in the past about the sponsorship of the conference and have urged them not to go unless they knew what they were doing, it seems to me improbable that it is mere window dressing.

In fact, reading this year's program makes me wonder why churches are not sponsoring more conversations on similar themes. Theologians may believe they have left the battle between science and theology far behind, but many young people—and many, many scientists—do not believe it at all. The turn of recent theology toward religious experience on the one hand, and social issues on the other, has left the vital issue of the relation between theology and science relatively unattended. Only the process theologians are pursuing it with much vigor. If the Moonie attempt to bridge the gap seems inept and heavy-handed, it should receive at least some credit for making the try. The only way to refute it is to do it better.

(3) *Spiritually guided secular order*. The critics of the Moonies are entirely right when they describe it as a political movement. Unification thought insists that its most important contribution is the idea of the "restoration" of God's original plan and the building of the Heavenly Kingdom on earth. It is a "social gospel" with a vengeance, based on a millenarian assurance that we are now living in the last days and a firm conviction that the Messiah will return when human beings have done their part to prepare the way. In Moon's theology the key institution in the transformation of any society is the *family*, since it forms the link between the individual and the larger institutions of a culture. Moonies believe that by purifying themselves and building new and holy families they are contributing to the reform of the whole. The restoration then proceeds to clan, tribe, nation and the world.

The question is, of course, about the ideological content

of the Unification ''social gospel'' and the theory of social change underlying its teaching. Here Moon makes no secret of his position. He is a militant anti-communist, a South Korean patriot who avidly defended Richard Nixon and a man who has publicly stated that one of his main reasons for coming to the US is to warn us about the Red Menace. Readers of the Unification Church's daily newspaper, *The News World,* can hardly miss its right-wing slant, its fondness for Ronald Reagan and its tendency to support conservative causes. On the weekend I was at the workshop the newspaper carried a letter to the editor demanding Carter's impeachment because of his pro-communist policies, and columns by such predictables as Michael Novak (supporting capital punishment) and Phyllis Schafly (denouncing the Panama Canal ''giveway''). Another Moon-sponsored publication, *The Rising Tide,* is even more vehemently right-wing. The August 1977 issue featured a front-page photo and article on Dr. Fred Schwartz, director of the Christian Anti-Communist Crusade. The cartoon depicted North Korean soldiers helping to get an American soldier out of Korea. The publisher of *The Rising Tide* is Neil A. Salonen, who is also president of the Unification Church of America.

''True Socialism''

Admittedly, this does not seem a very promising social gospel. My own experience with the Unification Church, however, suggests that its political profile may be a bit more complex than these facts suggest. Remember that Ted Patrick, the famous deprogrammer, made his original case against the Moonies by insisting that they represented a communist plot to subvert the youth of America. The lecturer at the workshop I attended frequently referred to capitalism as an example of the institutionalized selfishness which the Divine Principle is designed to eradicate. (His comment on communism: It's better than capitalism ''in principle'' since it looks to the whole rather than the individual, but its advocates have used ''wrong methods'' to introduce it, i.e., force.) The lecturer often used the term ''true socialism'' to describe the coming Kingdom of God on earth. The workshop attenders I talked to did not appear to be devout anti-communists. They seemed politically naive and not very well informed. A lovely African Moonie woman told me that although she came from Kenya, she actually preferred the "African socialism" of Tanzania as a more ideal social order. The main political errors of the Moonies are confusion, ignorance and innocence. Like most mainstream Americans, they are against communism and pornography, for the family and God. Making all the connections is left to someone else.

The Moon movement has been accused of being fascist or proto-fascist. Since these terms are often used very loosely, it is hard to be sure just what the accusation means. If it refers to avid anti-communism, an authoritarian ethos and a blatant kind of patriotism, then those ingredients are surely there. But there are other parts of the Moon organization and ideology which do not fit into any recognizable profile of "fascism." Moon himself says the two Americans he admires most are George Washington and Martin Luther King, Jr., one because he brought freedom to America, the other because he wanted to make America a place where all colors and nationalities could unite to form a world culture. The "God Bless America Rally" in Washington in 1976 ended with a tableau including a living Statue of Liberty—who was black. Unification thought is passionately anti-racist. Many of the marriages the leaders arrange among the members are across Oriental-Occidental lines, symbolizing the coming unification of East and West. A favorite Unification hymn puts it this way:

> Hope of a New Age is the power of the world
> Song of establishing the true ideal
> Resounding all over the world
> Eastern and Western together hand in hand
> Let us accomplish a united world.

The real political challenge of the Moonies is not, I believe, that they are a proto-fascist movement or a secret part of a vast right-wing conspiracy. Those would be relatively easy to deal with. The real challenge is that Unification presents to idealistic young people a social vision aimed at peace, racial amity, ecological balance and economic justice based on stories and symbols drawn directly from the biblical sources they have heard since they were young and from the American civil religion that still—despite Watergate, Viet Nam and all the rest—maintains a grip on their imaginations. This seems especially telling since sociologists who have studied the Moon movement tell us a large proportion of its adherents come from second-generation American families where the American dream is still more vital than it is in other sectors. Furthermore, this vision of a Heavenly Kingdom that will start in America is presented as something the members can begin to work and sacrifice for right now. And they do.

I believe the attraction of the Moon movement to naive idealistic youth is not a result of sinister brainwashing but an inevitable consequence of the utter vacuum that now exists on what might be called the "Christian left." The theory that the only things young people are interested in today are beer-guzzling and careerism is simply untrue. Many are looking for a credible, religiously grounded social vision. But little is offered them. The black movement, though it now appears to be stirring again, for years has seemed to be either moribund or suspicious of non-black participation. The peace movement is dead. Feminism, which has a powerful appeal to many women, hardly presents an inclusive social program. Everywhere else we see only fragmentation, confusion and appeals to support revolutions in the Third World, which—as essential as these revolutions are—rarely give a young person something to do here and now for a just and peaceful world. Moon offers toil and martyrdom for a world that must be built anew. The mainline churches seem to offer school and career in a world expected to stay pretty much the same.

I am convinced that the only real "answer" to the Unification religious/political challenge is to provide something better. It must be a political vision based on Judeo-Christian values, open to insights from the Orient, aware of the critical factor of class (which is rarely mentioned by the Moonies) and willing to utilize Marxist analyses without falling into sectarian bickering or authoritarianism. It is time for a rebirth of a biblically based socialism with a real program. Young people whose parents and older brothers and sisters marched at Selma and flocked to the mass peace rallies search in vain for comparable opportunities to invest their energies today. Moon's appeal is a reflection of the death of social action in churches and synagogues and the failure of theology to provide a credible basis for the struggle for the Kingdom. We should not underestimate youth's willingness to accept sacrifice and discipline in the interest of an ideal.

Beyond Ideology

At about 10 o'clock Saturday night, as the lecturer was finishing his presentation, he began talking—apparently with great feeling—about the "heart of God," a central symbol in Unification thought. "God," he said, "is a brokenhearted God, one who has suffered for thousands of years, waiting for us to do our part to serve him and build the Kingdom." And he began to weep. Soon most of the young Moonies around me were also praying and weeping, asking God to forgive them for contributing to his suffering, dedicating themselves to him anew.

At this point, in an atmosphere that reminded me of pentecostal and charismatic meetings, I became aware that the appeal of the Moon teaching is not *just* ideological. There is a part of it which does not come through in Sontag's book and is even more badly overlooked by press reports about brainwashing. The full name of the group is, after all, the Holy Spirit Association for the Unification of World Christianity. Here is a movement which manages to combine religious universalism, pentecostal immediacy, a warmly supportive "family" and a program for allegedly building the Kingdom of God on earth. Such a potent admixture cannot be dismissed lightly.

I left the workshop early Sunday afternoon. The door was open. No one tried to keep me from leaving. I had not been brainwashed; in fact, if anything, I had been a bit bored. My hosts and hostesses seemed genuinely sorry to see me go, but I attribute this to the kind of affection which always develops among people who spend a weekend together, not to some insidious strategy of deception. It was clear after the hours of lectures and discussions that Moon's theology is not my cup of ginseng tea—something I had really known all along. Still, as I looked at the other churches grouped around the Boston Common—Congregational, Catholic, Unitarian, Episcopal—I could not help wondering what, if anything, they would do that day to offer a discipline, a vision, a devotion and a strategy to the millions of young contemporaries of those I left behind at the Unification headquarters. I am still wondering.

The Study of New Religious Consciousness: A Black's Reflections

Archie Smith, Jr.

The new religious movements in America suggest not only a continuation of the Protestant and Catholic reforms, but also new promising stirrings in the depths of Western consciousness which imply "a new era in religion and the birth of the new social order." This common thesis is questioned by Archie Smith, because most scholars who formulate it tend to discuss the new religious movements as if the adherents represent the broad spectrum of society in the United States, whereas, in fact, they are mostly white, middle-class, educated, urban. In the search for "truth" in the new religious consciousness, how can one overcome racism, "endemic to white religion in America, and a reality in determining the real priorities in the everyday activities of this society"? Furthermore, argues this Associate Professor of Religion and Society at the Pacific School of Religion in Berkeley, California, "the Black experience is also part of the new religious phenomenon in America. But there is a difference for why Blacks are not turning to the same new forms of religion as whites." Smith concludes, "The new spiritual quest in America may be a sign of new and creative possibilities on the horizon, but such a quest will not be authenticated by ignoring personal and systemic sources of color, sex, and class oppression." In June 1977, the Graduate Theological Union of Berkeley, of which the author's school is a member, inaugurated its Program for the Study of New Religious Movements in

America with a major conference. The conference report and essays, plus several responses to them including this one by Archie Smith, Jr., are published in *Understanding the New Religions,* edited by Jacob Needleman and George Baker (New York: Seabury Press/A Crossroad Book, 1978).

There is a growing awareness among many scholars that we stand in witness of a great transition in Western culture, and the dawning of a new religious era. Jacob Needleman has written that

> Significant though it is, the revolution that is striking the established religious institutions of the West is only part of a spiritual phenomenon that promises to transform everything modern man has thought about God and human possibility. The contemporary disillusionment with religion has revealed itself to be a "religious" disillusionment [1].

Something new and liberating is stirring in the depths of Western religious consciousness which promises to be the source of a new vision for a new society. The religious focus is shifting and new interpretations of religion, conscience, God, and the role of the person in social life are emerging. The new religious consciousness is a symptom of a complex process of revolutionary changes going on in traditional roles and Western institutions. True, the current trend in universities by students seems to be more and more towards materialism. Many want to become doctors and lawyers for the money and prestige. Yet hundreds of thousands of Americans are turning East and towards the mystical core of all religion.

The new religious consciousness suggests that new themes of ultimate significance are emerging, further contributing towards a crisis in a materialistic culture premised upon modern capitalism, secularism, technology, and individualism. White scholars have been drawn to this movement, assessing its meanings and sharing their insights. It is too early to tell what will emerge from this new religious ferment. But while we stand in the presence of something new that promises liberation, we also stand in the presence of something old and enduring—which has made its impact in American society and the world.

W. E. B. DuBois, around the turn of the century, argued that the problem of the twentieth century is the problem of the color line:

> ... we must remember that living as the blacks do in close contact with a great modern nation, and sharing, although imperfectly, the soul-life of that nation, they must necessarily be affected more or less directly by all the religious and ethical forces that are today moving the United States. These questions and movements are, however, overshadowed and dwarfed by the (to them) all-important question of their civil, political, and economic status. They must perpetually discuss the "Negro Problem,"—must live, move, and have their being in it, and interpret all else in its light or darkness [2].

DuBois' point may be more relevant today than it was then. The problem of color is rooted in an even greater problem of economic oppression—supported by apathy and antipathy of the affluent towards their disinherited compatriots. The twin problems of racism and poverty conspire to form the basis of black victimization.[1] With the growing backlash of such hate groups as the American Nazi party, the increased interest and growth of the Ku Klux Klan, and other hate groups, one must ask: Can the new religious consciousness generate a new spirit of social commitments and a vision of society profound and heroic enough to effectively counter economic oppression, racism, and its subsequent effects?

I

With few exceptions, white scholars of the "New Religious Consciousness" have failed, so far, to perceive racism as a significant factor worthy of their attention in the study of the new religious movements. Yet racism has been endemic to white religion in America, and a reality in determining the real priorities in the everyday activities of this society. Racism, born of capitalism, continues to be a dominant form of oppression as well as a source of meaning in America. Yet it was ignored or trivialized when the white scholars who met at Berkeley assessed the meaning of the "new religious consciousness."

The relationship of race and racism to the new religious consciousness did not occupy a significant place in their deliberations. Indeed, the new religious consciousness was discussed without significant reference to "the problem of the color," and discussed as if the new forms of religious consciousness were of universal significance in an otherwise pluralistic society. I suspect that if a group of Black or ethnic scholars had met to discuss the new religious consciousness and its significance, racism and its effects upon social and religious life would be of central importance. Why, at this point in history, is racism not more central in the hierarchy of concerns of first-world scholars who study new, predominantly white, religious movements? Is it that racism and color oppression are completely absent from the "new consciousness" and therefore, simply "not there" to be investigated?

The search for "truth" in the new religious consciousness may be seriously compromised when those who study it trivialize or ignore the fact that racism is endemic to American intellectual and religious life. While sex and age, alienation and anomic conditions, conformity and dissent, truth, guilt, salvation, and the search for meaning were discussed, everyday realities of racism and social and economic oppression were left largely untreated.

The problem is one of relevance. Relevance is concerned with the investigator's interest, particular angle of observation and selective mapping of experienced reality. The interest of the investigator is critical. Interest selects what is an important area of study and what is to be ignored as unimportant. It plays a central role in the development of our stock of knowledge about the new religious movements and those who study them. The relevant task of social theory and scholarship is not only to codify data, but interpret social reality and help give society expressions that are truly creative and life-enhancing.

The problem of relevance in studies of the new religious

consciousness cannot be settled by simply adjusting Afro-American concerns within the current scope of scholarship. Our understanding will be enhanced when non-white scholars and women make significant contributions from their perspectives and experiences, and when white Western scholarship is brought into dialogue and challenged beyond its traditional perspective.

The new religious consciousness was largely treated at the Berkeley conference as a universal affecting young people in general, i.e., W.A.S.P., rather than youth from certain ethnic backgrounds and particular social strata. Recruits to the new religious movements tend to be urban white youth, well-educated and from middle- and upper-class families. Their disaffection is with the inability of established white religious traditions and materialistic strivings of family life to yield depth of meaning in living.

II

The literature on the "new religious consciousness" is growing, and suggests that the "new religious consciousness" is indeed a complex phenomenon. The new religious consciousness has arisen both within and outside of main-line religious traditions; some have taken more of a political emphasis, while others have emphasized individual salvation. The reasons for joining and methods of recruitment vary considerably. Initiates themselves are drawn to the new movements for reasons that range from sheer curiosity to a profoundly personal or spiritual quest for acceptance and growth towards wholeness. Many recruits lacked little in the way of material possessions in their family of origin. They are, after all, products of a powerful and wealthy economy and have been among its chief benefactors. They have been exposed to the best our society affords in terms of health care, education, homes equipped with the latest in modern technology, travel, and sophisticated psychotherapies. Many were participants in the antiwar movement of the 1960s and early 70s, and maintain their commitment to radical political action for a just society. Yet some perceive through disillusionment, that politics alone cannot achieve justice in society, or bring about the necessary social transformation apart from religion. Politics alone cannot satisfy the deeper strivings of the human spirit, or meet the moral requirements for justice. Neither can the requirements for social and spiritual justice be met by domesticated pietism, which abdicates risk and responsible self-conscious participation in the construction of a new society. The rational and prophetic dimensions in religious commitment can help pave the way to a more human social order.

Other recruits were among the uncommitted youth of the 1960s who participated in the hippie, dropout, and psychedelic drug cultures. Still others are from homes where real intimacy and emotional gratification were overshadowed by materialistic pursuits and search for security. They have not found fulfillment in the religious traditions in which they have been raised and are turning to non-traditional, often non-Western, forms of spirituality.

The personal forces that drive the youth to the new movements are a sense of alienation from main-line Protestant, Catholic, and Jewish traditions which some perceive to be decadent, and a search for an identity that has its roots in the conscious and unconscious strivings of the human soul. Some do not perceive that such a spiritual quest can be meaningfully fulfilled in the established religious traditions of the parent generation. Many come to the new movements as a part of an inner search for happiness, for friendship, communal living, authority, a personal sense of integration and intimate contact with a higher power. The new religious movements promise to be, for many, an alternative way of life, a more acceptable way of living in this society—where inner happiness and friendship can develop in community through sacrifice, purification rites, and where contact can be achieved with the sacred—a living reality more personal and powerful than any combination of people.

Individualism or personal transformation is a pervasive theme in the new modern religious movements. In some groups there is an emphasis upon diet and nutrition; forms of mysticism, trance behavior or altered states of consciousness, other forms of meditation; a stress upon separation from non-devotees; and a search for new social roles as ways to transform society. There is also a strong political element in the new religious consciousness among those who continue to be committed to (root) economic, political, and social structural transformation in America. What is new in this complex religious phenomenon is an unparalleled turn from the values of utilitarian individualism and established white religious traditions towards new forms of religion by white, urban, well-educated, and affluent youth from middle-class American families.

The Graduate Theological Union conferees did not address themselves to the question of "Black Religion,"[2] its impact upon social reality in America, and its implications for their own life and work. Religious movements such as the Black Muslims, Black Holiness and Pentecostals, Black sects and cults, the Ras Tafari movement, development within Black Christian theologies of liberation, and their impact upon Black main-line church persons and denominations. Black Jehovah's Witnesses and Seventh-Day Adventists—were not addressed at the conference, or recognized as significant aspects of the new religious consciousness in America. Perhaps these white scholars felt unprepared to address these topics. But if this were the case, then their own studies of the new religious consciousness should be qualified—as studies of a particular aspect of the new phenomena, especially if the groups studied are predominantly white. We argue that the Black experience is also part of the new religious phenomenon in America. But there is a difference for why Blacks are not turning to the same new forms of religion as whites.

While Black Americans experience more or less the same forces that contribute to disillusionment with the American dream, their experiences are nevertheless profoundly different because they are *Black* in America. Black Americans share a common culture with all other Americans, but due to African origins, the heritage of slavery, long-standing and complex patterns of oppression, Black Americans have evolved a different perspective and set of norms and values that have enabled them to survive in a hostile environment. Black people in America have been victimized because they are Black, and Blacks continue to be the nation's largest impoverished group of urban Americans. Forty-point-four percent unemployment (August 1977) among young urban Blacks is one indication of structural impoverishment; the subeducation received by many inner-city youth in large metropolitan areas is another indication; the increasing welfare roles, and imprisonment among inner-city Blacks is yet another indication of structural oppression with its subsequent permanent effects.

The Black experience in America is epitomized in the Black struggle for survival in a hostile white society. Their sole struggle centers in survival, and what they have to defend is their life. Historically, it has been out of conditions of brutal oppression and cultural alienation, not affluence, that has been the creative ground of Black religious consciousness and radicalism. Sometimes out of necessity that consciousness found radical expressions in the culture of the street as well as in the Black Church. Sometimes it turned to cynicism, resignation, and despair or rage. But always the underlying theme in Black religious consciousness has been liberation from oppression in white America [3,4,5,6,7,8].

When white scholars ignore racism, they legitimize covert violence in a racist society and contribute to problems of interpretation in the study of predominantly white new religious movements. The challenge for them is to show how the new religious consciousness can overcome the problems of racism so deeply embedded in white established religious traditions. Scholars are in a unique position not only to identify and interpret various forms of innovative folk religions, but also to provide the new movements with a reflexive, self-critical perspective regarding their own claims to be beyond racism, as well as a perspective for authentic liberation in society. The sign of authentic liberation in America is when the oppressed are set at liberty and the blind can see. No group is free as long as their compatriots are humiliated and oppressed . . . and so the struggle goes on

Harvey Cox, reflecting upon the new religious consciousness, wrote:

The spiritual crisis of the West will not be resolved by spiritual importations or individual salvation. It is the crisis of a whole civilization, and one of its major symptoms is the belief that the answer must come from elsewhere. The crisis can be met only when the West sets aside myths of the Orient, and returns to its own primal roots [9].

Those roots extend deep into the history of Black oppression. Scholarship cannot adequately address the issue of salvation and release from guilt in the new religious consciousness by ignoring the strivings in the souls of Black folk, and the corresponding search for meaning in the souls of white folk. When scholarship ignores the problem of the old in the search for the new, I suspect that we compound rather than shed meaningful light upon our destiny and common spiritual pilgrimage in this country.

III

I have been arguing that "the problem of the color line" has been ignored by white scholars in the study of the new religious consciousness, while it continues to be a pervasive theme in American life and in the everyday reality for Black Americans. By ignoring the problem of color, the experiences of young educated white and middle-class Americans tend to function as the norm for what is going on in the new religious movements. This has permitted a partial vision of religious experience to function as a universal in a pluralistic society. The problem of the color line, echoed by the eminent sociologist W. E. B. DuBois, needs to be reaffirmed as "a problem" to be addressed by white scholars.

The problem of the color line in the study of the new religious consciousness is broadened beyond traditional boundaries of Black, native, and white Americans with the emergence of Asian and Chicano presence, especially on the West Coast. The problem of the color line has implications for the conscious and unconscious strivings of white North Americans in general, and the souls of white scholars in particular.

The problem is not who is studied, but the integrity or quality of the dialogue among scholars from different ethnic backgrounds and perspectives. All are needed to assess the meaning of the new religious consciousness in North America, and to move us beyond partial frames of reference towards new concepts which will release our reality from a narrow point of view generated by a small minority of white scholars.

Racism was cited in the 1968 Kerner Commission Report as a pervasive American problem, and referred to by the late Reverend Dr. Martin Luther King, Jr., as "the corrosive force that may well bring down the curtain of Western civilization." Racism was the force that brought his own life and the lives of countless other Black Americans and Jews in Europe to an end. Black Americans have perceived the problem of racism and oppression to be far more deepseated and fatal to American life than has been generally appreciated by white Americans. Racism is a reality deeply rooted in American social history, intellectual life, and consciousness. It can no longer continue to be ignored or trivialized by white scholars in their study of the "New Religious Consciousness." If the new religious consciousness is "new," and if it is able to adequately counter the disruptive effects of racism and imperialism, then this is important data. Ought not this data be an object of investigation for white scholars in their pursuit of truth? Perhaps the "new religious consciousness" is a reaction or response to the failure of the older religious orientations to give meaning, to establish justice, and to live out the great covenant of this nation—as one nation in diversity, under God with authentic liberty and justice for everyone— especially the oppressed.

The new quest in America is but the ancient quest of the human spirit for wholeness and Truth, personal and social integration and transformation. These are manifestations of a genuine spiritual-moral quest. To be whole is, in part, a quest for union with the primal source which lies in the depths of our own nature. The journey inward must lead outward and affirm life comprehensively, intentionally, and for everyone. The mark of maturity in religious commitment is vulnerability manifest in faith and action within specific social processes. Spiritual-moral resignation or political activism alone lack the moral depth, breadth, and vision to liberate the Self or a social order from an exploitative, self-serving system of capitalism. Political apathy or activism alone cannot liberate persons from oppressive exterior pressures and interior psychic forces. The real transforming energy in the new religious movements will need to transcend (not deny) self- and class-interest, and will move towards the full realization of social and economic justice as a manifestation of liberation and authentic Selfhood. The new spiritual quest in America may be a sign of new and creative possibilities on the horizon, but such a quest will not be authenticated by ignoring personal and systemic sources of color, sex, and class oppression.

NOTES

1. Definitions of "racism" abound. Some readers may argue that "racism" is now an over-used term and has little heuristic value to warrant further use. Many may take exception to the author's angle of vision and use of the term "racism" and wish to replace it with some other, less volatile term, such as "ethnocentrism" or "cultural differences." This author, however, maintains that racism is the more accurate term to use. Mine is the viewpoint of a minority group member whose perception of reality has been shaped within a society without fundamental acceptance of Blacks. Hence, this essay is not written from a dispassionate, scientifically objective perspective. The author is involved and writes from a point of interest within this society. Consequently, my experience and perception as a racial minority group member will vary significantly from the dispassionate observer and from that of dominant group members. Unlike racism, ethnocentrism is a universal phenomenon. It is the tendency of human groups with similar characteristics to think of their cultural and social heritage as superior to others. Ethnocentrism is a sense of group pride and a source of self-esteem. However, in encounters with other groups, ethnocentric justifications of superiority are subject to modification in the process of intergroup interaction. Ethnocentrism may lead to racism when human groups fail to give up their claim to superiority and seek to impose their institutionalized definitions of reality upon those who are racially and culturally different. Black skin color is not the only criterion for invidious distinctions between groups in a racially heterogeneous society. But Blackness is as significant a criterion for exclusion as is sex and class and age. Black is a highly visible color in white America, and endowed with pejorative attributes. Blacks continue

to be singled out for differential and unequal treatment both as individuals and as a group. Unequal and differential treatment of Black people in America has decisively shaped American social and religious history. Although Blacks are not the only ethnic group to be singled out for special treatment in America, they are the largest racial minority group which has had a difficult time coming out of poverty and overcoming institutionalized discrimination—as a group. "Cultural differences," as a more acceptable explanation, fails to address the fact that those few Black Americans who participate in white institutionalized structures often do so at the price of denying their Blackness and African heritage. Blackness and African traditions are more often perceived as pathogenic deviations from acceptable white norms, or perceived as impediments to success within white institutional arrangements. Even when Blacks become culturally similar to whites, they are still Black and vulnerable to unequal and differential treatment. Many Black Americans, especially since the turbulent 1960s and Alex Haley's *Roots,* have had to face the fact that Black self-consciousness must be redefined in terms of its African heritage. Many Black Americans are responding to white racism by affirming their Blackness, their African heritage and cultural uniqueness. These responses are essential themes in the burgeoning religious consciousness among younger Black Americans. This essay is written with these ideas in mind.

2. Scholars are not agreed upon the precise meaning of the term "Black Religion" or whether it exists apart from white religion in America. This paper argues that there is a difference. Although the ultimate or primal source that underlies religion is One, the experiences of a people who confess it (religion) are located within the framework of a particular social history and culture which gives shape to their experiences and ways of apprehending the fundamental nature of Reality. Suffering from racial oppression in America, experience of a God who can make a way out of no way, and the continuation of African cultural residuals in Black experience have been distinctive sources of Black Religion in America.

REFERENCES

1. Jacob Needleman. *The New Religions,* preface. Garden City, N.Y.: Doubleday, 1970.

2. W. E. B. DuBois. *The Souls of Black Folk,* p. 148. New York: Fawcett ed., 1961.

3. C. Eric Lincoln, editor. *The Black Experience in Religion.* Garden City, N.Y.: Doubleday, 1974.

4. Joseph R. Washington, Jr. *Black Sects and Cults.* Garden City N.Y.: Doubleday, 1972.

5. James H. Cone. *God of the Oppressed.* New York: Seabury, 1975.

6. Albert B. Cleage, Jr. *Black Christian Nationalism.* New York: William Morrow, 1972.

7. Gayraud S. Wilmore. *Black Religion and Black Radicalism*. Garden City, N.Y.: Doubleday, 1973.

8. Clifton H. Johnson, editor. *God Struck Me Dead*. Boston: Pilgrim Press, 1969.

9. Harvey Cox. "Eastern Cults and Western Culture: Why Young Americans Are Buying Oriental Religions." *Psychology Today*, July 1977, p. 42.

Selected Bibliography of Books in English

Of books on this subject—especially since 1965—there is no end. A comprehensive guide to the literature is *Christian Faith Amidst Religious Pluralism: An Introductory Bibliography,* edited by Martha B. Aycock, Donald G. Dawe, S. Eleanor Godfrey, and John B. Trotti (Richmond, Va.: Union Theological Seminary Library, 1981). Since that substantial reference work is already available, we judge it more useful in this volume to provide a very limited and selective reading list of only 30 books in English, published since 1970, that are of prime value to introduce students to fresh thinking and crucial issues in this field.

Anderson, Gerald H. and Thomas F. Stransky, eds. *Christ's Lordship and Religious Pluralism.* Maryknoll, N.Y.: Orbis Books, 1981

Anderson, J. N. D. *Christianity and Comparative Religion.* Downers Grove, Ill.: InterVarsity Press, 1970.

Bria, Ion, ed. *Martyria/Mission. The Witness of the Orthodox Churches Today.* Geneva: World Council of Churches, 1980.

Bühlmann, Walbert. *The Search for God. An Encounter With the Peoples and Religions of Asia.* Maryknoll, N.Y.: Orbis Books, 1980.

Carmody, Denise Lardner. *Women and World Religions.* Nashville: Abingdon, 1979.

Clasper, Paul. *Eastern Paths and the Christian Way.* Maryknoll, N.Y.: Orbis Books, 1980.

Cragg, Kenneth. *The Christian and Other Religion. The Measure of Christ.* London: Mowbrays, 1977.

Davis, Charles. *Christ and the World Religions.* New York: Herder and Herder, 1971.

Dawe, Donald G. and John B. Carman, eds. *Christian Faith in a Religiously Plural World.* Maryknoll, N.Y.: Orbis Books, 1978.

Hallencreutz, Carl F. *Dialogue and Community. Ecumenical Issues in Inter-religious Relationships.* Geneva: World Council of Churches, 1977.

_____. *New Approaches to Men of Other Faiths, 1938–1968: A Theological Discussion.* Geneva, World Council of Churches, 1970.

Hick, John, ed. *Truth and Dialogue in World Religions: Conflicting Truth-Claims.* Philadelphia: Westminster Press, 1974.

_____ and Brian Hebblethwaite, eds. *Christianity and Other Religions: Selected Readings*. London: Collins/Fount, 1980.

Hillman, Eugene. *Polygamy Reconsidered. African Plural Marriage and the Christian Churches*. Maryknoll, N.Y.: Orbis Books, 1975.

Lausanne Committee for World Evangelization. *How Shall They Hear? Proceedings and Reports from the Consultation on World Evangelization, Pattaya, Thailand, 1980*. Minneapolis: World Wide Publications, 1981.

Mbiti, John S. *New Testament Eschatology in an African Background. A Study of the Encounter between New Testament Theology and African Traditional Concepts*. London: Oxford University Press, 1971; SPCK paperback edition, 1978.

McCurry, Don M., ed. *The Gospel and Islam*. Monrovia, Calif.: MARC/World Vision International, 1979.

Needleman, Jacob and George Baker, eds. *Understanding the New Religions*. New York: Seabury Press, 1978.

Neill, Stephen. *Salvation Tomorrow*. Nashville: Abingdon, 1976.

Newbigin, Lesslie. *The Open Secret. Sketches for a Missionary Theology*. Grand Rapids, Mich.: Wm. B. Eerdmans Publishing Co., 1978.

Richardson, Don. *Peace Child*. Glendale, Calif.: Regal Books, 1974.

Samartha, Stanley J., ed. *Faith in the Midst of Faiths. Reflections on Dialogue in Community*. Geneva: World Council of Churches, 1977.

Sharpe, Eric J. *Comparative Religion: A History*. New York: Scribners, 1975.

Smith, Wilfred Cantwell. *Towards a World Theology*. Philadelphia: Westminster Press, 1980.

Stott, John R. W. and Robert T. Coote, eds. *Down to Earth: Studies in Christianity and Culture*. Grand Rapids, Mich.: Wm. B. Eerdmans Publishing Co., 1980.

Swearer, Donald K. *Dialogue: The Key to Understanding Other Religions*. Philadelphia: Westminster Press, 1977.

Thomas, M. M. *Man and the Universe of Faiths*. Madras: Christian Literature Society, 1975.

Verkuyl, J. *Contemporary Missiology: An Introduction*. Grand Rapids, Mich.: Wm. B. Eerdmans Publishing Co., 1978.

World Council of Churches. *Christians Meeting Muslims. WCC Papers on Ten Years of Christian-Muslim Dialogue*. Geneva: World Council of Churches, 1977.

_____. *Jewish-Christian Dialogue. Six Years of Christian-Jewish Consultations*. Geneva: World Council of Churches, 1975.

MISSION TRENDS NO. 1

Contents

ISBN: 0-8091-1843-2

MISSION TRENDS NO. 2

Contents

MISSION TRENDS NO. 3

Contents

I. THEOLOGY IN CONTEXT

II: LATIN AMERICAN PERSPECTIVES

III. AFRICAN PERSPECTIVES

IV. ASIAN PERSPECTIVES

SELECTED BIBLIOGRAPHY OF BOOKS IN ENGLISH

(Paulist ISBN: 0-8091-1984-6) (Eerdmans ISBN: 0-8028-1654-1)

MISSION TRENDS NO. 4

Contents

I. MISSION AND LIBERATION

0467

II. BLACK EXPERIENCE

III. FEMINIST EXPERIENCE

IV. ASIAN AMERICAN EXPERIENCE

V. NATIVE AMERICAN EXPERIENCE

VI. HISPANIC AMERICAN EXPERIENCE

SELECTED BIBLIOGRAPHY OF BOOKS IN ENGLISH
(Paulist ISBN: 0-8091-2185-9) (Eerdmans ISBN 0-8028-1709-2)